The Future
of the
Welfare State

Edited by
Torben M. Andersen,
Karl O. Moene
and
Agnar Sandmo

The Future of the Welfare State

Previous titles in this series:

The Future of the Welfare State

Edited by
Torben M. Andersen

Karl O. Moene
and
Agnar Sandmo

BLACKWELL
Publishers

First published 1995

HB
846
.F88
1995

Blackwell Publishers
108 Cowley Road, Oxford OX4 1JF, UK
and
238 Main Street,
Cambridge, MA 02142, USA

British Library Cataloguing-in-Publication Data

A catalogue record for this book is available from the British Library.

Library of Congress Cataloguing in Publication Data applied for

ISBN 0-631-19576-9

Printed in Great Britain by Page Bros, Norwich

Contents

Contents

Editors' Preface

Even though the welfare state is a well-established economic institution in most Western European countries, it may face a troubled future. The challenge is how to ensure a welfare state which can adapt flexibly to internal and external changes. The present collection of articles takes as a starting point that creating a future for the welfare state requires a better understanding of how it works. These papers were originally presented at *The Scandinavian Journal of Economics*'s conference on "The Future of the Welfare State", held in Ebeltoft, Denmark, in September 1994. Financial support from the Aarhus University Research Fund, the Danish Social Science Research Council, the Norwegian Research Council and the Swedish Council for Research in the Humanities and Social Sciences is gratefully acknowledged.

Torben M. Andersen
Karl O. Moene
Agnar Sandmo

Introduction: The Welfare Economics of the Welfare State

Agnar Sandmo *

Norwegian School of Economics and Business Administration, Bergen, Norway

I. Introduction

Outsiders to economics might be forgiven for thinking that welfare economics provides the theoretical underpinnings for the welfare state. But although the language is suggestive, the link between theoretical welfare economics and policy recommendations concerning the role of the public sector, the optimal degree of redistribution and social insurance, etc. is not obviously a very strong one. Economists who use a welfare theoretic framework for thinking about economic and social problems might be led to advocate a "night watchman state" which would mainly be concerned with the provision of public goods or, alternatively, to argue for a crucial role of the public sector as a redistributive system, as in the welfare state.

What is the welfare state? It is always tempting to avoid issues of definition, but in this case it seems appropriate to point out that the concept is in fact used in at least two different ways. Some use it to denote a subsection of the public sector, concerned with redistribution (via social security and social assistance) and the provision of those social goods which have a strong redistributive element, like health care and education. Others use the term in a much wider sense to characterize the economic and social policies of a country that gives high priorities to equality and individual protection against social hazards. To illustrate the difference in usage, according to both definitions unemployment insurance would definitely come under the heading of welfare state policies, whereas macroeconomic policies that are designed to prevent or reduce unemployment would be included in the second definition of welfare state policies, but not in the first. I am inclined to take the wider view of the welfare state, primarily because I feel that the more narrow definition introduces a number of rather awkward borderlines between the various areas of economic policy.

In the following I first consider what bearing the neoclassical version of welfare economics has on the design of welfare policy. I then discuss various modern developments that have led economists to revise some of their views about the costs and benefits of the welfare state.

II. Welfare Economics: Changing Perspectives

Developments in welfare economics during the 1930s and 1940s were admirably integrated and summarized in Samuelson (1947) and further developed and restated by Arrow (1951). The most important insight of the theory was the two equivalence theorems about Pareto optima and competitive equilibria. A competitive equilibrium in which all consumer prices are equal to marginal costs is a Pareto optimum, but the allocation of resources (income, for short) among individuals will not in general correspond to the maximum of a social welfare function. To combine the efficiency property of the competitive equilibrium with an equitable and fair allocation of resources requires a system of lump sum transfers. Lump sum taxes are taxes that do not affect individual decisions except through pure income effects; thus, they lead to no substitution effects as between leisure and work, between different kinds of consumption goods, between consumption at different points in time, etc. Lump sum subsidies must have the same properties. The revenue from lump sum taxes will have to exceed the expenditure on subsidies because of the revenue requirement associated with the supply of public goods.

This theoretical insight could easily lead to a rather optimistic view of the possibility of establishing a redistributive public sector on a large scale. With lump sum transfers there does not exist any efficiency-equity trade-off. Redistributive policy can be carried out without creating price distortions and efficiency losses. True, the requirements for taxes and subsidies to be truly lump sum are very stringent, but in much of the older literature one finds statements which seem to imply that in practice the income tax is a good approximation; see e.g. Hotelling (1938). Thus, redistribution can occur within a system that satisfies, at least as an approximation, the conditions for social efficiency or Pareto optimality.

The standard version of welfare economics used to be silent on the time and uncertainty dimensions of the model, although an old insight was that the concept of a commodity could be thought of as being time-dated. Later on, Arrow (1953) and Debreu (1959) showed how this idea could be extended to include state-contingent commodities, so that commodities would be characterized by both the time period and "state of the world" in which they would be available. This led naturally to the study of redistributive transfers that are both time and state dependent; see Sandmo (1970).

The formulations of neoclassical welfare economics were in most cases so general that they did not carry any visible implications for the question of who the beneficiaries of and contributors to the redistributive system should be. References were sometimes made to the idea that someone with egalitarian beliefs would like to redistribute income from the rich to the poor. But how do you know who is rich and who is poor? This may seem like a frivolous question, but it is in fact a serious one when it comes to the design of a redistributive system. Such a system has to be based on a set of rules about the duty to pay taxes and the right to receive benefits, and these rules have to refer to observable characteristics of the individuals concerned. Let us first consider the problems that this raises for the tax system.

The ideal basis for a rational redistribution policy would be information about individuals' needs and resources. But in general this is private information for the individuals concerned and not directly observable by the government agencies in charge of the redistribution scheme. The most obvious observable criterion for deciding who is rich and who is poor is income, or perhaps consumption, which is income minus saving. But if the lump sum tax is related to income, it is simply an income tax in disguise, and a rather thin disguise at that. Theory tells us that an income tax will have substitution effects in both labour and capital markets, so that the benefits to the needy in this case will be financed through a tax system that imposes efficiency losses on the economy. Taxes on wealth and indirect taxes on consumer goods suffer from the same shortcomings. In brief, apart from Pigovian taxes on externality-generating goods, all feasible tax systems lead to a less efficient allocation of resources. In a realistic setting for the problem of tax system design, where proper account is taken of the asymmetric information between private individuals and the government, there is indeed a tradeoff between efficiency and equality.

Once one accepts this view of the second best setting of redistributional policy, it immediately follows that policy instruments which would be ruled out under first best conditions could indeed be employed to increase welfare. For instance, while a classical result is that transfers in cash are always better than transfers in kind, this is not necessarily the case when there are constraints on the use of other instruments of redistribution. This is demonstrated in the paper by Blomquist and Christiansen in this issue, which analyses transfers in kind as a means of inducing individuals to reveal their true needs. Another implication of this view is that when the productivity of workers is only partly observable by the government, as in the paper by Maderner and Rochet, it could be optimal to subsidize workers of low qualifications.

Let us now look at the receiving end of the redistributive system. A typical feature of the redistributive systems of the welfare state is that they combine principles of insurance with time and state dependent redistribution. The most important parts of the social security system are old-age pensions and disability and employment insurance. Now these benefits would be truly lump sum if the probabilities of occurrence of the various states were exogenous, but in reality they can frequently be influenced by the individual's own actions. For example, the probability of unemployment is partly determined by the worker's choice of education and training, by his work effort and by the intensity of his search for a new job if he should become unemployed. Generous unemployment benefits could be attractive from an egalitarian point of view, but they could also lead to less efficient educational decisions, lower effort and less search for a new job. Similarly, sickness and disability insurance could lead to less care being taken in work and leisure activities and to more absenteeism on the grounds of minor health complaints. The general problem is, of course, that of moral hazard, which induces efficiency problems also at the receiving end of the redistributive system. Here too there is a tradeoff between equality and efficiency.

However, at this point we should pause to consider whether, even from the point of view of pure theory, there is *always* a tradeoff between efficiency and equality. Might it be the case that the institutions and redistributive arrangements of the welfare state make a positive contribution to the efficiency of the economy? The discussion above focused on the properties of a redistributive system with reference to a perfectly functioning market economy. But to be realistic we should look at models of market economies that have a stronger resemblance to real economies. Much of the redistribution in the welfare state can be seen as socialized insurance. In order to pass judgement on the strengths and weaknesses of the redistributive system of the welfare state, we ought to take a closer look at the performance of private insurance markets.

Since the path-breaking paper by Akerlof (1970), it is by now a well-established insight that many insurance markets suffer from problems associated with adverse selection. If the insurance company only has statistical information about the risk properties of individuals, it will offer insurance at a premium that reflects the average risk in the population. But this will lead only the high-risk individuals in the population to buy insurance. It is easy to see that this could give rise to a situation where some insurance markets would vanish altogether — or, more realistically, never emerge. This implies that the economy would be undersupplied with coverage against a number of risks, and this is a problem that social insurance could overcome because of its compulsory nature. To some extent, therefore, social insurance and redistribution — the two concepts are sometimes hard to distinguish — could be seen as attempts at improving market performance; this aspect of the welfare state has been stressed by Barr (1987) and is also prominent in Sinn's contribution to this issue. From this point of view, then, types of redistribution that by many would be regarded as ethically desirable would also improve the allocative efficiency of the economy; there is then no tradeoff between efficiency and equality. It has also be pointed out by Varian (1980) that progressive income taxation has aspects of social insurance if people's abilities and wages have elements of luck in them; risk averse individuals who did not know their ability *ex ante* would then favour progressive *ex post* taxation as an insurance against low wages.

It is worth emphasizing that while the problem of adverse selection provides an argument for compulsory and possibly social insurance, the same does not apply to the other reason for failure of insurance markets, viz. moral hazard. Adverse effects on behaviour from insurance against risks that are partly under the individual's control are common to both private and social insurance. They do not in general provide any strong argument for socializing private insurance — or for privatizing social insurance.

One problem of welfare state policies that has risen to prominence in recent years concerns the effect of increasing international economic integration on the scope for redistributive policies within the single nation state. This was e.g. pointed out in a much cited article by Sinn (1990), who argued that increased international mobility of labour might lead to the "death of the insurance state". This type of problem is taken up in the paper by Wildasin, who points out that economic integration may also reduce some of the *need* for national redistribution.

One general message from the more recent welfare analyses of the welfare state is obviously that although redistributive taxes and transfers do lead to price distortions and efficiency losses, not all effects of welfare state activities point in the same direction. Someone who wants to estimate the social cost of the welfare state in efficiency terms needs to be clear as to what the alternative is, against which that cost is being measured. The Arrow–Debreu economy with a complete set of markets is not a very meaningful comparison, nor is the unregulated *laissez-faire* market economy. The fact that it is difficult to identify an obvious standard of comparison should be a reason for some caution in making too sweeping statements about the welfare state.

Another message is that a meaningful welfare economics of the welfare state must be empirical. This is because in a second best world we are constantly trading off efficiency gains against distributional benefits or considering the benefits of alternative distributional policies, and we have to know how large they are, not only whether they are positive or negative; see Atkinson (1987) and Moffitt (1992) for extensive surveys of empirical studies in this area. This is in contrast to the older variety of welfare economics, in which the magnitude and behavioural effects of the lump sum transfers required to achieve a just distribution of income were not of much intrinsic interest. But this also means that welfare theory must be closely tied to theories of individual behaviour in the welfare state.

III.   Individual Behaviour in the Welfare State

Studies of individual behaviour in the welfare state have traditionally focused on the effects of taxes and social security on labour supply and savings behaviour, as in the paper by Aaberge, Dagsvik and Strøm on taxation and labour supply. The emphasis in such studies is on the distortions of individual behaviour that the welfare state carries with it. This is, of course, right and proper, and we will no doubt be able to look forward to many more studies of this kind. But there are also reasons why this type of research has its clear limitations. For instance, in the area of labour supply, empirical work has concentrated on a fairly narrow range of questions, like the effects of changes in tax rates on overtime work and labour force participation. These are important issues which can be studied by means of cross-section or time-series data covering fairly short periods. But such studies do not quite capture the more systemic effects of the welfare state on work incentives, which may be harder to measure and have more long-run effects. This is discussed more fully in Lindbeck's paper, which takes up the intriguing and neglected issue of the possible feedbacks from policies to preferences and behaviour patterns.

Individual behaviour in the welfare state must in principle be seen as influenced not only by taxes and social security charges, but also by items on the expenditure side of the public budget. Among such items the main focus in the literature has been on price subsidies and cash transfers, whereas effects of the provision of social goods — both private and public — have not received the attention that they probably deserve, at least not in the mainstream literature on public finance. The provision of health care is discussed in the paper by Currie; a look through her list of references seems to indicate that this is a topic which has not exactly filled up the economics journals. An important theoretical point is that although a high level of average and marginal tax rates may discourage labour supply in quantitative terms, tax financing of public expenditure on health and education will presumably increase the quality of the labour force, so that an assessment of the effects of welfare state policy on labour supply in efficiency terms ought to consider these effects jointly.

Although an ideal egalitarian redistribution policy should aim at equalization of the standard of living, attention has typically been focused on the somewhat more narrow indicator of the distribution of income. Has public policy in the welfare state actually managed to reduce inequality? This is not an easy question, for published statistics tell us only part of the story; e.g. they do not tell us anything about the incidence effects of the redistributive instruments on *gross* incomes. Another shortcoming of published statistics in relation to the distribution of *welfare* is that they do not take account of the general equilibrium effects on resource allocation within the family, which might change the role and importance of income as an indicator of welfare. Konrad and Lommerud, in their paper, discuss some interesting aspects of this problem.

IV. The Political Economy of the Welfare State

What are the driving forces behind the emergence and continued growth of the welfare state? To some extent the answer to this question may be sought in the propositions of welfare economics. Income redistribution and spending on social goods like health and education are at high levels because there is a social concern with equality and justice; in addition, an extensive social security system is required to overcome the failures of private insurance markets. This answer is not entirely convincing, however; it implicitly interprets welfare economics as a positive theory of the political process. Perhaps the most popular explanation as to why welfare state policies may tend to overshoot their targets lies in the asymmetry between costs and benefits of redistributive policies. Much of redistribution goes from majorities to minorities of the population; from the employed to the unemployed, from the healthy to the disabled, from the urban to the rural population, etc. This implies that for each redistributive measure, the average burden on those who pay is significantly less than the average benefit for those at the receiving end, and this fact may bias political decision-making towards carrying redistribution — in cash or in kind — too far.

Other explanations of the overshooting phenomenon are also possible. One interesting observation is e.g. that in the Scandinavian welfare state, there is not only a high degree of equality of disposable income; gross incomes are also more equally distributed than in other countries. Given this achievement, one would perhaps think that the importance of continued equalization would diminish, but this appears not be the case. One explanation for this is offered in Lindbeck's paper in terms of a feedback from egalitarian policies to tastes and political attitudes. At a more formal level, Persson analyzes this issue by means of positive models of income taxation in which a crucial role is assigned to the notion of relative income.

Attempts to explain the growth of the welfare state would be incomplete without a consideration of the role of paternalistic attitudes in designing economic institutions. While economists have a fondness for the concept of consumer sovereignty, this feeling has not been shared by all proponents of the welfare state. Much of the motivation for the emergence of

8   *A. Sandmo*

state pensions was certainly the feeling among many politicians as well as among many academic writers that people were not rational enough to understand what would be in their own best interests in the long run. Both in the area of pensions and in that of family policy, it was often maintained that welfare gains could actually be made by *restricting* people's range of choices. This was not because of any side effects from behaviour on social efficiency in the ordinary sense of the word, but because people would benefit from constraints imposed by those who knew better; see e.g. the references to the work of the Myrdals in Sandmo (1991).

The economics of the welfare state offers a fascinating field of study for both the theorist and the empirical researcher, inviting contributions from many fields of economics and encouraging collaboration with our colleagues in the other social sciences. This will certainly not be the last conference to offer a range of interesting papers on this set of issues.

References

Akerlof, G.: The market for "lemons": Quality uncertainty and the market mechanism. *Quarterly Journal of Economics 84*, 488–500, 1970.
Arrow, K. J.: An extension of the basic theorems of welfare economics. In J. Neymann (ed.), *Proceedings of the Second Berkeley Symposium on Mathematical Statistics and Probability*, University of California Press, 1951.
Arrow, K. J.: Le rôle des valeurs boursières pour la répartition la meilleure des risques. *Econométrie*, CNRS, Paris, 1953; republished as The role of securities in the optimal allocation of risk-bearing. *Review of Economic Studies 31*, 91–96, 1963.
Atkinson, A. B.: Income maintenance and social insurance. In A. J. Auerbach & M. Feldstein (eds.), *Handbook of Public Economics*, vol. 2, North-Holland, Amsterdam, 779–908, 1987.
Barr, N.: *The Economics of the Welfare State*. Weidenfeld and Nicolson, London, 1987.
Debreu, G.: *Theory of Value*. Wiley, New York, 1959.
Hotelling, H.: The general welfare in relation to problems of taxation and of railway and utility rates. *Econometrica 6*, 242–69, 1938.
Moffitt, R.: Incentive effects of the U.S. welfare system: A review. *Journal of Economic Literature 30*, 1–61, 1992.
Samuelson, P. A.: *Foundations of Economic Analysis*. Harvard University Press, Cambridge, MA, 1947.
Sandmo, A.: Equilibrium and efficiency in loan markets. *Economica 37*, 23–38, 1970.
Sandmo, A.: Economists and the welfare state. *European Economic Review 35*, 213–39, 1991.
Sinn, H.-W.: Tax harmonization and tax competition in Europe. *European Economic Review 34* (2/3), 489–504, 1990.
Varian, H. R.: Redistributive taxation as social insurance. *Journal of Public Economics 14*, 49–68, 1980.

Welfare State Disincentives with Endogenous Habits and Norms

Assar Lindbeck

University of Stockholm and Industrial Institute for Economic and Social Research, Stockholm, Sweden

Abstract

It is assumed in this paper that habits and social norms constrain the influence of economic disincentives on individual behavior, but that these constraints themselves may subsequently be influenced by the very same disincentives. It is also assumed that an individual is more likely to obey such habits and norms if many individuals in society do so. Though such constraints on economic behavior usually recede only gradually in response to changes in economic incentives, it is argued that major macroeconomic shocks may drastically speed up the process (a "ketchup effect"). These features may generate multiple equilibria and vicious dynamics.

I. The Basic Idea

The basic idea of this paper is that various disincentive effects of welfare-state arrangements on economic behavior, and related economic distortions, are often delayed because habits and social norms constrain economic behavior. It will also be argued that these constraints themselves may *subsequently* be influenced by the very same disincentives. This is assumed to be the case not only for private agents but also for public-sector administrators. As a result, generous welfare-state arrangements may generate multiple equilibria and vicious, or "hazardous" dynamics.

One reason for confining the discussion to disincentive effects, and hence to various costs of welfare state arrangements, rather than covering both benefits and costs, is simply a lack of space. Another reason is that an

---

*I am grateful for useful comments on an earlier draft by Kenneth Arrow, Anders Björklund, Peter Hedström, Dennis J. Snower, Martin Paldam, Robert Zeckhauser and two anonymous referees, without implying any shared responsibility for the somewhat unconventional analysis.

understanding of disincentive effects, and related hazardous welfare-state dynamics is essential if we want to avoid that the welfare state, over time, undermines its own economic foundations by way of disincentive effects on the national economy and therefore also on the tax base; for discussions of benefits and costs of the welfare state, and of virtuous as well as hazardous dynamics, see Lindbeck (1993, 1994, 1995).

The paper is limited to what may be regarded as the "core" of the welfare state, namely cash transfers to households, including both social-insurance benefits and social assistance, and public-sector subsidies and the provision of various social services. I concentrate on the disincentive effects on a few broad economic activities — work, saving, asset choice and entrepreneurship. Considering the complexity of the issues to be discussed, my ambition is mainly exploratory. This is the reason for the informal, essayistic nature of the paper. I leave the task of theoretical formalization and empirical verification, or falsification, to future work; for a theoretical formalization of some aspects of the paper, see, however, Lindbeck, Nyberg and Weibull (1995).

II. Habits and Social Norms

Habits are usually defined in the sociological and psychological literature as routine behavior without much cognition or evaluation; cf. Verheller and von Raaij (1985, p. 5).[1] *Social norms* are usually characterized in the same literature as "required", or (by others) expected behavior, without much explicit purpose and calculated concern for the consequences, except for the expected discomfort associated with breaking such norms; see discussions in Parsons (1952), Lewis (1969), Scott (1971), Opp (1979), Elster (1989) and Bicchieri (1990). Individual behavior in conformity with habits and social norms is often contrasted to behavior based on instrumental rationality ("rational choice"), which is distinctively future oriented, purposeful, calculating and hence outcome oriented. The usual distinction between habits and social norms is that the latter are shared by others and sustained by their approval of compliance and disapproval of non-compliance, while habits (like "private norms") are regarded as more individualistic phenomena and not enforced by others to the same extent.[2] This distinction is somewhat blurred, however, by the observation that

---

[1] Compare the following characterization of habitual behavior by Katona (1973, pp. 218–19): "People act as they have acted before under similar circumstances without deliberating and choosing. Routine procedures and an application of rules of thumb by consumers as well as business exclude the weighing of alternatives".

[2] Coleman (1990, p. 243) takes this position strongly: "I will say that a norm concerning a specific action exists when the socially defined right to control the action is held not by the actor but by others". For a similar view, see Elster (1989).

social norms are often assumed to be "internalized" in the sense that an individual develops an "internal sanction system"; cf. Scott (1971) and Coleman (1990). Once such an internalization has occurred, individuals are asserted to conform to social norms even when there are no external sanctions; cf. Hoffman (1983).[3]

In terms of utility theory (which has traditionally not been used to any large extent by sociologists), an individual who breaks an internalized social norm will experience a utility loss not only through external sanctions and related losses of reputation, but also through internal sanctions in the form of subjectively felt discomfort. Borrowing Etzioni's (1989, p. 46) characterization of the "internalization of moral", we may say that the internalization of social norm turns constraints into preferences. Thus, social norms that emphasize socially acceptable behavior, or "community values", are assumed to mould preferences and constrain the effects of a deterioration in economic incentives. The individual, therefore, feels guilt, i.e., pays a psychological price, for having broken previously obeyed social norms. This guilt may, or may not, dominate over the direct material benefits of breaking the norm.[4]

In game-theoretic approaches, social norms are treated as equilibria of strategic interaction, reflecting clusters of self-fulfilling expectations of rationally calculating agents; for early attempts along these lines, see Lewis (1969) and Ullmann-Margalit (1977). Each individual's strategy is then a best reply to the others' strategies, where the latter are taken as given. Or, according to Bicchieri (1990, p. 841): "A norm is there because everyone expects everyone else to conform, and everyone knows he is expected to conform, too". The adherence to a social norm reflects, in this view, a *conditional choice* based on expectations about other peoples' behavior and beliefs; this means, of course, that conformity to a social norm is not a dominant strategy.[5]

---

[3] Such an internalization has been described by Kohlberg (1968, p. 483) as a socialization process in which a person learns to "conform to rules in situations that arose impulses to transgress and that lack surveillance and sanctions". The distinction between external and internal sanctions goes back (at least) to the classical discussion of norms by Parson (1951).

[4] Compare formulations by Akerlof (1980): "... social customs may act as a constraint on economic activity, preventing trades that would occur in the absence of such a code" (p. 756), and a "custom that is too costly to follow, in terms of lost utility, will not be followed and therefore will disappear" (p. 772). Moffitt (1983) also assumes that the individual suffers a utility loss if breaking a social norm.

[5] The term "convention" often seems to cover aspects of both habits and norms. A typical game-theoretic formulation of a convention, by Young (1993, p. 57), is "A convention is a pattern of behavior that is customary, expected and self-enforcing. Everyone conforms, everyone expects others to conform, and everyone wants to conform given that everyone else conforms". Formally, Young defines a convention as an absorbing state expressed as a number of repetitions of a strict, pure strategy Nash equilibrium. For a similar formulation, see Sugden (1986).

12   A. Lindbeck

The most difficult question when analyzing habits and social norms is probably to determine how they emerge and are sustained. A standard answer among sociologists is learning ("socialization"), which in evolutionary game theory is expressed by e.g. Sugden (1986) as repetition and imitation of successful behavior, as well as the disappearance of agents who use inappropriate strategies — an idea that harks back, at least, to Adam Smith (1758). Other (complementary) explanations for the emergence and sustenance of habits and social norms are the value-creating effects of law, the dominance of some people over others, membership in voluntary organizations that expect certain types of behavior of their members, and "metanorms" that require people to express disapproval of those who violate social norms; cf. Axelrod (1986).

These considerations are, of course, relevant also for understanding specific social norms that constrain the disincentive effects of various welfare-state arrangements. For instance, if work and saving during a prolonged period have been economically rewarding — perhaps even necessary for survival — it is likely that habits and social norms develop which encourage such behavior, illustrating the hypothesis that successful behavior tends to be repeated and imitated. Such behavior is also favorable for other individuals, who usually do not have to support those who work and save themselves. Other examples of the role of habits and social norms in connection with welfare-state arrangements are that citizens often abstain from applying for benefits to which they are entitled, presumably to avoid stigmatization and related loss of reputation, and that many citizens spontaneously comply with legislated benefit codes and tax codes even when the risk of being caught is negligible — an example of the internalization of habits and norms that are defined by law.

Norms against living on *selective social assistance* ("welfare" in US terminology) would be expected to be particularly strong, because of the stigmatization of such support; this stigmatization is accentuated by the inconvenience of losing one's personal integrity *vis-à-vis* the social-assistance administrators. Such stigmatization has, in fact, been amply documented in the sociological literature; see interview studies by Horan and Austin (1974) and Rainwater (1979).[6] An econometric study by Moffitt (1983, pp. 1030 and 1032-4) suggests that the stigma is connected with the act of welfare recipiency *per se*, but that it does not vary with the amount of the benefit once on welfare. Most likely, individuals are less hesitant to live on, and adjust their lives to, *general social security benefits*, such as sick pay, work-injury pay, unemployment benefits, early retirement

---

[6] In the U.S., as much as 30–60 per cent of the citizens who are eligible for welfare do not apply; cf. Moffitt (1983).

(disability) pensions and old-age pensions. After all, such benefits are often described today as "citizens' rights" and "entitlements", based on contributions paid previously.

It is reasonable to assume that the adherence to habits and social norms subsides only gradually if new institutions emerge that make such adherence more expensive than before, for instance because of more generous benefit systems and higher marginal tax rates, or because of softer control of the misuse of benefit and tax systems. Invoking a general concept introduced by Loury (1987), we may regard social norms as "social (collective) capital" which, like other kinds of capital, accumulates or decumulates over decades and centuries, partly in response to institutional arrangements including economic incentives and government control systems. Honesty is one example of such collective capital; cf. Lindbeck (1988, pp. 32–3).

I do not take a strong position in this paper on alternative explanations for the emergence and continuation of habits and social norms *in general*. I limit myself to habits and norms that are important for the functioning of various welfare-state arrangements. I then simply assume (i) that today's habits and social norms are influenced by institutions, including economic incentives and government control systems of the past; (ii) that an individual is more likely to conform to certain habits and social norms, the more individuals in society do so (a "critical mass" effect); (iii) that earlier acquired habits and social norms tend to survive also after the incentive or control systems have changed; but (iv) that a sufficiently large increase in economic disincentives, or a sufficiently large softening of government controls, creates a conflict between habits and social norms, on the one hand, and economic incentives and government control on the other, and that this will induce some (particularly entrepreneurial!) individuals to stop adhering to earlier obeyed habits and norms, with others following suit. I will also assume (v) that major macroeconomic shocks to the national economy may drastically speed up the process by which earlier obeyed habits and norms are abandoned.

The first three assumptions imply that the national economy is protected for a while from the effects of a deterioration in economic incentives — perhaps for as much as one or several decades in some cases. As a result, welfare-state policies easily "overshoot", in the sense that politicians would have chosen to offer citizens less generous welfare-state arrangements if it had been possible to anticipate the long-term consequences for individual behavior, including less compliance with traditional habits and social norms. The fourth assumption implies that sufficiently large deteriorations in economic incentives may gradually overcome the inertia generated by initially existing habits and norm, while the fifth assumption means that a major macroeconomic shock may result in a sudden 'ketchup effect' by generating a drastic rise in the number of citizens who depend on various types of government support programs, such as unemployment benefits, public works programs, social assistance and subsidized early retirement. Such a shock may, therefore, weaken the hesitation among individuals to live on benefits; it may also reduce the efficiency of government control of beneficiaries.

Interpersonal dependence may, of course, be analyzed without constructs such as habits and social norms. We may, for instance, simply assume that the behavior of others influences the benefits or costs, or both, of the actions of an individual with given preferences. This is the approach in e.g. Schelling's (1971, p. 167) "tipping model", in which an individual with given preferences is no longer willing to reside in a certain neighborhood if the percentage of residents of another ethnic origin exceeds a certain limit, as then the (economic and psychological) costs of living there start to exceed the benefits.

In a similar vein, Granovetter assumes that when the number (or proportion) of people who behave in a certain way exceeds a certain "threshold level", an individual with given preferences changes his own actions accordingly because the benefits of that behavior start to exceed the costs — with different "threshold levels" for each individual; cf. Granovetter (1978) and Granovetter and Soong (1989). For instance, as the size of a rioting crowd increases, the costs for an individual (with given preferences) of joining the riot fall, because of a reduced risk of being detected and arrested; moreover, the expected benefits of rioting may rise because of a greater likelihood that the rioters' targets will be achieved.

While such models may be useful for the analysis of housing segregation and rioting, and several other social phenomena, I believe that models with "conditional habits and norms", as applied in this paper, are also useful for analyzing the long-term consequences of welfare-state arrangements. It is true that the expected pecuniary costs of moral-hazard behavior and cheating with welfare-state benefits and taxes tend to decline when many others behave in the same way, simply because the risk of being detected tends to fall — as in the case of a growing riot. But as will hopefully be clear from the subsequent discussion, it is also useful to assume that the hesitation of an individual to engage in such behavior depends on the psychological costs of deviating from previously established habits and social norms in society — *either* because of external sanctions and related losses of reputation, *or* as a result of the individual's own internal sanction system. Thus, it may be analytically useful to make a distinction between rational responses to changes in the costs and benefits of certain behavior, for individuals with given preferences, and induced changes in these preferences due to changes in habits and (internalized) social norms.

III. Work Disincentives and Government Controls

The fact that tax wedges create disincentives on work (substitution effects against hours as well as intensity and quality of work) does not require elaboration. The reason why various welfare-state benefits do the same is, of course, that they reduce the difference in income when people work and when they are out of work. This effect arises *both* because benefit systems are seldom actuarially fair, partly due to ambitions to redistribute income and wealth, *and* because contingencies that qualify individuals to receive benefits cannot be perfectly monitored by the authorities, which is bound to create moral hazard and cheating.

A good humanitarian case can, no doubt, be made for generous welfare-state benefits in connection with contingencies such as sickness, disability, unemployment, single motherhood, etc. A basic dilemma for the welfare state, however, is that generous benefits tend to create many beneficiaries due to moral hazard and in some cases also benefit cheating. *Ceteris paribus*, the higher the sick-pay benefits, the more people will call in sick; the more favorable the conditions for disability pension, the more people will find it attractive to live on such pensions; the more generous the unemployment benefits, relative to after-tax wages, the more people will in the long run choose to stay unemployed; and the higher the benefits for single mothers, the more single mothers we would expect, as such support is an implicit subsidy to birth "out of wedlock", divorce, runaway fathers, and separate living quarters for formally unmarried couples.

Moral hazard and cheating look rather similar on the surface. But there is a distinction. If, because of generous sick pay, I choose to call in sick on Monday because I feel tired after drinking heavily on Sunday night, this would be classified as moral hazard. If I go to Copenhagen for a long weekend, but in fact pretend that I have stayed away from work because of (insured) illness, this is, of course, plain cheating. Similarly, while it is an example of moral hazard if I do not search for a job very energetically when I receive generous unemployment benefits, I would certainly be characterized as a cheater if, while receiving such benefits, I work in the underground economy.

Disincentive effects on work are, most likely, stronger in the long run than in the short and medium run because of the inertia created by habits and social norms. Obvious examples when we would expect this to be the case are decisions by individuals regarding their allocation of time between work and leisure (including "on-the-job-leisure"), the choice between household service production and purchases of services in the market, and decisions about the division of work among family members. Other examples are decisions to apply for social assistance, support for single motherhood, unemployment benefits or disability pension (early retirement). The hesitation to live on such benefits would be expected to recede only gradually, in particular when others decide to do so — an illustration of evolutionary adjustments by way of learning and imitation. Long-term benefit dependency among individuals may, therefore, develop only gradually.

We may schematically differentiate between two types of benefit dependency. One type is when individuals become "pacified", in the sense that they lose the energy to look for jobs and to improve their skills. Such developments are analytically highlighted by the branch of modern psychology that deals with so-called "learned helplessness", according to which the individual is unable to control his own situation; see Seligman (1975) and Magnusson (1980). Casual evidence suggests that such pacification of individuals has occurred on a much broader basis in the former socialist countries than in the welfare states of Western Europe.

The other type of benefit dependency implies that some citizens actively and rationally adjust, in a calculated way, to living at the expense of taxpayers' money. We may say that they acquire subjectively felt property rights to other citizens' incomes and tax payments. This type of behavior has been observed, in particular, in some countries that are characterized by a combination of high long-term unemployment and generous social assistance and social security benefits, such as Denmark and the Netherlands. The issue has recently been analyzed empirically by four Dutch sociologists through interviews with people living on social assistance, disability pensions and unemployment benefits in three Dutch cities; cf. Enbersen *et al.* (1993). They found that about 55 per cent of the long-term unemployed in their sample had, effectively, stopped looking for work, and that more than half of these asserted that they had stopped because they had found "other activities to give meaning to their lives: hobbies, voluntary work, studying, or working in the informal economy". These observations are in line with the assertions by the American sociologist Murray (1984), to the effect that some citizens tend, after a while, to choose quite rationally and actively to live on social benefits.

We would, of course, also expect habits and social norms to limit the frequency of tax avoidance, tax evasion and benefit cheating, not to speak of various types of criminal activities (including work in the "black economy") for which income is usually tax free, except for a stochastic "tax" in the form of punishment if caught. There is also evidence that peoples' willingness to pay taxes is favorably influenced by positive attitudes to the government's spending programs; see Lewis (1982). But there must also be a "price" on honesty, in the sense that habits and social norms that encourage such behavior may be undermined if honesty becomes sufficiently expensive because of high marginal tax rates and generous benefit levels, or because taxpayers become less supportive of government spending programs. Such developments would counteract the often hypothesized tendency of welfare-state arrangements to mitigate criminal cultures in potentially poor neighborhoods; cf. Freeman (1995). The *types* of crimes that are stimulated and mitigated, respectively, as well as the individuals who commit them will, of course, differ substantially in the two cases.

Changes in habits and norms are perhaps particularly likely to occur when a new generation that forms its values on the basis of a new incentive system enters working life.[7] Immigrants who have moved to a country largely because of generous benefits may also be relatively quick to utilize the existing benefit system.[8]

It is a commonplace that adjustments of individual behavior to welfare-state arrangements depend not only on the generosity of the benefits but also on the conditions for receiving benefits and on the administrative controls of beneficiaries. From a normative point of view, it is indeed useful for the government to strive for an optimum combination of incentives, on one hand, and conditionality and controls, on the other: the stricter the conditionality and the tighter the controls, the more generous benefits are possible without serious problems of moral hazard and cheating; cf. Lantto (1991).

An example of the importance of *conditionality* is that welfare-state induced reductions in labor force participation, because of tax and benefit wedges, may be mitigated if future eligibility for benefits is tied to previous work and income, which is a typical feature in the Nordic countries, even though the benefit systems are far from actuarially fair.[9] Another example is that long-term benefit dependency of single mothers may be limited by strict work or training requirements for the beneficiaries. The enforcement of such requirements, in combination with the provision of child care, is most likely an important explanation for the more modest problems of long-term benefit dependency among unmarried mothers in the Nordic countries than in the U.S., where unconditioned cash support dominates; see Jäntti and Danziger (1994). But the basic dilemma that generous support to single mothers tends to expand their numbers cannot be avoided, even with the "Nordic model".

An illustration of the importance of government *controls* is that the strictness of "work requirements" in the unemployment benefit system, i.e.,

---

[7] In a regression analysis, Moffitt (1983, p. 1032) reaches the conclusion that the distaste for living on social assistance ("welfare") rises with age.

[8] In some suburbs of Stockholm, more than 50 per cent of the immigrants from certain countries lived on social transfers of different types in 1994.

[9] In the case of decisions about labor-force participation, it is average rather than marginal benefits that matter, as the choice set is not convex — the decisions being taken at the extensive rather than the intensive margin.

the requirement that the individual should accept work offers, seems to influence how many employees choose to live on such benefits. But it may be difficult for public-sector administrators to cut off unemployment benefits in situations of heavy unemployment — as illustrated by the experience in several countries during the 1980s and early 1990s; see Layard, Nickel and Jackman (1991). Another illustration of the difficulties in enforcing strict government controls is that the number of people living on subsidized disability (early retirement) pensions has recently "exploded" in some countries, in particular in periods when layoffs of elderly workers and unemployment have increased. In the Netherlands, 12 per cent of the population of working age had such a pension in 1993; the corresponding figure in Sweden was 8 per cent.

Public-sector administrators may also, after some time, simply find that it is unpleasant to be harsh toward benefit applicants. It is particularly tempting for individual administrators to become more lenient if they find out that other administrators have become more permissive. Similarly, physicians may hesitate to be strict with people who ask for a disability pension (early retirement) because of asserted physical or psychological health problems. After all, the costs to public-sector administrators and physicians themselves of being "humane", i.e., generous with taxpayers' money, are very small. Indeed, some physicians may even make a living by writing "humane" testimonies to the effect that individuals are disabled. Thus, endogenous changes in habits and social norms may develop over time not only among potential beneficiaries but also among the administrators and experts of the systems.

Moreover, if a major macroeconomic shock has shifted large groups of citizens onto various safety nets, there may simply not be enough administrative resources for efficient control. And with less efficient controls, it becomes even more tempting for potential beneficiaries to exploit and abuse the systems, etc.

The punchline of this discussion is that benefit systems which function reasonably well under prolonged periods may subsequently go out of control either because of endogenous behavior adjustments over time, or because of macroeconomic shocks that increase the number of beneficiaries substantially.

It is tempting to analyze mechanisms like these in terms of models with multiple equilibria (as in the earlier mentioned tipping model) — one equilibrium with widespread adherence to social norms, strict administrative control and few beneficiaries, another with less adherence to social norms, lax administrative control and many beneficiaries.[10] Such develop-

---

[10] For an analysis of the unemployment benefit system in terms of multiple equilibria — though without concern for social norms — see Ljungquist and Sargent (1994). In an

ments may also be described in terms of *vicious circles*, or hazardous dynamics, in order to emphasize the dynamic process by which the number of beneficiaries may increase over time in connection with changes in habits and social norms among beneficiaries, administrators and experts. The ensuing fall in the tax base may subsequently force the government to increase tax rates, which tends to reduce the tax base even further because of new disincentive effects, and so on. Developments like these imply that the equilibrium position of the economy is path dependent in the sense that the behavior of a certain individual, at a specific point in time, depends on the previous behavior of others.

Models in which, because of the influence of habits and norms, disincentive effects only gradually harm the national economy, until a sudden shock abruptly "activates" the disincentives, are analytically quite similar to dynamic models of "natural disasters" in modern ecology: to begin with, pollution only moderately and gradually damages the ecological system until a sudden major disturbance (such as a meteorological shock) abruptly shifts the system into a new and strongly inferior state, or creates a vicious circle without apparent end.

This discussion raises somewhat of a welfare-state paradox. The welfare state has largely been motivated as a way of shielding the individual from the consequences of macroeconomic shocks and related market risks. It is possible, however, that exactly such shocks may undermine the welfare state itself by pushing large fractions of the labor force onto various safety nets for prolonged periods, and by undermining the financial position of the government.

More generally, while a generous welfare state presupposes a national economy with high productivity and a large fraction of the population at work in the market system, forces may emerge in advanced welfare states that undermine both these prerequisites — either endogenously or as a result of exogenous shocks, or a combination of both. Neither politicians nor economists, or other social scientists, seem to have been much aware of such long-term dynamic adjustments.

A neglect of the risks of such hazardous long-term dynamics is also apparent in many contemporary suggestions for welfare-state reform. An example is the popularity among economists of the idea to replace means-tested benefits with a "negative income tax", i.e., a combination of a fixed (unconditional) cash grant to everybody and an income tax rate. In spite of the elegance of such a system, as well as of its administrative simplicity, it has serious flaws precisely because it neglects the possibility of long-term

---

analysis of wage setting and unemployment, Akerlof (1980, p. 756) derives two equilibria, one where almost everybody adheres to social customs about wage setting, another where almost nobody does.

adjustments in habits and social norms. Not only will people with high preferences for leisure be *systematically* subsidized by a negative income-tax system, as there would be no discretionary examination of individuals, but individuals who originally do not belong to this category may also acquire such tastes and habits after a while. As a consequence, earlier obeyed habits and social norms against such behavior may be eroded. There is, therefore, a risk that a negative income tax, in particular among young people, will over time create a large group of "drifters" who abstain from work in the official labor market, and who instead live permanently on grants from the government, possibly combined with occasional incomes from underground work and, in some cases, also criminal activities.

It may be retorted that similar incentive problems arise in the case of means-tested income support, i.e., social assistance. An important difference, though, is that in the case of a negative income tax (in its pure form) it is, in principle, impossible to prevent able-bodied beneficiaries from abstaining from work, while this is possible, at least to some extent, in the case of means-tested systems as the benefits are then tied to specific contingencies such as poor health, unemployment and old age.

More subtle, though rather speculative, long-term consequences of welfare-state policies may also arise by way of the influence of values and social norms. For instance, the egalitarian views that lie behind many welfare-state policies may feed back on, and strengthen, egalitarianism itself. Important social norms as to what are acceptable income differences may then change. One reason is that the political discussion in highly egalitarian welfare states tends to center on distributional issues: "who gains, who loses?" This may generate such a concentration on distributional issues in the public debate, not least in the mass media, that the tolerance for income differences will gradually fall, and that social and political conflicts, as a result, will rise in parallel with an equalization of disposable income. We may also speculate that the "respect" for existing distributions of income will decline when it becomes clear that this distribution is, to a considerable extent, determined by "arbitrary" political decisions rather than by anonymous market forces. As a result, the often hypothesized tendency for distributional conflict to subside along with greater equality of disposable income may not be a monotone relation; social and political conflicts may rise after the equalization of income, by means of government policies, has reached a certain state.

IV. Saving, Asset Choice and Entrepreneurship

We would expect that habits and social norms are also important for *saving behavior*. For instance, households have, at least until recently, "learned" that it is proper to save. Moreover, people have traditionally saved not only to be able to consume in the future, but also to avoid being dependent on their children or the government, and to enhance their reputation (status) and self-respect in general. Among many citizens it has probably been regarded as particularly improper to incur debt, except perhaps in connection with buying real estate. Indeed, "reluctance to being in debt" seems to be, or at least to have been, a strongly held habit and norm among households.[11]

It may, for these reasons, take considerable time before household saving is very negatively influenced by higher marginal capital-income tax rates and improved social security benefits. For instance, it would seem that households in some countries only gradually gave up their earlier acquired saving habits, including their reluctance to being in debt, during the post-World War II period, in spite of the fact that real after-tax interest rates (at least *ex post*) were often negative, and that the government provided more and more elaborate systems of social security and social assistance.

It is also likely that the consequences of tax-induced distortions of *asset choice* — often accentuated by inflation and various asymmetries in the taxation of different types of assets — develop only gradually. For instance, it was not until the second half of the 1980s that households finally seemed to have adjusted their behavior to the fact that borrowing for the purchase of various types of assets, including real estate, durable consumer goods and shares — was highly profitable. At that time, in a number of countries, households were also finally allowed to borrow freely in the wake of the deregulation of capital markets. Ironically, just when households had "learned" to borrow, real after-tax interest rates increased abruptly in the late 1980s and early 1990s because of tax reforms and lower inflation that were not fully reflected in lower nominal interest rates. It would seem that households adjusted their saving behavior to the new economic incentive much more rapidly this time, possibly because of the extraordinary size and abruptness of the rise in real after-tax interest rates, and perhaps partly also because of the simultaneous increase in economic uncertainty.

A more speculative point is that welfare-state egalitarianism may also influence policies towards *entrepreneurship*. As entrepreneurs often strive to become affluent, and in some cases also succeed, they may easily come to be regarded as "alien" figures in a highly egalitarian welfare state. This is, I believe, what happened in Sweden in the "egalitarian" 1960s and 1970s. One illustration is the strongly negative attitudes towards entrepreneurs in the mass media during that period. A concrete expression of

---

[11] For an attempt to integrate such reluctance towards indebtedness with standard microeconomic theory of households, see Lindbeck (1963, Chap. 2).

these attitudes is that policies in some highly egalitarian countries favor the plowback of profits at the expense of dividend payments, apparently in the belief that this limits the income (or at least consumption opportunities) of the owners. In some countries with highly egalitarian welfare policies, such as Sweden, the tax burden on small entrepreneurs also became amazingly heavy during this period, and the after-tax return extremely low (for those who were not willing to cheat on taxes). Attitudes in society toward entrepreneurs may also have more *direct* effects on the vitality of entrepreneurship. Entrepreneurship is likely to suffer if entrepreneurs do not feel that they are respected in society. The attitudes toward entrepreneurs — among politicians, the mass media and the general public — are perhaps no less important for small entrepreneurs than are the pecuniary rewards of their activities.

We may, with slight exaggeration, say that there has been a tendency in some countries with highly egalitarian welfare-state policies, Sweden being one example, to opt for "capitalism without capitalists", and "enterprises without entrepreneurs" — probably not a very efficient economic system. These experiences illustrate how values that originally stimulated the build-up of a welfare state, after a while, may penetrate other sectors of society.

V. Difficulties of Reform

The basic dilemma of the welfare state is that it partly disconnects the relationship between effort and reward by creating disincentives to work, saving, asset choice and entrepreneurship. It is, therefore, important to avoid pushing welfare-state disincentives into "dangerous territory", where disincentive effects seriously damage the national economy and erode the tax base, and hence undermine the economic foundations of the welfare state itself. In particular, it is important not to build up welfare-state arrangements on the assumption that private agents do not, over time, change their economic behavior in order to utilize, and perhaps even cheat with the system. It is also important to avoid creating welfare-state systems that get into serious difficulty if the national economy is hit by severe macroeconomic shocks that drastically increase the number of citizens who depend on various benefit systems.

It has been argued in this paper that some disincentive effects of welfare-state policies, and their financing, are delayed because of the influence of habits and social norms on individual behavior, and that these delays may induce politicians to offer more generous benefits to citizens than if induced changes in habits and norms had been anticipated. This problem is particularly serious if, after severe disincentive effects have emerged, it takes considerable time to restore previous habits and social norms by way of reduced benefit levels and tighter controls. It may then be necessary to be much more harsh toward citizens — by way of lower benefits and strict control — than if the benefits had been less generous to begin with.

It may also take a long time for researchers to discover the existence of serious welfare-state problems, partly because of the earlier discussed delay in the adjustment of basic behavior patterns of private agents. Empirical estimates of the effects of welfare-state policies suffer from a problem similar to that expressed by the Lucas critique of estimated econometric functions. Lucas pointed out that such estimates are contingent on the expectations among private agents of the behavior of politicians. The discussion above suggests that estimates of disincentive effects of contemplated welfare-state reforms are contingent on existing habits and social norms, which may change either gradually or drama-tically, subsequently generating "regime shifts" for individual behavior patterns. Indeed, this econometric problem may be much more serious than the one emphasized by the Lucas critique which can, in principle, be met either by explicitly introducing government behavior functions or by estimating so-called "deep structures" such as preferences and production functions. It is more difficult to design analytical procedures that solve the estimation problems in connection with welfare-state policies which result in changes in habits or social norms.

Ideological beliefs, which are mixtures of values and views of the world, also tend to block, or at least delay, the realization that incentive problems do exist. Information that indicates such effects is often neglected among adherents of existing welfare-state systems, while information pointing in the opposite direction is often accepted. Welfare-state sceptics tend to screen information in the opposite direction. Psychological research on "cognitive dissonance" gives strong support for the existence of this type of screening behavior; see e.g. Aronson (1979), Hirschman (1965) and Akerlof and Dickens (1982).

Serious problems necessarily arise when attempts are made to reform or rewind a welfare state that is believed either to be poorly designed or to have "overshot" reasonable limits. The most obvious example is perhaps that several welfare-state arrangements (such as pension rules) may be regarded as long-term contacts between the government and the citizens. As life is irreversible, the individual runs into serious problems if such contracts are broken by the government after several decades. Long-term changes in habits and social norms among beneficiaries may also con-tribute to the political difficulties of reforming or rewinding the welfare state. For instance, the subjectively experienced utility loss when a benefit is removed may be much greater than the "utility loss" of never having received it in the first place — a hypothesis that is consistent with Tversky and Kahneman's (1981) "prospect theory", according to which the utility function is steeper to the left of the initial point than to the right of it.[12] Alternatively, we may hypothesize that preferences are endogenous in the sense that the aspiration level of individuals increases by previous achievements — an application of the psychological theory of the "rising aspiration level"; see Lewin *et al.* (1944).[13] Applying this theory to welfare-state benefits may explain why individuals seem to develop social norms in the form of subjectively felt "property rights" in existing benefits, i.e., in other peoples' incomes and tax payments, which means that it is regarded as "natural" to be financed by the government.

There are, of course, other serious complications if welfare-state spending is cut substantially. First of all, it is difficult to avoid the breakdown of important achievements of the welfare state, such as increased economic security, income smoothing over the life cycle of the individual, redistributions of wealth in favor of low-income groups and the provision of various types of social services. It may also be difficult to avoid undermining some of the virtuous dynamics that are created by various welfare-state arrangements, such as increased productivity, improved neighborhoods and less street crime in connection with reduced poverty and better health and education among low-income groups, an expanded tax base due to higher labor-force participation among the poor, ethnic minorities and women, and perhaps also a more general acceptance of continuing economic change and related reallocation of resources, and possibly even greater sympathies for the market system as such.

The least risky way of mitigating various welfare-state distortions and of fighting vicious welfare-state dynamics, without damaging the achievements of the welfare state, is probably to concentrate spending cuts on entitlements and other transfers to the large middle-class. It would then be possible to maintain, and possibly even expand, public-sector spending with large elements of investment in human capital, in particular perhaps among potential low-income groups. The problem is the political feasibility of this strategy.

References

Akerlof, G.: A theory of social custom, of which unemployment may be one consequence. *Quarterly Journal of Economics 94*, 749–55, June 1980.

---

[12] See also Thaler (1980).

[13] Katona (1951) has applied this theory to different types of economic behavior, though without any attempt to integrate the analysis with traditional microeconomic theory of households. Such an attempt is made, however, in Lindbeck (1963, Chap. 2) for the case of wealth accumulation.

Akerlof, G. & Dickens, W.: The economic consequences of cognitive dissonance. *American Economic Review 72*, 307–19, June 1982.

Aronson, E.: *The Social Animal.* 3rd ed., W.H. Freeman, San Francisco, 1979.

Axelrod, R.: An evolutionary approach to norms. *American Political Science Review 80*, 1096–111, Dec. 1986.

Bicchieri, C.: Norms of cooperation. *Ethics 100*, 838–86, July 1990.

Coleman, J. S.: *Foundations of Social Theory.* Harvard University Press, Cambridge, MA, 1990.

Elster, J.: Social norms and economic theory. *Journal of Economic Perspectives 3* (4), 99–117, 1989.

Engbersen, G., Schuyt, K., Timmer, J. & Van Waarden, F.: *Cultures of Unemployment: A Comparative Look at Long-Term Unemployment and Urban Poverty.* Westview Press, Boulder, CO, 1993.

Etzioni, A.: *The Moral Dimension. Towards a New Economics.* Free Press, New York, 1989.

Freeman, R.: Crime and the employment of disadvantaged youths. In G. Peterson & W. Vroman (eds.), *Urban Labour Markets,* Urban Institute Press, Washington, DC, 1993.

Granovetter, M.: Threshold models of collective behavior. *American Journal of Sociology 83* (6), 1420–43, 1978.

Granovetter, M. & Soong, R.: Threshold models of diversity: Chinese restaurants, residential segregation and the spiral of silence. *Sociological Methodology 18*, 69–104, 1989.

Hirschman, A.: Obstacles to development: A classification and a quasi-vanishing act. *Economic Development and Cultural Change 13*, 385–93, July 1965.

Hoffman, M.: Affective and cognitive processes in moral internationalization. In E. T. Higgins *et al.* (eds.), *Social Cognition and Social Development,* Cambridge University Press, Cambridge, 1983.

Horan, P. & Austin, P.: The social bases of welfare stigma. *Social Problems 21*, 648–57, June 1974.

Jäntti, M. & Danziger, S.: Child poverty in Sweden and the United States. The effects of social transfers and parental labor force participation. Mimeo, Department of Economics, Åbo Akademi, April 1994.

Kohlberg, L.: Moral development. In *Encyclopaedia of the Social Sciences,* Macmillan and Free Press, 1968.

Katona, G.: *Psychological Analysis of Economic Behavior.* McGraw-Hill, New York, 1951.

Lantto, K.: *Optimal Deterrents to Malingering.* Ph.D. thesis, Department of Economics, University of Stockholm, 1991.

Layard, R., Nickel, S. & Jackman, R.: *Unemployment — Macroeconomic Performance and the Labor Market.* Oxford University Press, Oxford, 1991.

Lewin, K., Dembo, T., Festsinger, L. & Sears, P. S.: Level of aspiration. In J. McV. Hunt (ed.), *Personality and the Behavior Disorders,* vol. 1, Ronald Press, New York, 1944.

Lewis, A.: *The Psychology of Taxation.* Martin Robertson Press, Oxford, 1982.

Lewis, D.: *Conventions.* Harvard University Press, Cambridge, MA, 1969.

Lindbeck, A.: *A Study in Monetary Analysis.* Almquist och Wiksell, Stockholm, 1963.

Lindbeck, A.: Consequences of the advanced welfare state. *The World Economy 11*, 19–37, 1988; reprinted in the author's *Selected Essays,* vol. II, *The Welfare State,* Edward Elgar, London, 1993

Lindbeck, A.: Overshooting, reform and retreat of the welfare state. *De Economist 104*, 1–19, 1994.

Lindbeck, A.: Uncertainty under the welfare state. *Geneva Papers on Risk and Insurance Theory,* Geneva, 379–393, 1994.

Lindbeck, A.: Hazardous welfare state dynamics. *American Economic Review, Papers and Proceedings 84*, 9–15, May 1995.

Lindbeck, A., Nyberg, S. & Weibull, J. W.: A public transfer game. Mimeo, IUI, Stockholm, 1995.

Ljungquist, L. & Sargent, T.: Welfare states and unemployment. In *Reforming the Welfare State: The Swedish Model in Transition*, NBER-SNS, Stockholm, 1994.

Loury, G.: Why should we care about group inequality? *Social Philosophy and Politics 5*, 249–71, 1987.

Magnusson, D.: Learned helplessness. *Skandinaviska Banken Quarterly Review 9*, 67–74, 1980.

Moffitt, R.: An economic model of welfare stigma. *American Economic Review 73*, 1023–35, 1983.

Murray, C.: *Losing Ground, American Social Policy 1950–1980*. Basic Books, New York, 1984.

Opp, K.-D.: The emergence and effects of social norms. A confrontation of some hypotheses of sociology and economics. *Kyklos 32*, 775–801, 1979.

Parsons, T.: *The Social System*. Tavistock Publications, London, 1952.

Rainwater, L.: Stigma in income-tested programs. Paper presented at Conference on Universal vs. Income Tested Programs, University of Wisconsin, Madison, 1979.

Schelling, T.: Dynamic models of segregation. *Journal of Mathematical Sociology 1*, 143–86, July 1971.

Scott, J.: *Internalization of Norms*. Prentice Hall, Englewood-Cliffs, NJ, 1971.

Seligman, M.: *Helplessness: On Depression, Development and Death*. Freeman, San Francisco, 1975.

Smith, A.: *The Theory of Moral Sentiment*, 1758; Liberty Classics, Indianapolis, 1982.

Sugden, R.: *The Economics of Rights, Cooperation and Welfare*. Basil Blackwell, Oxford, 1986.

Thaler, R.: Towards a positive theory of consumer behavior. *Journal of Economic Behavior and Organization 1*, 39–60, 1980.

Tversky, A. & Kahneman, D.: The framing of decisions and the psychology of choice. *Science 211*, 453–8, 1981.

Ullmann-Margalit, E.: *The Emergence of Norms*. Oxford University Press, Oxford, 1977.

Verheller, T. & van Raaij, F.: A behavior cost-benefit approach to the explanation of prediction and behavior. Paper presented at the 10th Annual Colloquium of the International Association for Research on Economic Psychology, Linz, Austria, July, 1985.

Young, H. P.: The evolution of conventions. *Econometrica 61* (1), 57–84, 1993.

A Theory of the Welfare State

Hans-Werner Sinn*

University of Munich, Germany

Abstract

The welfare state can be seen as an insurance device that makes lifetime careers safer, increases risk taking and suffers from moral hazard effects. Adopting this view, the paper studies the trade-off between average income and inequality, evaluating redistributive equilibria from an allocative point of view. It examines the problem of optimal redistributive taxation with tax-induced risk taking and shows that constant returns to risk taking are likely to imply a paradox where more redistribution results in more post-tax inequality. In general, optimal taxation will imply either that the redistribution paradox is present or that the economy operates at a point of its efficiency frontier where more inequality implies a lower average income.

I. Redistribution and Insurance

While this may be the time to turn the welfare state around, it is also the time to warn against throwing the baby out with the bathwater. Economists have learned so much about the Laffer curve, Leviathan, and a myriad of disincentive effects brought about by government intervention that they have lost sight of the allocative advantages of the welfare state.

From an allocative point of view, the main advantage of the welfare state is the insurance or risk reducing function of redistributive taxation. To finance commonly accessible public goods and public transfers, governments take more taxes from the rich than from the poor, thus reducing the variance in real lifetime incomes. To the extent that this variance is not predictable when people are born, this activity can be regarded as welfare increasing insurance. Every insurance contract involves a redistribution of resources from the lucky to the unlucky, and most of the redistributive

*This paper is part of the NBER program on public economics and the CEPR project "Monitoring European Integration". The author wishes to thank the referees and the participants of *SJE's* conference on "The Future of the Welfare State" for useful comments. Research assistance by Marcel Thum is also gratefully acknowledged.

measures of the state can be interpreted as insurance if the time span between judging and taking these measures is sufficiently long. Redistributive taxation and insurance are two sides of the same coin.

It has been argued that the insurance function of the government budget can be privately provided and that redistributive taxation might simply crowd out private insurance; see Kaplow (1991, 1992) and Konrad (1991). This argument certainly has theoretical appeal for a number of specific risks. However, it does not seem applicable to the typical lifetime income risk. It is difficult to imagine endowing private agencies with the extensive monitoring and enforcement rights which the government needs in order to administer an income tax, and in the absence of such rights, moral hazard and adverse selection problems render a broad-based private solution impossible.[1] The insurance provided by the public tax and transfer system is an insurance against the randomness in career opportunities and in nature's lottery draw of innate abilities. Organizing this insurance privately would require signing a contract with a lifelong commitment at the time of birth of an individual; it would approximate bondage, a system long overcome by the course of history. In addition, as pointed out by Christiansen (1990), government insurance may well be cheaper than private insurance given that a system of fiscal taxation is considered inevitable. The marginal cost of making the existing tax system redistributive will, in all likelihood, be lower than the total cost of introducing private income insurance *ab ovo*. Regardless of which of these reasons dominated, the historical growth of the welfare state can, in part, be seen as a response to the inability of the private insurance system to offer the better solution.[2]

While the production of safety is an important function of the welfare state, the Domar–Musgrave effect of increased risk taking may be even more important. Protected by the welfare state, people engage in risky and profitable activities which they otherwise would not have dared to undertake. Risky occupations might not be chosen without the protection of the welfare state, and it would be difficult to find entrepreneurs willing to supervise risky investment if debtor's prison were all that society provided in the case of failure. Perhaps the most important function of the social welfare net is that it makes people jump over the dangerous chasms which would otherwise have put a halt to their economic endeavors.

---

[1] For an explicit adverse selection model where a positive role is left for insurance through the tax system, see Konrad (1992, pp. 126–8).

[2] An enlightening discussion of further reasons for the government's superior ability to absorb income risk is provided by Gordon (1985) and Gordon and Varian (1988). These reasons include intergenerational diversification in the absence of an operative bequest motive as well as diversification in the form of changing the supply of public goods.

It may, in fact, make them too eager to jump. Protected by the welfare state, people may neglect to take necessary care, may take too much risk, and end up in a worse situation than without such protection. This is the moral hazard problem that an overwhelming majority of policy advisors seems to fear. The paper offers a simple model that makes it possible to analyse the interaction between redistributive taxation and risk taking, distinguishing sharply between a desirable increase in risk taking and an overshooting in risk taking due to moral hazard effects.

The effect on risk taking has important repercussions for the observable degree of inequality in the economy, for, if a given set of people choose more risk *ex ante*, they will typically be more unequal *ex post*. Risk averse societies may exhibit relatively little inequality, and the more redistribution there is, the larger the pre-tax inequality tolerated may be. As suggested by Harsanyi (1953, 1955), Rawls (1971) and others, the social welfare function for evaluating the income distribution is taken to be identical with a representative individual's utility function for risk evaluations. However, unlike the argument brought forward by these authors, in the model, people really are behind the veil of ignorance when they make their decisions and evaluate the resulting income distribution. Their amount of risk taking *ex ante* determines their degree of inequality *ex post*.

The main focus here is on the policy trade-off between income equality and average income. It is not on the trade-off between equity and efficiency, because equity is an aspect of efficiency. Will redistributive taxation induce too much or too little risk taking? How does it compare with ideal insurance? Will the pie shrink when it is more evenly distributed? Will more redistribution result in less inequality? What are the characteristics of an optimal redistributive tax system that balances the marginal impacts on the size of the pie and the equality in the slices distributed? These are among the questions addressed in this paper.

While little is known about the issue, there are many important studies on the role of taxation under uncertainty. These include the literature on risk taking and taxation in the context of asset choice, savings or occupational decisions, e.g. Ahsan (1974, 1976), Allingham (1972), Atkinson and Stiglitz (1980, Ch. 4), Bamberg and Richter (1984), Domar and Musgrave (1944), Kanbur (1979), Sandmo (1977) and Sinn (1981), as well as the welfare theoretic literature studying optimal redistributive taxation in the case of income risks, e.g. Diamond, Helms and Mirrlees (1980), Eaton and Rosen (1980), Varian (1980) and Rochet (1991). This paper is an attempt to integrate some of the existing ideas by analyzing the problem of optimal redistributive taxation in the context of tax-induced risk taking. The first literature mentioned has not considered the problem of optimal taxation, and the other has not been concerned with the issue of risk taking. Combining the two issues may offer new insight into the nature of the welfare state and help derive new propositions about the trade-off between income and equality.

In considering the modern literature, it should not be forgotten that the paper's basic themes were first discussed in Friedman's (1953) "Choice, Chance and the Personal Distribution of Income" and Buchanan and Tullock's (1962) *Calculus of Consent*, Chapter 13. The analysis can be understood as an attempt to formalize, apply and develop these path-breaking approaches.

A technical feature distinguishing the present model from the existing literature and allowing new questions to be asked is the location and scale parameter methodology developed by Meyer (1987) and Sinn (1983, 1989) which makes it possible to represent the individual choice problem and the resulting income distribution in a (μ, σ) framework without imposing the usual restrictions on preferences and technologies. Despite the assumption of expected utility maximization, this methodology is based neither on quadratic utility nor on normal distributions. The use of an additional result concerning the required marginal compensation for risk taking reported in Sinn (1990) makes it possible to find strong implications of redistributive taxation while avoiding the familiar ambiguities in the relationship between taxation and risk taking pointed out by Feldstein (1969) and Stiglitz (1969) for the case of fiscal taxation.

II. The Model

A very simple model that is able to incorporate the issues discussed is the following. There is a large number of identical individuals, each facing the same choice problem under uncertainty. With stochastically independent income risks and identical choices, each person's probability distribution of income converts to the economy's frequency distribution of realized incomes. If, say, a single person's probability of having a lifetime income of between $500,000 and $510,000 is 1 per cent, then the law of large numbers will ensure that 1 per cent of the population will have an income in this range. Risk and expected income *ex ante* will turn out as inequality and average income *ex post*.

To reduce the dimensionality of risk, a broad-based definition of income including market income, non-market income (or leisure), public goods and public transfers is used. The risk occurs in the form of an uninsurable lifetime random income loss $L \geq 0$ whose magnitude depends on the random state of nature θ and the cost of self-insurance effort e in terms of foregone market and non-market resources. The variable θ may, for example, reflect the risk in unknown innate abilities or uncontrollable external events, and e may stand for working time or investment in physical and human capital limiting the risk of not reaching one's income goals. Let m and n be the maximum values of market and non-market income attainable if the individual makes no effort and the loss nevertheless happens to be zero, p be the value of transfers (monetary transfers and public goods) received, and T be the individual's tax liability which, among other things, also depends on θ and e. Then the individual's (post-tax) income is

$$Y = m + n - L(e, \theta) - e - T(e, \theta) + p. \tag{1}$$

Effort is chosen before nature has revealed θ. An increase in effort e reduces the size of the income loss for all states of the world, albeit with diminishing marginal returns. It is assumed that[3]

$$L(e, \theta) = \lambda(e)\theta, \qquad \theta \geq 0, \qquad \lambda > 0, \tag{2}$$

$$\lambda' < 0, \qquad \lambda'' \geq 0, \qquad \lambda'(0) = -\infty,$$

where λ is a twice continuously differentiable function reflecting the efficacy of *self-insurance* — to use a term first introduced by Ehrlich and Becker (1972).

There is a linear tax on market income. Let α be the fraction of self-insurance efforts consisting of foregone market income and $1 - \alpha$ the fraction consisting of foregone non-market income (or leisure). Then

$$T(e, \theta) = \tau[m - L(e, \theta) - \alpha e] \tag{3}$$

where τ is the tax rate. Note that, despite the linearity of the tax, the tax system is redistributive because the public transfer p is independent of the state of nature.[4] Lucky individuals are net payers and unlucky net recipients of public funds. While α is treated as an exogenous parameter throughout this paper, τ is endogenously determined in a social optimization problem in Section VI.

To balance the government budget, the public transfer is chosen so as to make it equal to the average tax liability:[5]

$$p = E[T(e, \theta)]. \tag{4}$$

---

[3] Note that this formulation differs significantly from that of Varian (1980) where the individual is assumed to be unable to affect his income risk through his own actions. In Varian's model, the (μ, σ) trade-off specified below would have to be represented by a vertical straight line.

[4] The formal structure of the redistribution mechanism is similar to the progressive linear tax used by Ahsan (1974, 1976) for a portfolio selection problem with fiscal taxation.

[5] Alternatively, it could have been assumed that $p = \Sigma_{j=1}^{x} T(e_j, \theta_j)/x$ where x is the number of individuals in the economy. Because of the assumption of identical choices and stochastic independence of the $\theta_j, j = 1, \ldots, x$, the transfer specified this way converges stochastically to $E[T(e, \theta)]$ as x goes to infinity.

It is assumed that the government can observe m, n and the individual realization of L, and that it learns the tax deduction αe legally claimed by each individual according to the specifications given in the tax law. The government has some statistical information on α which makes it possible to infer the underlying effort level chosen by the average taxpayer, but it may be unable to observe the individual effort level e or be unwilling to make it fully tax deductible.[6] Similarly, the government possesses the statistical information necessary for choosing the transfer p so as to satisfy its budget constraint (4), but it is unable to tailor each individual's transfer p to this individual's expected tax liability. Equation (4) holds in equilibrium without implying that the individual is able to change p through his own actions.

The formulation includes the extreme cases $\alpha = 0$ and $\alpha = 1$. In the case $\alpha = 0$, the opportunity cost of effort occurs exclusively in the form of foregone non-market income, and non-market income is unobservable and untaxed. This case can be interpreted in terms of the familiar labor-leisure distortion if leisure is, in fact, an activity producing non-market income and if the tax is imposed on labor income alone. The tax system discourages the self-insurance effort because this effort cannot be deducted from the tax base. In the case $\alpha = 1$, and only in this case, individual effort is fully observable. It occurs exclusively in the form of foregone market resources and will enjoy full tax deductibility. One may think in particular of pecuniary investment outlays or business expenses that are fully tax deductible. In an intertemporal context, an ideal cash flow tax would be an exact example for the case $\alpha = 1$ because it allows an immediate write-off of investment expenses.[7] A capital income tax with annual economic depreciation allowances would instead be equivalent to $0 < \alpha < 1$, because the present value of depreciation allowances falls short of the investment. It will be shown below that whenever $\alpha < 1$, there is a moral hazard effect in terms of reduced effort strong enough to imply an optimal tax rate less than unity.[8] Only in the theoretical case $\alpha = 1$ would it be optimal to fully develop the welfare state.

It is admissible to assume that there is a perfect private insurance market in the background that has already absorbed some of the risks the individual would otherwise have to bear. It simply had to be assumed that m and n are incomes net of the respective insurance premia where m is an

---

[6] The analysis abstracts from the problem of imperfect observability of losses as may be the case with health insurance; for a discussion of such issues see Diamond and Mirrlees (1978).

[7] The variables of the model would then have to be interpreted in terms of present values.

[8] Note that the case $\alpha < 1$ can also be interpreted as describing a situation where all self-insurance occurs in the form of foregone market resources, but where not all of these resources are tax deductible.

income net of tax deductible, and n an income net of non-deductible, premia.[9] Recall that L is the uninsurable risk in one's lifetime career which may largely result from the randomness in nature's draw of innate abilities.

The income distribution in the economy described is specified once the government has chosen τ and the individuals have chosen e. For the planned analysis of income distributions, it is convenient to describe this distribution in terms of its mean μ (the average income) and its standard deviation σ. It follows from (1)–(4) that

$$\mu = m + n - \lambda(e) E(\theta) - e \tag{5}$$

and

$$\sigma = (1 - \tau)\lambda(e)R(\theta) \tag{6}$$

where $R(\cdot)$ is the standard deviation operator.[10] Equations (5) and (6) show that, with any given amount of self-insurance effort e, redistributive taxation will not affect the average income, μ, but will reduce the deviation from the average, σ. Seen from an *ex-ante* perspective, this is the insurance aspect of redistributive taxation. The important question of how redistributive taxation will in turn affect the amount of effort chosen is postponed to later sections.

Figure 1 depicts the combinations of μ and σ attainable with an appropriate choice of e and for two alternative values of the tax rate: $\tau = 0$ and $\tau > 0$, where σ is the post-tax and σ_G the pre-tax standard deviation of income.

The opportunity set of (μ, σ) combinations attainable with $\tau = 0$ will be called the "self-insurance line" and the set attainable with a given $\tau > 0$ will be called the "redistribution line". Geometrically, the redistribution line can be constructed by shifting all points on the self-insurance line horizontally to the left where the percentage reduction of the distance from the ordinate equals the tax rate. The movements of A, B and C towards A', B' and C' are examples of this shift. It is unclear at this stage which amount of self-insurance effort and which pair of points on the two lines the individual chooses. However, whatever his choice, all attainable post-tax income distributions that satisfy the government's budget constraint (4) are represented by points on the redistribution line.

---

[9] See Rochet (1991) for a model that explicitly incorporates insurable and non-insurable risks where the redistributive tax system covers the latter.

[10] Throughout the paper E and R are used as expectation and standard deviation operators while μ and σ are the mean and standard deviation of post-redistribution income. Recall that

$R(X) = [E(X^2) - E^2(X)]^{1/2}$ and note that $E(a + bX) = a + bE(X)$ and $R(a + bX) = |b| R(X)$.

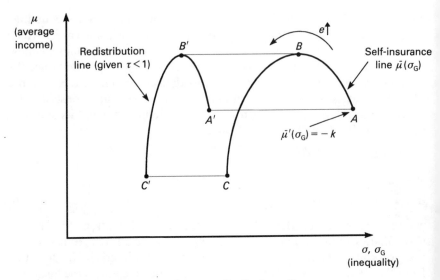

Fig. 1. The sets of feasible pre-tax and post-tax distributions of income.

The pre-tax standard deviation is given by

$$\sigma_G = \lambda(e)R(\theta). \tag{7}$$

Since $\lambda'(e) < 0$ implies that σ_G is a monotonically declining function of e, it is possible to treat σ_G as the choice variable of the individual. Accordingly (5) and (6) can be written as

$$\mu = \bar{\mu}(\sigma_G) \tag{8}$$

and

$$\sigma = (1 - \tau)\sigma_G \tag{9}$$

where

$$\bar{\mu}(\sigma_G) \equiv m + n - E(L) - e$$
$$= m + n - \sigma_G k - \lambda^{-1}[\sigma_G / R(\theta)] \tag{10}$$

is the function defining the self-insurance line with

$$\sigma_G k = E[L(e, \theta)] = \lambda(e)E(\theta) \tag{11}$$

and

$$k \equiv \frac{E(\theta)}{R(\theta)} = \text{const.} > 0. \tag{12}$$

It is easy to derive a boundary condition for the slope of the self-insurance line,[11]

$$\bar{\mu}'(\sigma_G) = -k \qquad \text{when } e = 0, \tag{13}$$

and to show that the line has a maximum where $\lambda'(e)E(\theta) = -1$ and is concave throughout:[12]

$$\bar{\mu}''(\sigma_G) \begin{Bmatrix} < \\ = \end{Bmatrix} 0 \qquad \text{when } \lambda''(e) \begin{Bmatrix} > \\ = \end{Bmatrix} 0. \tag{14}$$

To close the model, the representative agent's preference structure has to be specified. It is assumed that the agent is a globally and locally risk averse expected utility maximizer. Since the set of distributions implied by (1), (2) and (3) forms a linear class, any given von Neumann–Morgenstern function can be exactly represented in terms of (μ, σ) preferences without any loss of generality.[13] Neither quadratic utility nor normality in the distributions have to be assumed. As shown by Meyer (1987) and Sinn (1983, 1989), there exists a well-behaved utility function $U(\mu, \sigma)$ if the von Neumann–Morgenstern function is well behaved. Its properties can best be summarized by the properties of the function

$$i(\mu, \sigma) \equiv \frac{d\mu}{d\sigma}\bigg|_U = -\frac{U_\sigma}{U_\mu} \tag{15}$$

which indicates the indifference-curve slope — required marginal compensation for risk — at a particular combination of μ and σ:

(a) $i(\mu, 0) = 0$ (enter ordinate perpendicularly)
(b) $i(\mu, \sigma) > 0$ for $\sigma > 0$ (upward bending)

---

[11] Equation (13) follows from (5), (7) and the assumption $\lambda'(0) = -\infty$.

[12] It follows from (10) that $\bar{\mu}''(\sigma_G) = \lambda''(e)/[\lambda'^3(e)R^2(\theta)]$. Since $\lambda'' \geq 0$ and $\lambda' < 0$ the sign of this expression is zero or negative.

[13] To prove that the attainable distributions belong to the same linear class, it is necessary to show that the standardized distribution $Z = [Y - E(Y)]/R(Y)$ is independent of the model's choice variables and parameters e, τ and α. Inserting (2) and (3) into (1) gives

$$Z = \frac{m + n - \lambda\theta - e - \tau[m - \lambda\theta - \alpha e] + p - \{m + n - \lambda E(\theta) - e - \tau[m - \lambda E(\theta) - \alpha e] + p\}}{(1 - \tau)\lambda R(\theta)}$$

or, after a few simplifications,

$$z = \frac{-\theta + E(\theta)}{R(\theta)}, \qquad \text{q.e.d.}$$

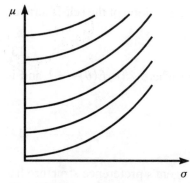

Fig. 2. Evaluating income distributions.

(c) $\left.\dfrac{di}{d\sigma}\right|_{U} > 0$ (strictly convex)

(d) $i_\sigma > 0$ (slope increases with σ, given μ)[14]

(e) $i_\mu \begin{Bmatrix} > \\ = \\ < \end{Bmatrix} 0$ for $\begin{bmatrix} \text{increasing} \\ \text{constant} \\ \text{decreasing} \end{bmatrix}$ absolute risk aversion (slope change with μ, given σ).

Figure 2 illustrates an example of the indifference-curve system for the case of constant absolute risk aversion. While the preference map of Figure 2 makes it possible to evaluate probability distributions, it allows an equally appropriate evaluation of the realized income distributions. Since people have identical risk preferences and since the probability distribution chosen translates into an identical frequency distribution of realized incomes, an unambiguous social welfare function is available.

III. *Laissez Faire* and the Social Optimum

Imposing the "indifference map" of Figure 2 on the "feasibility map" of Figure 1 gives two kinds of optima, illustrated by points T and Q' in Figure 3. Point T is the *laissez-faire* optimum without redistributive taxation and Q' is the optimum with redistribution at a given tax rate $\tau > 0$. Let T' and Q be the counterparts of these two points on the redistribution

---

[14] Condition (d) derives basic results of this paper. It has been proved under the condition that absolute risk aversion is decreasing, is constant, or does not increase faster than with the "fastest" quadratic utility function compatible with strictly positive marginal utility in the relevant range; see Sinn (1990). It is assumed that this extremely weak condition will hold.

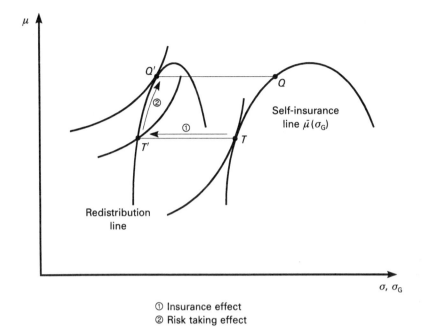

① Insurance effect
② Risk taking effect

Fig. 3. The socially optimal degree of risk taking, given the tax rate.

line and the self-insurance line, respectively.[15] Formally, the two solutions follow from the problem

$$\max_{\sigma_G} U(\mu, \sigma) \qquad \text{s.t. } \mu = \bar{\mu}(\sigma_G), \quad \sigma = (1 - \tau)\sigma_G \qquad (16)$$

which implies the first-order condition

$$i[\bar{\mu}(\sigma_G), (1 - \tau)\sigma_G] = \frac{\bar{\mu}'(\sigma_G)}{1 - \tau}. \qquad (17)$$

the l.h.s. of (17) is the indifference curve slope and the r.h.s. is the slope of the redistribution line. In general, (17) refers to a point like Q'; however, in the limiting case where $\tau = 0$ it also captures the *laissez-faire* solution T.

The solution illustrated in Figure 3 is a constrained Pareto optimum, defining the optimal level of self-insurance effort given the tax rate. It will not necessarily be reached by private actions, since the redistribution line

---

[15] Throughout the paper, points labelled with a prime are located on the redistribution line horizontally left of the respective points without a prime which are located on the self-insurance line. Points labelled by the same letter indicate the same self-insurance effort.

may not coincide with the opportunity set as perceived by the individual. It would, however, be attained in an ideal insurance market where individual actions can be monitored by the company and a fair premium is announced for each self-insurance strategy the individual may choose. It would also be attained if a strict equivalence principle of taxation could be met. The government would have to be able to monitor individual self-insurance activities and announce a separate value of the public transfer for every feasible action, obviously an unrealistic requirement.

Having made these reservations, two lessons can be learned from Figure 3.

Proposition 1. *Under laissez faire, or with ideal insurance, society operates at a point in its opportunity set where an increase in inequality would increase the average income.*

Proposition 2. *Redistributive taxation with individually tailored transfers creates two kinds of welfare gain. It increases welfare by increasing the equality of incomes, and it increases it even more when more risk is taken and some equality is sacrificed for a higher level of average income. The socially optimal level of pre-tax inequality is an increasing function of the tax rate.*

While Proposition 1 is obvious, Proposition 2 needs a

Proof: Assume that $0 < \tau < 1$ and let $r(\cdot)$, $i(\cdot)$, and $s(\cdot)$ denote the slopes of the redistribution line, the indifference curve and the self-insurance line at the respective points (in Figure 3) named in the brackets. By the definition of T, $s(T) = i(T)$ and, because of (8) and (9), $r(T') = r(T)/(1 - \tau) > i(T)$. Property (d) of the indifference curve system ensures that $i(T) > i(T')$. Thus $r(T') > i(T')$. Together with the convexity of the indifference curves and the concavity of $\bar{\mu}$, this implies $\sigma(Q') > \sigma(T')$ and $\sigma_G(Q) > \sigma_G(T)$.[16] While this proves that taxation increases risk taking and pre-tax inequality in the large, the marginal effect of τ on the optimal level of σ_G, $\sigma_G(Q)$, follows from implicitly differentiating (17):

$$\frac{d\sigma_G(Q)}{d\tau} = \frac{i + i_\sigma \sigma_G(Q)(1 - \tau)}{(1 - \tau)\{i_\mu \bar{\mu}[\sigma_G(Q)] + i_\sigma(1 - \tau)\} - \bar{\mu}''[\sigma_G(Q)]} > 0. \tag{18}$$

The denominator of this expression is strictly positive if the second-order condition of problem (17) is satisfied. This is the case since the indif-

---

[16] The notation should be self-explanatory. For example $\sigma(T')$ is the post-tax standard deviation at point T' which is the counterpart of $\sigma_G(T)$, the pre-tax standard deviation. Note that $\sigma(T') = (1 - \tau)\sigma_G(T)$.

ference curves are strictly concave and the redistribution line is convex. The numerator is strictly positive since all items occurring there are strictly positive. (Cf. property (d) of the indifference curve system.) **Q.e.d.**

Proposition 1 is the model's confirmation of the frequently expressed belief that the pie can grow when a more unequal distribution of its slices is tolerated. Risk aversion (or inequality aversion) requires a compromise between the goals of maximizing the size of the pie and minimizing the degree of inequality. It makes it wise to operate at a point on the efficiency frontier where a little more tolerance with regard to the latter makes it possible to come somewhat closer to the former.

Proposition 2 confirms the discussion in the introduction. Given that the government offers public insurance, the need for self-insurance is reduced. Redistributive taxation with individually tailored transfers increases the marginal post-tax return to risk taking (the slope of the redistribution line as compared to that of the self-insurance line) and lowers the marginal compensation for risk taking that the agent requires (the indifference curve slope). This makes it socially optimal to tolerate more risk and inequality in exchange for a higher level of average income. Under the protection of the welfare state, more can be dared.[17]

The risk taking effect of the welfare state may have far-reaching implications. In a broader context, risk can be seen as a factor of production, a necessary input for the economy without which a high level of productivity could not be achieved.[18] The factor "risk" is probably no less important than "waiting", the factor economists have familiarized themselves with under the name of capital. If the real rate of interest is a measure of the importance of waiting and if the unexplained remainder of the "return to capital" is in fact the reward for risk taking, then risk taking should be considered at least as responsible for economic prosperity as capital investment. The enhancement of risk taking may be the most important economic function the welfare state can perform.

IV. Redistributive Taxation and the Optimality of Individual Choice

While the preceding section demonstrated the potential for gains from redistributive taxation under rather unrealistic conditions, this section addresses the more interesting question of whether the exploitation of this

---

[17] Surprisingly, the benefits from increased risk taking have been largely ignored in the insurance literature. Often the insurance-induced increase in risk taking is confused with moral hazard resulting from a lack of observability of individual actions.

[18] See Pigou (1932, Appendix I, pp. 771–81), Sinn (1986) or Konrad (1992).

potential through individual choice can really be expected. The crucial assumption here is that the government transfer p is *not* tailored to the individual decision. The individual agent takes this transfer as exogenous to his own decisions, notwithstanding the fact that it will endogenously be determined in equilibrium through the government budget constraint, equation (4).

The individual opportunity set of decision alternatives is given by equation (1). Taking expectations, noting that $\bar{\mu}(\sigma_G) = m + n - E(L) - e$ from (10), and using (3) yields

$$\mu = \bar{\mu}(\sigma_G) - \tau\{m - E[L(e, \theta)] - \alpha e\} + p. \tag{19}$$

After a few algebraic manipulations making use of (11), equation (19) can also be written as

$$\mu = \bar{\mu}(\sigma_G)(1 - \alpha\tau) - \tau(1 - \alpha)(m - k\sigma_G) + \alpha\tau n + p. \tag{20}$$

The standard deviation as perceived by the individual follows from (1), (3) and (7):

$$\sigma = (1 - \tau)\sigma_G. \tag{21}$$

Since p was also non-stochastic in the social planning problem, this is the same as equation (9). Equations (20) and (21) imply an opportunity locus in (μ, σ) space that will be called the "individual opportunity line".

The agent's optimization problem is

$$\max_{\sigma_G} U(\mu, \sigma) \qquad \text{s.t.} \quad (20) \text{ and } (21). \tag{22}$$

Using (15), the first-order condition of this problem can be written as[19]

$$i(\mu, \sigma) = \bar{\mu}'(\sigma_G) \frac{1 - \alpha\tau}{1 - \tau} + \frac{\tau}{1 - \tau}(1 - \alpha)k. \tag{23}$$

The l.h.s. of equation (23) is the indifference curve slope, and the r.h.s. is the slope of the individual opportunity line.

A redistributive equilibrium is defined as a situation where the agent has chosen σ_G so as to maximize his utility and the government has chosen the public transfer p so as to satisfy its budget constraint (4). In equilibrium, therefore, (23) has to hold on the redistribution line (cf. Figures 1 and 3) which means that the indifference curve slope $i(\mu, \sigma)$ refers to a point where $\mu = \bar{\mu}(\sigma_G)$ and $\sigma = (1 - \tau)\sigma_G$.

---

[19] The second-order condition is satisfied since the indifference curves are convex and (20) and (21) define a concave curve in (μ, σ) space representing the individual opportunity set as perceived by the agent.

A comparison with (17) reveals that the equilibrium satisfying (23) is not in general identical with the constrained Pareto optimum characterized by the pair (Q, Q') in Figure 3. The next three subsections analyze the differences.[20]

Deductible Effects

Consider first the case $\alpha = 1$, where, as explained, the cost of self-insurance occurs exclusively in the form of foregone market resources and will therefore enjoy full tax deductibility (cash flow tax). The implications of (23) for this case are summarized in

Proposition 3. *When self-insurance efforts are fully tax deductible (as with investment under a cash flow tax), redistributive taxation is welfare increasing. In addition to the direct gain from insurance there is a gain from increased risk taking. However, risk taking and the resulting increase in inequality are less than what would be socially optimal.*

Proof: If $\alpha = 1$, condition (23) becomes

$$i[\bar{\mu}(\sigma_G), (1 - \tau)\sigma_G] = \bar{\mu}'(\sigma_G). \tag{24}$$

Assume that $\tau > 0$ and let $i(\cdot)$ and $s(\cdot)$ denote the slopes of the indifference curve and the self-insurance line at the respective points (from Figure 4) named in the brackets. Condition (24) defines a point V' on the redistribution line and its counterpart V horizontally to the right on the self-insurance line such that the indifference curve slope on the redistribution line equals the corresponding slope of the self-insurance line: $i(V') = s(V)$. From (17) it is known that $i(Q') = s(Q)/(1 - \tau) > s(Q)$. On the other hand, property (d) of the indifference curve system and the definition of T imply that $i(T') < i(T) = s(T)$. Continuity implies that a solution exists between T' and Q' on the redistribution line; i.e., $\sigma(T') < \sigma(V') < \sigma(Q')$ and $\sigma_G(T) < \sigma_G(V) < \sigma_G(Q)$, q.e.d.

The intuition for the suboptimality of individual risk taking can best be gained by inspecting (19). Suppose the individual had chosen the socially otpimal level of σ_G and considers a small variation by changing his self-insurance effort. This variation will, in general, change his expected tax liability, $\tau\{m - E(L) - \alpha e\}$. If the public transfer p is changed accordingly so as to satisfy the government budget constraint (4), then the variation in σ_G implies no change in the expected net payment to the government, and, by assumption, expected utility stays constant. However, if p stays constant despite the change in the expected tax liability, expected utility will change. The individual will have an incentive to deviate from the social optimum in

---

[20] The existence of equilibrium is also proved in these subsections.

the direction where the expected tax liability declines and where he can expect to become a net recipient of public funds. Assuming an endogenous change in p would require collective rationality. It is when only individual rationality is available that p has to be taken as exogenous, because the agent knows that his taxes will contribute only a negligible fraction to the government budget and will therefore not be able to affect the volume of public transfers returned.

For the case $\alpha = 1$, this argument implies that the representative agent takes less risk and chooses a lower degree of inequality than is socially optimal, optimality being judged by his own preferences. The expected tax base is $\{m - E(L) - e\}$. Since it differs from the expected income $\bar{\mu}(\sigma_G)$ only by the non-market component of income, n, which is a constant, the expected tax liability can be reduced by lowering income and enjoying the advantage of lower risk.

Figure 4 illustrates this reasoning. The broken line through Q' is the individual opportunity line, given the level of public transfers p that would be paid if the agents chose the socially optimal level of self-insurance effort. The individual believes that he will be able to reach a higher indifference curve by moving to the left of Q'; i.e., by reducing σ_G. In fact, however, if everyone does so, the transfer will have to be reduced and the

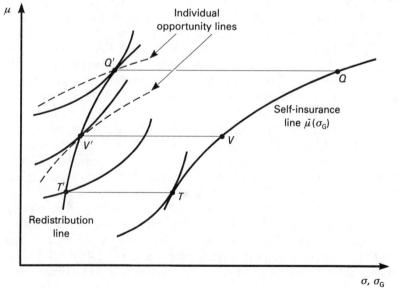

Fig. 4. Less than optimal inequality with full deductibility of self-insurance efforts (cash flow tax).

realized point in (μ, σ) space is pushed down, back to the redistribution line. The equilibrium is at a point such as V'. Here an indifference curve is tangent to an individual opportunity line, and the point of tangency is also on the redistribution line. The individual does not want to change his behavior, and the government budget is balanced.

It is important to note that, although the increase in risk taking is too small, there definitely is such an increase. Redistributive taxation without individually tailored transfers and with full deductibility of self-insurance efforts does not change the marginal post-tax return to risk taking (the slope of the individual opportunity line), but it lowers the required marginal compensation for risk taking (the slope of the indifference curve). This induces the individual to dare more in order to enjoy a higher level of expected income. There are no ambiguities of the kind Feldstein (1969) and Stiglitz (1969) pointed out for the case of fiscal taxation. As the balanced budget condition (4) requires a transfer level equal to the expected tax revenue, there are no income or wealth effects that could increase the size of the required marginal compensation for risk taking. Thus it is clear that there is an increase in risk taking that produces an additional welfare gain beyond the gain from a reduction in uncertainty and inequality that would occur if people did not react to the imposition of the tax system.

Non-deductible Efforts

Consider now the other extreme case $\alpha = 0$. Here, the opportunity cost of effort occurs exclusively in the form of non-market income or leisure foregone, and non-market income or leisure is untaxed (labor income tax).

Inspecting (19) shows that the expected tax base now reduces to $\{m - E(L)\}$. Since m is a constant, the base is smaller the greater $E(L)$ and hence the larger the amount of risk taking as measured by σ_G; cf. equation (11). Thus the intuitive argument raised above suggests that the individual will want to deviate to the right from the social optimum Q' in Figure 5 in order to become a net recipient of public funds. There is an individual opportunity line cutting through the redistribution line at point Q' from below such that a higher indifference curve seems to be attainable by increasing σ and σ_G. Again, however, if everyone behaves that way, the public transfer p will have to be reduced, and the individual's position will be pushed downward, back to the redistribution line. The equilibrium V' where an indifference curve is tangent to the individual opportunity line, and where the point of the tangency is, in addition, located on the re-distribution line, will be to the right of Q', possibly even to the right of the maximum as shown in the figure. This intuitive result is confirmed by

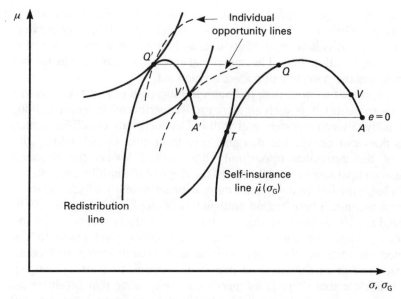

Fig. 5. Excessive inequality without deductibility of self-insurance (labor and income tax).

Proposition 4. *When self-insurance efforts are not tax deductible (as with a labor income tax), there will be some self-insurance effort but not enough: risk taking overshoots the social optimum, and too much inequality will result.*

Proof: In the case $\alpha = 0$, condition (23) becomes

$$\bar{\mu}'(\sigma_G) - i[\bar{\mu}(\sigma_G), (1 - \tau)\sigma_G](1 - \tau) = -\tau k. \tag{25}$$

Assume $0 < \tau < 1$ and let $r(\cdot)$ and $i(\cdot)$ denote the slopes of the self-insurance line and the indifference curve at the respective points (from Figure 5) named in the brackets. Let A be the end point of the self-insurance line where $e = 0$ and recall from (13) that $r(A) = -k$, k being a strictly positive parameter characterizing the distribution of θ (the state of the world). Recall furthermore from (17) that the social optimum is defined by $r(Q) - i(Q')(1 - \tau) = 0$. Equation (25) defines a point V' on the redistribution line and its counterpart V horizontally to the right on the self-insurance line such that $r(V) - i(V')(1 - \tau) = -\tau k$. Since $i \geq 0$, this implies $r(V) > r(A)$ which, because of the concavity of the self-insurance line, defines a point to the left of A. Moreover the concavity of the self-insurance line and the strict convexity of the indifference curves imply that $r(V) - i(V')(1 - \tau) < 0$ can only hold true to the right of the social optimum. Thus $\sigma(Q') < \sigma(V') < \sigma(A')$ and $\sigma_G(Q) < \sigma_G(V) < \sigma_G(A)$, q.e.d.

The General Case

Since $\alpha = 0$ implies too much and $\alpha = 1$ too little inequality relative to the social optimum, there should be an intermediate value of α where the right amount of inequality will be generated. Equating the r.h.s. of (17) and of (23) gives

$$\bar{a}(\sigma_G) = \frac{k}{\bar{\mu}'(\sigma_G) + k} \tag{26}$$

where $\bar{a}(\sigma_G)$ is a function that indicates the level of α that equates the slope of the individual opportunity line with the slope of the redistribution line at a given level of σ_G. Let $\sigma_G(Q)$ be the socially optimal level of σ_G. Then $\alpha = \bar{a}[\sigma_G(Q)]$ will ensure that the equilibrium coincides with the social optimum. Uniqueness of (26) and continuity of (23) imply that higher levels of α will induce too little, and lower levels too much, risk taking and inequality.

Note that the critical level of α depends on the size of the tax rate because the optimal amount of risk taking does so. From Proposition 2 and equation (18) it is known that $\sigma_G(Q)$ is a strictly increasing function of τ. Since $\bar{\mu}'' \leq 0$, the optimal level of α increases with τ where $\bar{\mu}'' < 0$ and stays constant where $\bar{\mu}'' = 0$.

It is known from property (a) of the indifference system that $i(\mu, \sigma) = 0$ when $\sigma = 0$. In the limit, where $\tau \to 1$, this property and equation (17) imply that the socially optimal amount of risk taking, $\sigma_G(Q)$, converges to that value of σ_G where $\bar{\mu}$ has its maximum and $\bar{\mu}' = 0$. The critical level of α will then converge towards unity such that, with any given $\alpha < 1$, there will be too much risk taking.

In fact, when τ goes to unity, effort e approaches zero and $\sigma_G(V)$ approaches $\sigma_G(A)$, the maximum feasible value of σ_G. To see this, rewrite (23) in the form

$$i[\bar{\mu}(\sigma_G), \sigma_G(1 - \tau)](1 - \tau) = (1 - \alpha)\left[\bar{\mu}'(\sigma_G)\frac{1 - \alpha\tau}{1 - \alpha} + \tau k\right]. \tag{27}$$

Clearly, $\tau \to 1$ implies that $\bar{\mu}'(\sigma_G) \to -k$, the condition characterizing point A. Conversely, if $\tau < 1$, an equilibrium at point A is impossible. For one thing, the l.h.s. of (27) is now strictly positive since $i > 0$ and $1 - \tau > 0$. For another, the r.h.s. of (27) would be negative if $\bar{\mu}' = -k$ and $\tau < 1$. This becomes immediately obvious by differentiating the r.h.s. of equation (27) with regard to τ. As the derivative is positive (namely $+k$), $\tau < 1$ implies a value less than zero.

These findings can be summarized as follows.

Proposition 5. *There is a critical value for the deductible proportion of self-insurance efforts greater than zero and smaller than one which generates an equilibrium with the optimal amount of risk taking and inequality. Higher values imply too little risk taking and inequality, lower values too much. The critical value is an increasing function of the tax rate and approaches unity as the tax rate does so.*

Proposition 6. *Assume that the deductible proportion of self-insurance effort is a constant less than one. Then there is always some self-insurance effort if the tax rate is less than one, but this effort will go to zero when the tax rate approaches one. In the limiting case $\tau \to 1$ there is no self-insurance effort and society will operate beyond the maximum of the self-insurance line where a higher average income could be reached by a reduction in pre-tax inequality.*

Proposition 6 confirms the scepticism of those who doubt that redistribution is an efficiency enhancing or even legitimate part of government activity. Since it is rarely the case in practice that all self-insurance efforts are tax deductible $(\alpha = 1)$, it is unavoidable that an ongoing growth of the welfare state will eventually push the economy to the wrong side of its risk-return opportunity space and will tend to eliminate all self-insurance efforts. When the government absorbs all risks, excessive risk taking is the obvious consequence.

The disincentive effects of the welfare state may indeed be so strong that society on the whole loses from the existence of this state. Figure 6

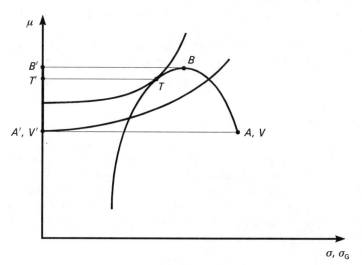

Fig. 6. The welfare loss from an overdrawn welfare state $(\tau \to 1, \alpha < 1)$.

demonstrates such a possibility. Without any protection of the welfare state a point like T is chosen which is located to the left of the maximum of the self-insurance line. With full protection, the redistribution line converges to a straight line on the ordinate which extends from B' to A'. Since the perfect welfare state eliminates all incentives for self-protection, individuals choose the lowest point on the redistribution line ($V' = A'$). In the case at hand, this point is located on a lower indifference curve than the *laissez-faire* point T.

While a, the proportion of self-insurance effort consisting of the consumption of market resources, has been treated as exogenous thus far, the model does have implications for the case where the government can manipulate its size. To be on the safe side it would be better to choose a high value of a rather than a low one.[21] Truly detrimental effects can only occur when a is too small. When it is too high, the welfare gain from redistributional taxation will not be maximal, but at least there will be some gain. The insurance effect will in this case be fully present, and part of the potential welfare gain from risk taking can also be exploited. For practical tax systems this means that a move from capital income taxes towards cash flow taxes on capital is advisable, as are all measures which the optimal tax literature recommends for minimizing the labor-leisure distortion. In particular, the investment in human capital which may be the most important self-insurance activity in a market economy should be made fully tax deductible.

V. The Redistribution Paradox

How redistributive taxation will affect the equality of incomes is an old economic question. With any pre-tax income distribution, the variance of post-tax incomes is clearly reduced by redistributive taxation. However, people may react by taking more risks so that the pre-tax inequality rises. How strong is this countervailing effect? Is it possible that it offsets the primary effect?

Section IV showed, among other things, that the introduction of a linear redistribution system will increase the equilibrium pre-tax inequality. Before the impact of a tax rate change on the post-tax distribution can be considered, the marginal analogue of that result has to be proved.

---

[21] Alternatively it may be advisable to make only a fraction of the income losses tax deductible. However, as can be seen from equation (3), such policy does not offer an additional degree of freedom beyond what can be achieved with an appropriate choice of a and τ.

Proposition 7. *A marginal increase in the tax rate will increase the equilibrium inequality of pre-tax incomes.*

Proof: Implicit differentiation of (23) yields

$$\frac{d\sigma_G}{d\tau} = \frac{i_\sigma \sigma_G + [\beta/(1-\tau)]}{\gamma - \delta} > 0 \tag{28}$$

where

$$\beta \equiv i - \alpha\bar{\mu}'(\sigma_G) + (1-\alpha)k, \tag{29}$$

$$\gamma \equiv i_\mu \bar{\mu}'(\sigma_G) + i_\sigma \cdot (1-\tau), \tag{30}$$

$$\delta \equiv \bar{\mu}''(\sigma_G)(1-\alpha\tau)/(1-\tau). \tag{31}$$

Here, the indifference curve slope i and its derivatives i_μ and i_σ are functions of μ and σ, where $\mu = \bar{\mu}(\sigma_G)$ and $\sigma = (1-\tau)(\sigma_G)$.

To sign (28) consider first the numerator. It is clearly positive. For one thing, property (d) of the indifference curves ensures that $i_\sigma \sigma_G > 0$. For another, if $\alpha\bar{\mu}' - (1-\alpha)k$ is subtracted from both sides of equation (23), it follows after a few algebraic manipulations that

$$\beta = (\bar{\mu}' + k)(1-\alpha)/(1-\tau). \tag{32}$$

Since it is known from Proposition 6 and the preceding discussion that $\bar{\mu}' + k$ is positive and will only in the limiting case $\tau \to 1$ approach zero, it follows that

$$\beta \begin{Bmatrix} > \\ = \end{Bmatrix} 0 \qquad \text{for } \alpha \begin{Bmatrix} < \\ = \end{Bmatrix} 1 \text{ and } \tau < 1, \tag{33}$$

a result that will also be needed below.

Consider the denominator next. The terms γ and δ measure the marginal changes of the slope of the indifference curve and the individual opportunity line, respectively, brought about by a rightward movement *along the redistribution line* (and along neither a given indifference curve nor a given individual opportunity line). It can be shown that $\gamma - \delta > 0$ is a stability condition for the equilibrium and that the existence of a stable equilibrium is ensured.[22] The correspondence principle therefore implies that $d\sigma_G/d\tau > 0$. **Q.e.d.**

Consider now post-tax incomes. Since $\sigma = (1-\tau)\sigma_G$ (from (9) and (21)) is the standard deviation of the income distribution net of taxes and public

---

[22] The complete proof is contained in the Appendix of an earlier version of this paper; see NBER WP 4856, 1994 and CES WP 65, 1994.

transfers, it holds that

$$\frac{\mathrm{d}\sigma}{\mathrm{d}\tau}=(1-\tau)\frac{\mathrm{d}\sigma_G}{\mathrm{d}\tau}-\sigma_G. \tag{34}$$

Using (28), (29) and (30) this expression can be transformed to

$$\frac{\mathrm{d}\sigma}{\mathrm{d}\tau}=\frac{\beta-\sigma_G i_\mu \bar{\mu}'(\sigma_G)+\bar{\mu}''(\sigma_G)[(1-\alpha\tau)/(1-\tau)]}{\gamma-\delta}. \tag{35}$$

The sign of (35) is ambiguous. Since $\gamma-\delta>0$, it equals the sign of the numerator.

Note first that $\mathrm{d}\sigma/\mathrm{d}\tau<0$ if $\bar{\mu}''$ is sufficiently strongly negative. A negative sign for $\bar{\mu}''$ indicates a curved self-insurance line and decreasing returns to risk taking. With a strongly negative value of $\bar{\mu}''$, the scope for individual reactions to a tax increase is small, and obviously the direct effect of a tax increase dominates.

A more interesting possibility is the one where $\bar{\mu}'$ is a positive constant in the relevant range such that $\bar{\mu}''=0$. In this case, equation (35) simplifies to

$$\frac{\mathrm{d}\sigma}{\mathrm{d}\tau}=\frac{\beta-\sigma_G i_\mu \bar{\mu}'}{\gamma-\delta} \quad \text{for } \bar{\mu}'=\text{const.} \tag{36}$$

Recalling property (e) of the indifference curve system and (33) this expression can easily be interpreted.

Proposition 8. *Suppose there are constant returns to risk taking in the relevant range. Then, with decreasing absolute risk aversion $(i_\mu<0)$, an expansion of the redistribution system will imply an equilibrium with more post-tax inequality. The same will be true with constant absolute risk aversion $(i_\mu=0)$ provided that less than 100 per cent of self-insurance efforts are tax deductible. With constant absolute risk aversion and full deductibility of self-insurance efforts, the equilibrium post-tax inequality will not be affected by the tax rate.*[23]

---

[23] The proposition is related to a result that had been derived in another context by Atkinson and Stiglitz (1980, p. 119). These authors studied redistributive taxation in the context of the standard two-asset portfolio problem (where the (μ, σ) trade-off is automatically constant) and found that taxation increases "private risk taking" if the wealth elasticity of demand for the risky asset is positive. There is also a similarity with a problem in traffic regulation where artificial impediments to traffic (like road bumps) lead to an overreaction of drivers, implying an increase in safety despite the deterioration of driving conditions; see Risa (1994). I am grateful to Kjell Erik Lommerud for leading me to this paper.

Proposition 8 describes a redistribution paradox because it specifies conditions under which the primary effect of increased taxes on equality will be overcompensated by the secondary effect of increased risk taking. This gives a deeper meaning to the statement made in the introduction that the risk taking effect of redistributive taxation may be more important than the insurance effect. In the cases considered, people transform more than 100 per cent of the increase in equality through redistributive taxation into income increases. Redistributive taxation does not improve the distribution of the pie's slices, but it makes the pie bigger.

An intuitive explanation of Proposition 8 can be given using Figure 7. This figure incorporates the cases of constant and decreasing absolute risk aversion and assumes that α equals unity (full deductibility of effort). The self-insurance line is linear in the relevant range, and so is the redistribution line. The equilibrium is characterized by a point on the redistribution line which is also a point of tangency between an indifference curve and the individual opportunity line. Depending on the level of government transfers, the latter can have a continuum of alternative positions. For the case at hand ($\alpha = 1$), it is known from (24) that the individual opportunity line has the same slope as the self-insurance line. The possible positions of the

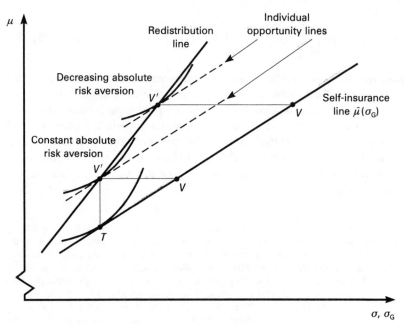

Fig. 7. More inequality through redistributive taxation.

individual opportunity line can therefore be constructed by parallel shifts of the self-insurance line to the left. When absolute risk aversion is constant, the indifference curve slope stays constant when μ increases, given σ ($i_\mu = 0$). The equilibrium point V' on the redistribution line will therefore be vertically above the *laissez-faire* point T, while the point characterizing the pre-tax distribution shifts from T to V on the self-insurance line. The advantage of the protection that the redistribution scheme offers is entirely translated into a higher average income.

On the basis of this neutrality result, it is easy to see under which conditions the equilibrium point V' will be to the right of the *laissez-faire* point T. A first and obvious possibility is the case where, vertically above T, the indifference-curve slope is lower than at T. This case prevails under decreasing absolute risk aversion. For any given level of post-tax inequality, pre-tax inequality and average income rise with an introduction of the redistribution scheme. The rise in average income lowers the required marginal compensation of risk taking, $i(\mu, \sigma)$. The actual marginal compensation perceived by the individual, $\bar{\mu}'$, is constant, on the other hand. Hence, an equilibrium with a higher level of post-tax inequality will result. Figure 5 illustrates this with the upper of the two solution points labelled V'.

The second reason (not shown in the figure) for an equilibrium with a higher inequality in post-tax incomes is incomplete deductibility of self-insurance efforts ($\alpha < 1$). Incomplete deductibility means that the decision maker perceives an additional incentive to reduce his effort and to move along the self-insurance line towards higher values of pre-tax inequality. In Figure 7, the individual opportunity line would have a higher slope than the self-insurance line and so the solution point V' would be to the right of T even in the case where absolute risk aversion is constant ($i_\mu = 0$).[24]

The conditions under which the redistribution paradox emerges are not implausible. From an empirical point of view, there can be little doubt that decreasing absolute risk aversion and less than full deductibility of self-insurance efforts are realistic assumptions. So the assumption of constant returns to risk taking is crucial. With the specifications of this model, this assumption is only a limiting case. However, other model specifications may rather give the impression that constant returns to scale are an intermediate case in the spectrum of possibilities. For example, when there are decreasing returns to self-insurance while, at the same time, it is possible for an agent to add up independent income risks, then it is entirely unclear whether there will be increasing or decreasing returns to risk taking, since adding up independent income risks in itself implies increas-

---

[24] This effect is operative even when $\bar{\mu}' = 0$. Cf. the next section, in particular equation (40).

ing returns to risk taking. Increasing returns to risk taking would strengthen the mechanism underlying the redistribution paradox.

VI. The Optimal Welfare State

Up till now it has been assumed that the government is a fairly passive
agent satisfying itself with adjusting the public transfer so as to balance the
government budget. What if the government chooses the tax rate so as to
maximize the representative individual's expected utility? What are the
characteristics of the optimal welfare state?

To make the problem interesting it has to be assumed that $\alpha < 1$ so that
at least some moral hazard effect is present. With $\alpha = 1$ the model would
predict an optimal tax rate of one, since successive tax increases would
always generate welfare increasing insurance and risk taking effects.
Assuming that at least part of the agent's effort results in a loss of non-
market income (i.e., leisure or goods produced and consumed during
"leisure" time) is common to the optimal tax literature. Without this
assumption the optimal tax problem would not yield an intermediate
solution.

The problem of optimal taxation is illustrated in Figure 8. For every tax
rate τ, there is an equilibrium as described by equation (23). Starting from
the *laissez-faire* point T, an increase in the tax rate will therefore induce a
movement to the right along the self-insurance line (Proposition 7). In
addition, the tax increase will move the redistribution line (cf. Figure 1) to
the left. The net effect on the equilibrium combinations of μ and σ
attainable through successive tax rate changes is illustrated by the arrowed
curve in Figure 8 which will be called the "equilibrium line". It is known
from Proposition 6 that the equilibrium line ends at point A' on the
ordinate when the tax rate approaches one. (A' is the counterpart of A on
the self-insurance line which is characterized by an absence of self-
insurance effort.) The optimal tax rate is determined by a point like Z'
where an indifference curve is tangent to the equilibrium line. Z' and its
counterpart Z on the self-insurance line coincide with points like V' and V
in Figure 5 if that figure is drawn for the optimal tax rate. The magnitude
of the tax rate equals the distance $Z'Z$ relative to the distance between Z
and the ordinate.

Let $\bar{\sigma}_G(\tau)$ be a function that summarizes the relationship between the
equilibrium amount of pre-tax inequality and the tax rate as calculated
with (28). Then the problem of optimal taxation can be stated as follows:[25]

---

[25] This formulation incorporates the government budget constraint through the assumption
$\mu = \bar{\mu}(\sigma_G)$.

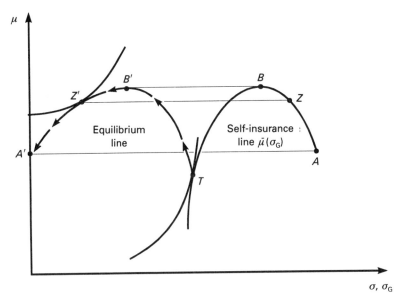

Fig. 8. One version of the optimal tax problem.

$$\max_{\tau} U(\mu, \sigma) \quad \text{s.t. } \mu = \bar{\mu}(\sigma_G), \quad \sigma = (1 - \tau)\sigma_G, \quad \sigma_G = \bar{\sigma}_G(\tau). \tag{37}$$

Let $(\mathrm{d}U/\mathrm{d}\tau)/U_\mu$ denote the tax-induced welfare change in terms of certainty equivalents or what Atkinson (1970) called "equally distributed equivalent incomes". Differentiation of $U(\mu, \sigma)$ yields:

$$\frac{\mathrm{d}U/\mathrm{d}\tau}{U_\mu} = i\sigma_G + \bar{\sigma}'_G(\tau)[\bar{\mu}'(\sigma_G) - i(1 - \tau)] \tag{38}$$

where $i = i(\mu, \sigma)$ is the indifference curve slope as defined in (15). A change in the tax rate generally alters μ and σ. The r.h.s. of equation (38) evaluates these alterations. The term $i\sigma_G$ is the direct gain from redistribu- $\bar{\sigma}'_G(\tau)[\bar{\mu}' - i(1 - \tau)]$ is the welfare change resulting from the increase in risk taking: it consists of a change in per capita income, $\bar{\sigma}'_G\bar{\mu}'$, and a change in post-tax inequality evaluated at the individual's "price of risk" (the indifference curve slope), $\bar{\sigma}'_G i(1 - \tau)$.

From (17) it is known that, if risk taking is at the socially optimal level given the tax rate, then $\bar{\mu}' - i(1 - \tau) = 0$. As this includes the *laissez-faire* situation where $\tau = 0$, the first bit of redistributive taxation must increase welfare through the direct gain from redistribution; i.e., $(\mathrm{d}U/\mathrm{d}\tau)/U_\mu = i \cdot \sigma_G > 0$ at $\tau = 0$. At $\tau = 1$, according to Proposition 6, effort is zero so that $\bar{\mu}' = -k < 0$. Since, in addition, $i = i(\mu, \sigma) = 0$, from property (a) of the indifference curve system, the marginal increase in welfare approaches $(\mathrm{d}U/\mathrm{d}\tau)/U_\mu = -\bar{\sigma}'_G(\tau)k < 0$ as $\tau \to 1$. This implies that there is an interior solution for the optimal tax rate such as the one illustrated in Figure 8.

In the optimum, it is necessary that $(\mathrm{d}\mu/\mathrm{d}\tau)/U_\mu = 0$, which means that the welfare gain from the insurance effect is outweighed by a welfare loss resulting from excessive risk taking:

$$i\sigma_G = -\bar{\sigma}'_G(\tau)[\bar{\mu}'(\sigma_G) - i(1-\tau)] > 0. \tag{39}$$

Since $i\sigma_G > 0$ and $\bar{\sigma}'_G > 0$, it is necessary for (39) to be true that $\bar{\mu}'/(1-\tau) < i$. A comparison with (17) shows that this condition implies an equilibrium point on the redistribution line to the right of the constrained social optimum Q'. The result can be summarized as follows.

Proposition 9. *When self-insurance efforts are not fully tax deductible, there is an interior solution for the socially optimal tax rate. In the optimum, risk taking and inequality overshoot the constrained social optimum, given a tax rate at the level of the optimal rate.*

The overshooting of risk taking may be substantial. In the case considered in Figure 8, it even implies moving to a point to the right of the maximum of the self-insurance line, where the marginal return to risk taking is negative.

Figure 8 does not, however, depict the only possible case. An alternative possibility is illustrated in Figure 9. Here the equilibrium line performs a loop, and the optimal size of the redistributive system is found before the maxima of the self-insurance line and the equilibrium line are reached. The solution is now located in the range of positive marginal returns to risk taking (albeit still in the range where the marginal return to risk taking is unable to compensate for the resulting marginal increase in inequality).

Since σ_G is a monotonically increasing function of τ, and μ is a concave function of σ_G, a necessary and sufficient condition for a loop in the equilibrium line is that, at the maxima of the two curves, a redistribution paradox is present; i.e., it is necessary that, in the neighborhood of the point where $\bar{\mu}' = 0$, post-tax inequality rises with an increase in the tax rate.

To check whether and under what conditions this can be the case, insert (29), (30) and (31) into (35). If $\bar{\mu}' = 0$, this expression becomes

$$\frac{\mathrm{d}\sigma}{\mathrm{d}\tau} = \frac{i + (1-a)k + \bar{\mu}''[(1-a\tau)/(1-\tau)]}{i_o(1-\tau) - \bar{\mu}''[(1-a\tau)/(1-\tau)]}. \tag{40}$$

Equation (40) shows that the curvature of the self-insurance line, $|\bar{\mu}''|$, is essential for the existence of a loop. If the self-insurance line is sufficiently

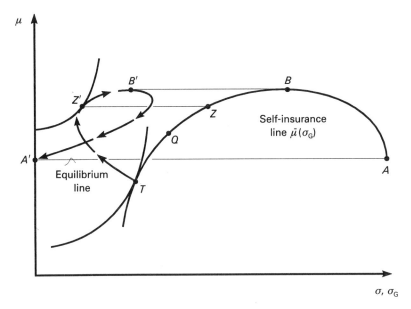

Fig. 9. Optimal taxation and the redistribution paradox.

curved, then $d\sigma/d\tau < 0$ and there will be no loop. If it is sufficiently flat, there will be one. General continuity arguments imply that $d\sigma/d\tau$ will be strictly positive in the neighborhood of the maximum of $\bar{\mu}(\sigma_G)$ if $|\bar{\mu}''|$ stays sufficiently small in that neighborhood.

The interesting aspect of the solution illustrated in Figure 9 is that the redistribution paradox is present when the size of the welfare state has been optimized. A marginal increase in the tax rate increases average income, but this advantage is outweighed by an increase in post-tax inequality.

The nature of the two kinds of solution becomes apparent when equation (34) is inserted into (39). The resulting version of the optimality condition,

$$\frac{d\sigma_G}{d\tau}\,\bar{\mu}'(\sigma_G) = i\,\frac{d\sigma}{d\tau}, \tag{41}$$

shows that $\bar{\mu}'$ and $d\sigma/d\tau$ will have the same sign. In the case depicted in Figure 9, the common sign is positive; in the case depicted in Figure 9 it is negative. The following proposition emphasizes the interesting aspects of this result.

Proposition 10. *With an optimal size of the redistributive tax system, one of the two following conditions will hold. Either the economy operates at a point on its self-insurance line where, given the tax rate, more inequality results in a smaller average income, or more redistribution causes more inequality in post-tax incomes and a higher average income.*

Although it contradicts popular views, Proposition 10 is a very natural and straightforward implication of a preference for equality when — as in the present model — the inequality of pre-tax incomes is an increasing function of the tax rate. Obviously, in the optimum, a marginal tax change must not induce adverse movements of average income and post-tax inequality for, if it did, a tax reform could be designed that increases welfare. Instead a marginal tax change must either decrease post-tax inequality and average income or have precisely the reverse effect. In the former case, a fall in average income coincides with an increase in pre-tax inequality; thus, given the redistribution scheme, the economy's technology implies a positive relationship between the size of the pie and the equality in the distribution of its slices. In the latter case, more redistribution increases the pie, but makes its distribution more unequal.

VII. Concluding Remarks

This analysis has countered popular views concerning the role of the welfare state. It is not true that the welfare state will always reduce inequality and it is not true that it will always make the pie smaller. The paper has studied cases confirming the conventional wisdom, but it has also emphasized the important role of the welfare state as a device for stimulating risk taking, thereby liberating productive forces and increasing aggregate income. Under constant returns to risk taking, the stimulus is likely to be so strong that more than 100 per cent of the risk consolidating effect of the welfare state is being translated into an income increase. Thus, the welfare state would make people richer, but not necessarily more equal and not necessarily happier. In fact, the moral hazard effect resulting from a likely imperfect deductibility of individual effort produces a welfare loss which needs to be subtracted from the welfare gain which under ideal circumstances could be achieved.

One of the less satisfactory aspects of this paper concerns the way the risk-return trade-off has been modeled. There are certainly alternatives to the self-insurance specification chosen here. Pigou (1932) once called risk a "forgotten factor of production", alluding to the prominent role classical economists had attributed to risk taking. Indeed it seems that theoretical and empirical research on the productive effects of risk taking would be highly rewarding.

References

Ahsan, S. M.: Progression and risk-taking. *Oxford Economic Papers 26*, 318-28, 1974.
Ahsan, S. M.: Taxation in a two-period temporal model of consumption and portfolio allocation. *Journal of Public Economics 5*, 337-52, 1976.
Allingham, M. G.: Risk taking and taxation. *Zeitschrift für Nationalökonomie 32*, 203-24, 1972.
Atkinson, A. B.: On the measurement of inequality. *Journal of Economic Theory 2*, 244-63, 1970.
Atkinson, A. B. & Stiglitz, J.: *Lectures on Public Economics*. McGraw-Hill, New York, 1980.
Bamberg, G. & Richter, W. F.: The effects of progressive taxation on risk-taking. *Zeitschrift für Nationalökonomie 44*, 93-102, 1984.
Buchanan, J. M. & Tullock, G.: *The Calculus of Consent*. University of Michigan Press, Ann Arbor, 1962.
Christiansen, V.: Subsidization of risky investment under income taxation and moral hazard. Warwick Economic Research Paper 357, 1990.
Diamond, P. H., Helms, L. J. & Mirrlees, J. A.: Optimal taxation in a stochastic economy. *Journal of Public Economics 14*, 1-29, 1980.
Diamond, P. H. & Mirrlees, J. A.: A model of social insurance with variable retirement. *Journal of Public Economics 10*, 295-336, 1978.
Domar, E. & Musgrave, R. A.: Proportional income taxation and risk-taking. *Quarterly Journal of Economics 58*, 388-422, 1944.
Eaton, J. & Rosen, H. S.: Optimal redistributive taxation and uncertainty. *Quarterly Journal of Economics 95*, 1980, 357-64, 1980.
Ehrlich, I. & Becker, G. S.: Market insurance, self-insurance, and self-protection. *Journal of Political Economy 80*, 623-48, 1972.
Feldstein, M.: The effects of taxation on risk taking. *Journal of Political Economy 77*, 755-64, 1969.
Friedman, M.: Choice, chance, and the personal distribution of income. *Journal of Political Economy 61*, 277-90, 1953.
Gordon, R. H.: Taxation of corporate capital income: Tax revenues versus tax distortions. *Quarterly Journal of Economics 100*, 1-27, 1985.
Gordon, R. H. & Varian, H.: Intergenerational risk sharing. *Journal of Public Economics 37*, 1988, 185-202, 1988.
Harsanyi, J. C.: Cardinal utility in welfare economics and the theory of risk-taking. *Journal of Political Economy 61*, 434-5, 1953.
Harsanyi, J. C.: Cardinal welfare, individualistic ethics and interpersonal comparisons of utility. *Journal of Political Economy 63*, 309-21, 1955.
Kanbur, R.: Of risk taking and the personal distribution of income. *Journal of Political Economy 87*, 769-97, 1979.
Kaplow, L.: A note on taxation as social insurance for uncertain labor income. NBER WP 3708, 1991.
Kaplow, L.: Income tax deductions for losses as insurance. *American Economic Review 82*, 1013-17, 1992.
Konrad, K.: Risk taking and taxation in complete capital markets. *Geneva Papers on Risk and Insurance Theory 16*, 167-77, 1991.
Konrad, K.: *Risikoproduktivität*. Springer, Berlin, Heidelberg, New York, 1992.
Meyer, J.: Two-moment decision models and expected utility maximization. *American Economic Review 77*, 421-30, 1987.
Pigou, A. C.: *The Economics of Welfare*. McMillan, London, 1932.

Rawls, J.: *A Theory of Justice.* Harvard University Press, Cambridge, MA, 1971.

Risa, A. E.: Adverse incentives from improved technology: Traffic safety and regulation in Norway. *Southern Economic Journal 60,* 844–57, 1994.

Rochet, J.-C.: Incentives, redistribution and social insurance. *Geneva Papers on Risk and Insurance Theory 16,* 143–65, 1991.

Sandmo, A.: Portfolio choice, asset demand and taxation. *Review of Economic Studies 44,* 369–79, 1977.

Sinn, H.-W.: Die Grenzen des Versicherungsstaates. Theoretische Bemerkungen zum Thema Einkommensumverteilung, Versicherung und Wohlfart. In H. Göppl & R. Henn (eds.), *Geld, Banken und Versicherungen,* Athenäum, Königstein; 907–28, 1981; reprinted in G. Rolf, P. B. Spahn & G. Wagner (eds.), *Sozialvertrag und Sicherung — Zur ökonomischen Theorie staatlicher Versicherungs- und Umverteilungssysteme,* Campus, Frankfurt and New York, 65–84, 1988.

Sinn, H.-W.: *Economic Decisions under Uncertainty.* North Holland, Amsterdam, New York and Oxford, 1983.

Sinn, H.-W.: Risiko als Produktionsfaktor. *Jahrbücher für Nationalökonomie und Statistik 201,* 557–71, 1986.

Sinn, H.-W.: Two-moment decision models and expected utility maximization: Comment. *American Economic Review 79,* 601–2, 1989.

Sinn, H.-W., Expected utility, μ, σ preferences, and linear distribution classes: A further result. *Journal of Risk and Uncertainty 3,* 277–81, 1990.

Stiglitz, J. E.: The effects of income, wealth, and capital gains taxation on risk taking. *Quarterly Journal of Economics 83,* 263–83, 1969.

Varian, H. R.: Redistributive taxation as social insurance. *Journal of Public Economics 14,* 49–68, 1980.

Factor Mobility, Risk and Redistribution in the Welfare State

David E. Wildasin *

Vanderbilt University, Nashville TN, USA

Abstract

Economic integration reduces the costs of factor mobility, producing efficiency gains and contributing to equalization of net factor returns. This raises the *cost* of income-redistribution policy, thus threatening a basic function of the welfare state. A simple model of costly factor mobility under uncertainty shows that greater factor mobility enables factor owners to pool industry-specific, region-specific or occupation-specific risks (due to uncertain technology or terms of trade). Economic integration may thus reduce some of the potential social insurance *benefits* of redistributive policy.

I. Introduction

Economic integration is not easy to define a precise way, but in general it is clear that technological and political change over the past half-century or more has lowered the cost of many types of transactions among spatially separated agents. Better communication and transportation, the spread of knowledge about market opportunities and commercial practice, the liberalization of many types of economic policy through such institutions as the European Union and the North American Free Trade Agreement, and the collapse of the planning mechanisms of the state-dominated

---

* Earlier versions were presented at meetings of the Regional Science Association, Niagara Falls, and Allied Social Science Associations, Washington, DC, at the *SJE's* conference on "The Future of the Welfare State" and at conferences on "Topics in Public Ecnomics", Tel Aviv University, and "Distributional Aspects of Fiscal Policy: The Implications of Economic Integration", University of Essex. I am grateful to J. Burbidge, R. Musgrave, J. Rust, R. Schoeb, Y. Weiss and other participants, G. Eskeland, P. Mieszkowski, two anonymous referees and the editors for many useful comments. This reseach was initiated during a visit to the Norwegian School of Economics and Business Administration and continued at the Public Economics Division of the World Bank. I am grateful to these institutions for their hospitality and support.

economies of Eastern Europe and the former Soviet Union all exemplify and contribute to this trend. Goods and services now flow more freely within and among regions, businesses can attract capital from more fully developed and interlinked capital markets, and workers can move more freely among different jurisdictions. Increased interjurisdictional linkages of markets for goods and factors change significantly the economic environment within which government fiscal and other policies are implemented. In particular, income redistribution and social insurance policies, which more than any others define the modern welfare state, directly impinge upon and attempt to alter the equilibrium outcomes of factor markets.[1] Their effects are likely to depend sensitively on the nature of these markets. How does factor market integration affect income inequality and risk and what are its implications for social policies that deal with inequality and risk?

It may be noted, first, that increased integration of factor markets can impose new constraints on the ability of governments to engage in income redistribution. The potential mobility of factors of production in response to fiscal differentials underlies traditional arguments for centralization of the redistributive functions of government; see e.g. Oates (1972). Increased internationalization of factor markets implies that such a "central" government, i.e., one whose geographical extent coincides with that of the relevant factor market, cannot ordinarily be understood as a "national" government. The redistributive function of government has become increasingly decentralized over time due to the expanded geographical scope of the ambient factor markets within which redistributive policies are executed. However, while greater factor mobility may add constraints to the ability of governments to redistribute income, it can also in itself provide a form of market insurance against income risk. Access to "external" factor markets limits the extent of factor price variation through spatial arbitrage and may, to some degree, obviate the need for public sector insurance of such risks. Here, this aspect of increasing factor market integration is investigated for the insurance and redistributive role of the public sector. Recent macroeconomic literature (e.g. analyses of optimal currency areas; see De Grauwe (1992) and Eichengreen (1993) and references therein) have emphasized the possibility of risk *pooling* through centralized fiscal systems with immobile factors of production. The analysis here emphasizes risk *shifting*, and changes in the welfare costs of

---

[1] In a "short-run" and *ex post* sense, many welfare-state policies are redistributive in nature. From a "long-run" and *ex ante* perspective, however, they can also be viewed as insurance programs. Many authors have commented on the "social insurance" view of government income redistribution policy, and this view may indeed be one of the foundations of the modern welfare state; see e.g. Atkinson (1987, Section 2.3) and references therein to work by Harsanyi, Buchanan, Rawls, Varian and others.

redistribution, due to the increased mobility of some but not all factors of production.

Section II develops a model in which one immobile and one potentially mobile factor of production are employed together in a risky production process. The degree of integration of the market for the potentially mobile factor is parameterized by a mobility cost parameter. Section III investigates the impact of variations in this parameter to show how changes in factor mobility affect factor pricing and income risk, with or without government redistributive policies. While many of the most important results are quite general, the analysis is worked out in particular detail for a special case in which the possible consequences of factor market integration are especially striking. Section IV identifies some questions for further research.

II. The Model

It is helpful to begin by illustrating some of the basic ideas of the model with a simple parable. Imagine a group of specialized regions, in each of which workers produce a region-specific commodity for export, and suppose that regional weather conditions and the prices of export goods on external markets vary randomly and, to at least some degree, independently. If workers are unable to leave their native regions for alternative types of employment, the regional market-clearing wages will depend on region-specific weather and price realizations, so that, in a given year, some workers will experience high incomes while others have low incomes. If all of these regions were within the jurisdiction of a single government, it would be possible, in principle, to devise a system of taxes and transfers that would pool some or all of this income risk. If there is no such government and no market mechanisms through which to insure against these risks, however, the workers must simply absorb their regional income shocks.

Now suppose that it becomes possible for workers to move from one region to another after they observe the weather and the market price for the goods produced in each region. As long as the random shocks to each region are not perfectly correlated, the returns to workers will be higher in some regions than in others, and workers will tend to move from low-wage to high-wage regions. In doing so, they carry out a form of spatial arbitrage that brings wages in different regions closer together. They also improve the efficiency of resource allocation, increasing the total value of production. In the limit, if migration is costless, wages must be equalized among regions, so that all region-specific risk is perfectly pooled and the *ex post* distribution of income among workers is perfectly equal. In short, *the integration of labor markets can itself insure workers from income risk, obviating the need for any explicit private or public insurance.* Indeed, whereas such insurance might be valuable when the regional labor markets are completely isolated from each other, it might be harmful in the case where the markets are integrated. At least it would reduce the incentives for workers to relocate from low- to high-wage regions.

This parable suggests how the integration of factor markets can bring about both greater efficiency of resource allocation as well as greater equality in the distribution of income. It suggests that government policies that attempt to mitigate income risk may be more harmful to the efficiency of resource allocation as markets become more integrated, and it also suggests that the benefits of those policies may diminish as well. Perhaps, then, increased factor mobility associated with economic integration weakens the rationale for some of the traditional redistributive functions of the welfare state, both by making those functions more costly and by reducing whatever insurance benefits they might have provided.

Although the parable is suggestive, it is both imprecise and incomplete. Equilibrium models of factor mobility most naturally are based on the existence of some *immobile* factor. The presence of immobile factors implies that production in each region exhibits diminishing returns to mobile factors, giving rise to equilibrating adjustments of factor prices in response to factor migration.[2] The presence of immobile factors is also important in the analysis of income redistribution policy, since some degree of immobility is necessary for such policies to have any real effects on income distribution. If the existence of immobile factors is acknowledged, one must ask how the increasing mobility of some factors interacts with the pricing of other, less mobile factors and the income risk to which they are exposed. How do the incidence and allocative effects of redistributive policies depend on the presence of multiple factors with simultaneously determined prices? The interplay between mobile and immobile factors features prominently in the following analysis and differs from many macro models which assume complete factor immobility (e.g. models of optimal currency areas with centralized fiscal systems that pool risk among regions).[3]

---

[2] In the absence of fixed factors, there is no mechanism to stop the flow of factors from low-to high-return locations, other than *a priori* given migration costs. While such migration costs are certainly important, they do not in themselves offer a very complete or insightful theory of interregional factor allocations.

[3] See e.g. De Grauwe (1992), Bureau and Champsaur (1992), Drèze (1993) and Persson and Tabellini (1993) and, for a survey and additional references to the literature, Eichengreen (1993). Factor mobility, and the relationship between factor mobility, general equilibrium factor pricing, and the sharing of risk through factor markets are not generally considered in these discussions. By assuming a given degree of factor market integration, previous analyses take underlying income risks as given, whereas the impact of integration on the

To address these questions, a more formal analysis is necessary. Thus, consider an economy in which a single homogeneous output x is produced using one potentially variable factor of production, m, and one or more fixed factors. The production technology is subject to uncertainty, represented by a random variable θ, and is characterized by diminishing returns to m:

$$x = f(m, \theta), \qquad f_m > 0 > f_{mm}. \tag{1}$$

Note that the model is fundamentally static, with production occurring once after the realization of a single random shock. Factor markets are perfectly competitive and the price of the variable factor is determined after the state of the world is known. Expressing all prices relative to the homogeneous output, the return per unit of the variable factor is thus

$$w = f_m(m, \theta), \tag{2}$$

which, in general, is random. The returns to the fixed factors are given by

$$r = f(m, \theta) - wm \tag{3}$$

and are random, in general. It is assumed here that *factor owners are unable to buy private insurance against factor price fluctuations, so that they do bear income risk when factor prices vary.* Some of the issues that arise in the presence of such insurance are briefly discussed in the conclusion.

Factor supplies are perfectly inelastic at the level of individual households, so that labor/leisure, consumption/saving, and human capital investment decisions are ignored. The initial domestic endowment of the variable factor is denoted by $\bar{m}$. When this factor is mobile, the amount of the input used in local production, m, may differ from $\bar{m}$ either because of imports from external sources $(\bar{m} < m)$ or because of exports to the external market $(\bar{m} > m)$; mobility is the only source of factor variability. As one central case, the variable factor could be labor, with $\bar{m}$ the initial native population of mobile workers, and the fixed factor could be land and capital owned by other (non-mobile worker) native residents. In this case, movement of the variable factor corresponds to immigration or emigration. The analysis does not, however, require factors of production to be owned by (initial) domestic residents.

---

magnitude and distribution of these risks is a central issue here. Bureau and Richard (1994) provide a recent analysis of some of the implications of factor mobility for public insurance mechanisms. Analyses of convergence among regions, e.g. Barro and Sala-i-Martin (1991), have drawn attention to the potential importance of factor mobility but tend to focus on total per capita income variation among regions rather than the implications of partial factor mobility for the distribution of income and income risk within regions by type of factor. The analytical framework of Boadway and Wildasin (1990) is similar to that presented here but the focus there is on centralized rather than decentralized redistributive policy.

The domestic government may drive a wedge between gross and net factor returns through the use of (source-based) taxes and transfers. Let t denote a tax (or transfer, if negative) paid by (or to) the owners of the variable factor, so that its net domestic return is $w - t$. In general, t is allowed to depend on the state of nature or (equivalently) to depend on the realized income of the variable factor. The government budget constraint requires that taxes paid by the owners of one factor be transferred to the owners of the other factor, so that the net return to the owners of the immobile factors is given by $r + tm$.[4]

The level of employment of the variable factor is determined by factor mobility, which may be costly. Let $\bar{w}$ denote the certain net return to the variable input on external markets, taken as exogenously fixed. Let c be the per-unit cost of moving the variable factor into or out of the domestic economy. Migration equilibrium requires that the net return to the variable factor be equalized across locations, net of migration costs, i.e.,

$$\bar{w} - c \leq w - t \leq \bar{w} + c \tag{4a}$$

$$m > \bar{m} \rightarrow w - t = \bar{w} + c \tag{4b}$$

$$m < \bar{m} \rightarrow w - t = \bar{w} - c \tag{4c}$$

$$\bar{w} - c < w - t < \bar{w} + c \rightarrow m = \bar{m}. \tag{4d}$$

Substituting from (2), equations (4) determine the equilibrium value of m conditional on the state of the world θ and on the tax/transfer policy t.

A special case. Given the state of the world and the redistributive policy of the domestic government, the system of equations and inequalities in (2) and (4) constitutes a simple general equilibrium model that can be used to

---

[4] It is trivial to allow for other exogenously fixed government expenditures or revenues, but since none of the results are affected by ignoring such policies, they are omitted for ease of exposition. If provision levels are held fixed, expenditures on pure or non-rival public goods would not vary with factor movements. Differences in levels of provision among regions, like differences in climate and other amenities, would give rise to compensating differentials in equilibrium wages in the presence of full factor market integration, a fact that many authors have exploited to estimate revealed valuations of amenities and public goods. Allowing explicitly for such differences among regions would complicate the details of the following analysis but not its essential features. The benefits from provision of rival or congestible public goods, including cash subsidies as well as various in-kind transfers and public services, are captured in the model through the fiscal variable t. This variable should be interpreted to represent the fiscal contribution per unit of the variable factor, net of any costs incurred for the provision of rival public goods and services. There is some loss of important detail in this interpretation insofar as the value of the benefits provided by public expenditures differ from the cost of provision, but once again the analysis would be complicated, although not affected in its essential features, by explicit inclusion of congestible public goods in the model.

determine equilibrium levels of the variable factor and output, equilibrium gross and net factor prices, and the distribution of income. It would be possible to study this model in its most general form, and the anlaysis below contains several results that apply in the general case. However, the nature and mechanics of equilibrium in the model are most easily understood by considering an illustrative special case.

The special case involves restrictions on the production function and on the distribution of the random variable θ. First, the production function is assumed to be quadratic in m with a marginal product for the variable factor that is subject to additive uncertainty, i.e., $f(m, \theta) = (a + \theta)m - bm^2/2$, so that $f_m = a + \theta - bm$. For the sake of brevity, let us call this the *additive-quadratic* production technology. Second, suppose that θ is a discrete random variable, taking on only the values θ_1, θ_2 with equal probability. Without loss of generality, assume that $\theta_1 > \theta_2$ (so that θ_1 is a "good" state of the world) and that $\theta_1 + \theta_2 = 0$ (that is, the parameter a is adjusted so that the θ_i's have zero mean). Figure 1 shows the linear downward-sloping marginal productivity curves for the variable factor for each of the two states of the world. Moreover, assume that $a - b\bar{m} = \bar{w}$, so that the mean domestic marginal product of the variable factor, when only the domestic endowment of the factor is employed, is equal to its external net rate of return. This assumption provides a reference point or normalization for the analysis, by anchoring the expected return to the variable input to that obtainable externally.[5] To depict the equilibrium, suppose first that there is no government redistributive policy so that $t = 0$. If c is sufficiently large — specifically, if $c > \theta_1 = |\theta_2|$ — there will be no movement of the variable factor in either state of the world. Hence $m = \bar{m}$ in equilibrium, and the equilibrium price of the variable factor is $\bar{w}_i \equiv f_m(\bar{m}, \theta_i)$ in state θ_i, as shown in Figure 1. This corresponds to the equilibrium condition (4d). Total output and the return to the fixed factor are given by $O(a + \theta_1)A\bar{m}$ and $(a + \theta_1)A\bar{w}_1$, respectively, for the good state, and by $O(a + \theta_2)D\bar{m}$ and $(a + \theta_2)D\bar{w}_2$ for the bad state.

If $c < \theta_1$, factor migration will occur in each state of the world. In the extreme case where $c = 0$, migration will occur in either state of the world, with $m = m_{max}$ if $\theta = \theta_1$ and $m = m_{min}$ if $\theta = \theta_2$, as shown in Figure 1. The net domestic return to the variable factor will be equal to that on the external market, $\bar{w}$, independently of the realization of θ. Total output and the return to the fixed factor will be $O(a + \theta_1)Bm_{max}$ and $(a + \theta_1)B\bar{w}$ in the good state and $O(a + \theta_2)Cm_{min}$ and $(a + \theta_2)C\bar{w}$ in the bad state. More

---

[5] If the mean domestic return is higher or lower than that in the external market, the owners of the variable factor would obtain a higher or lower expected return, respectively, when factor markets are integrated.

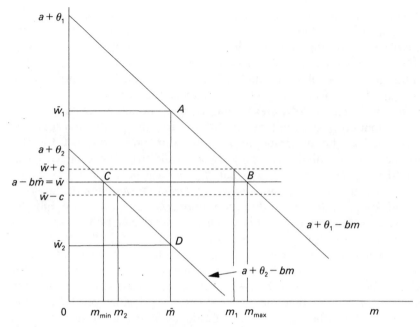

Fig. 1.

generally, if $0 < c < \theta_1$, the equilibrium domestic price for the variable factor is $\bar{w} + c$ in the good state (corresponding to equilibrium condition (4b)) and $\bar{w} - c$ in the bad state (corresponding to equilibrium condition (4c)). The equilibrium level of employment of the variable factor is m_i in state i, with $m_{\min} < m_2 < \bar{m} < m_1 < m_{\max}$, as shown in the figure. Total output and the return to the fixed input can be read from the figure as before.

It is straightforward to show how taxes or transfers are incorporated into this model. If, for instance, the variable factor is subject to a positive per-unit tax of t in the good state, the curve $a + \theta_1 - bm$ in Figure 1, shifted down by the amount t, would show the *net* return to the variable input as a function of the level of employment. The level of m at which this net return is equal to $\bar{w} + c$ would determine the equilibrium level of m in the good state, assuming that it exceeds $\bar{m}$. If the variable input receives a subsidy (i.e., $t < 0$) then the curve would be shifted upward by the appropriate amount to determine the equilibrium. The level of employment of the variable input generally depends on the tax-transfer policy t.

Although this special case of the model entails quite restrictive assumptions, it illustrates clearly the essential elements of the determination of equilibrium. Most importantly, it shows how the equilibrium level of employment and gross and net factor prices depend on the state of nature, government redistributive policies and the level of migration costs. If migration costs are sufficiently high, the variable factor is effectively immobile and external factor prices do not affect domestic factor prices. If migration costs are sufficiently low, domestic factor prices are linked by spatial arbitrage through factor mobility to external prices. These are important and *general* properties of the model, not dependent on specific assumptions about the form of the production function or the nature of uncertainty.

In closing the description of the basic model, it is worth noting some possible interpretations and extensions. First, the underlying source of risk in the economy, the random variable θ, could refer to technological uncertainty in an economy where the homogeneous output is "corn", an all-purpose commodity in which incomes are denominated and which is used directly for consumption. Alternatively, one might suppose that the domestic economy is small and open with respect to commodity trade and that it is specialized in the production of particular goods which trade on world markets at uncertain prices. This corresponds to the special case of (1) where θ enters f multiplicatively and is interpreted as the world price of the domestically produced good relative to the price of "corn;" "corn" itself could be a Hicksian composite commodity that encompasses all other tradeable goods for which world relative prices are fixed.

The fixed input(s) could include land, natural resources and public infrastructure such as transportation and communication systems. Depending on the desired application, either labor or private capital, or specific types of each, might be either fixed or variable. Just to name three possibilities: (i) all private capital could be mobile while all labor is fixed, more or less corresponding to the view of many commentators when evaluating the "southern tier" EU countries in relation to existing EU members, (ii) labor could be mobile while capital is fixed, more or less corresponding to the situation in Germany in the "short run" following unification, or to eastern Europe in relation to western Europe if border controls on labor movement were to be removed or greatly eased, and (iii) skilled (or young) labor could be mobile while unskilled (or old) labor and capital are immobile, as in "brain drain" models. The degree of factor mobility in general depends on time horizons and on policy restrictions as well as on intrinsic mobility costs.

It is straightforward to extend the model to allow explicitly for other traded factors of production or for many traded goods, provided that these commodities trade at fixed external prices and that they are not the subject of any fiscal policies or other distortions. Adding extra inputs to the production process at fixed prices does not change the nature of factor price determination for the two inputs described already; see Sandmo and

Wildasin (1994) for further discussion. Trade in goods can lead to factor price equalization, in which case "commodity movements and factor movements are substitutes"; cf. Mundell (1957). Although factor price equalization could obviate much of the present analysis by eliminating migration incentives, it is worth recalling that the underlying assumptions of identical production technologies among jurisdictions and free inter-sectoral factor mobility are quite strong.[6] In the present model, the random variable θ can be interpreted as random departures from the production technology prevailing in the rest of the world. Under this interpretation, factor-price equalization is precluded by jurisdiction-specific production technologies built directly into the model. Alternatively, one could think of θ as a terms-of-trade shock which affects factor prices because some factors of production are not only interjurisdictionally but intersectorally immobile (at least over the relevant time horizon). At the empirical level, observed factor mobility as well as (binding) constraints on factor mobility (such as immigration quotas or capital controls) testify to the existence of spatial variations in net factor returns, suggesting the value of models in which factor price equalization does not hold.

III. Economic Integration and Income Risk

Income Risk in the Absence of Income Redistribution Policy

Consider now the nature of income risk in the foregoing model. We begin with the case where the government does not intervene to change the distribution of income.

Suppose first that migration costs are prohibitively high, so that no factor reallocations occur in any state of the world. Domestic factor prices and incomes will in general be stochastic, with distributions that depend both on the distribution of the underlying random variable θ and on the way that uncertainty enters the production technology. When the production function is additive-quadratic, the gross price of the variable factor has a variance equal to the variance of θ itself, while the gross return to the fixed input is non-stochastic.[7] This is illustrated for the particular case of a two-point distribution of θ in Figure 1, where the return to the fixed factor

---

[6] Indeed, any plausible theory of technological uniformity requires an explanation of technological diffusion; since technology is frequently embodied in either human or non-human capital, factor mobility may actually contribute importantly to the establishment of identical production technologies in different regions or countries.

[7] Given $f(m, \theta) = (a + \theta)m - bm^2/2$, the equilibrium price of the variable factor with no migration is $a - b\tilde{m} + \theta$. Since $E(\theta) = 0$, the expected return to the variable factor is just $a - b\tilde{m}$ and the variance is $E(a - b\tilde{m} + \theta - [a - b\tilde{m}])^2 = E(\theta)^2 = \text{Var}(\theta)$. From (3), $r = (a + \theta)\tilde{m} - b\tilde{m}^2/2 - ([a + \theta]\tilde{m} - b\tilde{m}^2) = b\tilde{m}^2/2$, which is indepenent of the value of θ.

is the area under the marginal product curve for m and above its equilibrium price, i.e., the triangular area $(a + \theta_1)A\bar{w}_1$ in the good state and $(a + \theta_2)D\bar{w}_2$ in the bad state. These triangles are clearly equal in size, showing that the return to the fixed factor is state independent.

In the opposite extreme case where migration costs are negligible, the equilibrium domestic factor price for the variable input is equal to the price fixed on external markets and is thus completely certain. Income risk for the owners of the variable factor disappears in this case. It does not disappear for the economy as a whole. Rather, all risk is shifted to the owners of the immobile factor. A complete opening of the economy to the external market for the variable input does not merely imply that the fixed factor absorbs all risk, however. It also changes the mean return to the fixed factor. In the special case illustrated in Figure 1, for example, the mean return to the variable input is unchanged when it becomes perfectly mobile, but the mean return to the fixed input becomes $0.5(a + \theta_1)B\bar{w} + 0.5(a + \theta_2)C\bar{w}$, in contrast to a mean return of $0.5(a + \theta_1)A\bar{w}_1 + 0.5(a + \theta_2)D\bar{w}_2$ when the variable input is completely immobile. Moving from complete immobility to perfect mobility of the variable input thus increases the mean return to the fixed input by the amount $\bar{w}_1AB\bar{w} - \bar{w}CD\bar{w}_2 = (\bar{m} - m_{min})\theta_1$. There is an "efficiency gain" that results from an increase in the mobility of the variable input, in the form of an increase in the mean income accruing to the factor owners in the domestic economy.

Although the comparison of the polar extreme cases of complete immobility and complete mobility of the variable input is informative, the process of economic integration does not occur all at once, as represented in the model by a reduction in c from some very high level to 0. A more realistic view of the process is that the variable input is partially mobile initially, but that it becomes increasingly mobile over time. What happens to income and income risk for each type of factor as the domestic market for the variable input becomes *increasingly* integrated with the external market? This amounts to asking for a comparative-statics analysis of the effect of a reduction in c on the distribution of returns to both factors.

When the variable input is immobile (e.g. if c is infinite), the cumulative distribution of w is given by

$$\Pr\{w \le w_0\} = \Pr\{f_m(\bar{m}, \theta) \le w_0\}$$

for any $w_0 \ge 0$, a distribution that can be determined for any given production technology and distribution of θ. For instance, in the additive-quadratic case, the distribution of $w - a + b\bar{m}$ is identical to that of θ. Reductions in c truncate the distribution of w at both tails, such that

$$\Pr\{w = \bar{w} + c\} = \Pr\{f_m(\bar{m}, \theta) \ge \bar{w} + c\} \equiv P_1 \tag{5a}$$

$$\Pr\{w = \bar{w} - c\} = \Pr\{f_m(\bar{m}, \theta) \leq \bar{w} - c\} \equiv P_2 \tag{5b}$$

$$\Pr\{w \leq w_0\} = P_2 + \Pr\{\bar{w} - c \leq f_m(\bar{m}, \theta) \leq w_0\} \ \forall \ w_0 \in [\bar{w} - c, \bar{w} + c]. \tag{5c}$$

In particular, if θ is symmetrically distributed and if $\bar{w} = a - b\bar{m}$, reductions in c trim the tails of the distribution of w without changing its mean, so that *the only effect of increased integration on the return to the variable factor is to reduce its risk.* If the external rate of return to the variable factor were higher or lower than $a + b\bar{m}$ or if θ were not symmetrically distributed, greater integration would raise or lower its mean return while still limiting the range of its variation.

The effect of reductions in c on the distribution of returns to the immobile factor is more difficult to ascertain in general. However, analysis of a useful special case — that of an additive-quadratic production technology and uniformly distributed technology shocks — confirms what the polar cases of complete immobility and complete immobility suggest should be true. First, as shown in Figure 2, *reductions in the cost of factor*

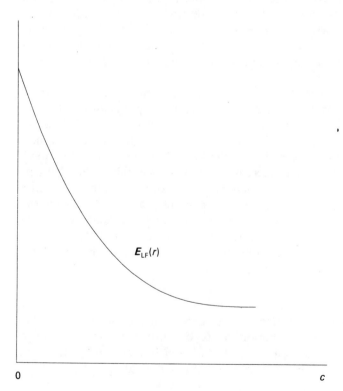

0   c

Fig. 2. Expected return to fixed factor.

mobility raise the expected return to the fixed input. That is, there is an "efficiency gain" from improved mobility of the variable input and the fact that it can be allocated more easily where its productivity is higher. (The subscript LF in these figures denotes *laissez-faire*, in reference to the absence of government redistributive policy.) Second, *the variance of the return to the variable input diminishes as its mobility improves,* as shown in Figure 3. Third, *the variance of the return to the fixed factor rises as the mobility of the variable input increases.*

Economic Integration, Risk, and Income Redistribution

Let us now consider now the impact of government redistribution policy as the mobility of the variable factor changes.

Full insurance for the variable factor. Begin with the case where the variable factor is completely immobile. As noted above, the gross income

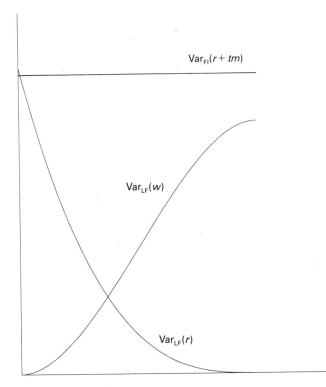

Fig. 3. Variances of factor returns.

of this factor varies with the state of nature in this case; the income of the immobile factor may not. Government policy cannot eliminate income risk under the assumptions that we have made, but it can change how that risk is distributed. For instance, it would be possible to impose a tax/transfer policy such that the net income of the variable input would be the same in all states of the world, the case of *full insurance* for the variable factor. This outcome can be achieved by setting $t = f_m(\bar{m}, \theta) - \bar{w}$, in which case the net income of the variable input would be equal to $\bar{w}$ in every state while the income of the fixed input would be equal to $f(\bar{m}, \theta) - \bar{w}\bar{m}$, thus absorbing all income risk. Income redistribution policy has no effect on the physical allocation of resources in this case.

Now suppose that the variable input is potentially mobile, at a cost of c per unit, and that the government continues to use redistributive policies that keep the net income of the variable input fixed at $\bar{w}$. As long as this policy is in place, there is no incentive for domestic or foreign owners of the variable input to incur the cost of removing it from or bringing it to the domestic economy, i.e., this policy forestalls any factor mobility for any positive value of c. Under this policy, then, changes in the level of c have no effect on input or output levels or on gross or net incomes in any state of the world. By comparison with the *laissez-faire* case, for each value of c, the mean return to the variable input is the same, but its variance is lower (specifically, zero) in the presence of this government policy. On the other hand, the mean return to the immobile factor is lower because the efficiency gains from factor mobility, identified in (7) above, are not exploited. This is an "efficiency loss" from the imposition of the government's redistributive policy.

How does this policy of full insurance for the variable factor affect the variability of the net return to the fixed factor? The answer is clear in general terms: the fixed input absorbs all income risk in the economy and this risk is independent of the level of c (because the allocation of resources is independent of c in the presence of full public insurance for the variable input). This is illustrated by the horizontal line in Figure 3 labelled $\mathrm{Var}_{LF}(r)$ for "full insurance". Interestingly, it is possible that the variability of the return to the fixed factor can be lower in the full insurance case than under *laissez-faire* for sufficiently small values of c. In the case illustrated in Figure 3, however, this occurs only at very low values of c.

Partial insurance of the variable input. An extreme policy of using taxes and transfers to shift all income risk from the variable to the fixed factor destroys all incentives for the variable factor to relocate after the state of nature is known. This policy thus completely negates any allocative gains from reductions in the cost of factor mobility. While this extreme case is illustrative, it is clearly quite special; *a priori*, findings for this case may not extend to more interesting intermediate cases. For instance, suppose that the government imposes a proportional tax or subsidy on deviations from the mean return of the variable input, such

$$t = \alpha(w - \bar{w}), \qquad \alpha \in [0, 1]. \tag{6}$$

This policy encompasses the *laissez-faire* and perfect insurance policies as polar extremes, corresponding to $\alpha = 0$ and $\alpha = 1$, respectively. More generally, a policy with $\alpha \in (0, 1)$ proportionally shrinks the variation in w, and can be viewed as a proportional income tax/negative income tax scheme with a constant marginal tax rate of α and a break-even level of income of $\bar{w}$. The net return to the variable input under this policy is a simple weighted average of the gross return w and the mean return $\bar{w}$:

$$w - t = \alpha\bar{w} + (1 - \alpha)w. \tag{7}$$

Although it is quite difficult to derive general conclusions about the effects of increased factor mobility on factor allocations and income distribution under this policy, results can be obtained computationally for the simple special case where the production technology is additive-quadratic and θ is uniformly distributed. A policy of partial insurance for the variable input implies that the gross and net returns to each factor diverge, due to the presence of the taxes and transfers through which the insurance is implemented. For any *given* value of the cost of migration c, one can show that (i) the expected gross and net return to the variable input is equal to $\bar{w}$ in the presence of partial insurance (by construction), (ii) the variance of the net return to the variable input is less than the variance of the gross return, (iii) the expected net return to the fixed input is less than its expected gross return, and (iv) the variance of the net return to the fixed input exceeds that of the gross return.[8] What is of most interest for present purposes, however, is how these moments of the factor price distributions change as the cost of mobility changes. Essentially, the results parallel those for the *laissez-faire* case. As economic integration proceeds, the variance of both the gross and net return to the variable input falls. In the extreme case of perfect mobility, both variances drop to zero as a result of perfect arbitrage between the internal and external factor markets. Reductions in c raise the expected gross and net return to the fixed factor and also raise the variance of both the gross and the net return. These impacts are qualitatively in the same direction as for the *laissez-faire* case, though of course their quantitative magnitudes are different.

---

[8] Details and illustrations of the calculations are omitted to save space. These properties are as expected: (ii) implies that the partial insurance policy actually does lower the variance of net relative to gross income for the "insured" factor, (iii) implies that there is an "efficiency loss" from the policy, and (iv) implies that the policy shifts risk from the variable to the fixed input.

Economic Security in the Welfare State

The welfare states of the advanced democracies face an increasingly liberalized economic environment. In part this is a result of more or less deliberate policy choices, and in part it is a result of long-run technological and other trends. One aspect of this liberalization is an increase in factor mobility. Freer markets generally create incentives for greater responsiveness to shocks, with resulting gains in efficiency. The analysis of Sections II and III bears this out: as factor mobility increases, expected income rises. Shocks give rise to larger fluctuations in input and output levels, with higher levels of employment in high-productivity states of the world and lower levels in states where productivity is low. Efficiency is improved and expected returns rise. In the specific model used, the increase in efficiency of resource allocation accrues only to the immobile input, while the expected return to the variable input remains unchanged. These efficiency gains may be lost if government redistributive policies dull the incentives for state-contingent reallocations of the variable input, however. In the extreme case of full insurance, none of the potential efficiency gains from greater factor mobility may be realized.

What are the distributional implications of greater factor mobility? Do the efficiency gains of greater factor mobility come at the cost of equity? These questions are by their nature not easily resolved due to the difficulty in defining what is equitable. Still, some useful lessons can be drawn from the foregoing analysis by considering different possible scenarios.

Suppose, for example, that there are only two factors, labor and capital, and that labor is the variable input. In the *laissez-faire* economy, greater labor mobility raises the expected return to capital. Workers do not, on average, obtain higher incomes. They do, however, experience reduced income risk, as greater mobility provides them with better access to external market opportunities. Capital income becomes increasingly risky as labor mobility improves. Government policies that pool income risk bring about efficiency losses but also shift income risk from labor to capital. If protection of labor income through market mechanisms is infeasible, then there may be substantial benefit from government redistributive policies in a relatively closed economic environment where workers in unproductive regions have very few opportunities to escape to more rewarding pursuits. However, the benefit from these policies is diminished, and their cost is increased, when labor mobility increases. These policies now inhibit state-contingent factor reallocations that both increase efficiency and reduce income risk for workers. Although a more open economic environment may limit the ability of policymakers to redistribute income and cause some retrenchment of programs aimed at insuring wage incomes, it does not necessarily follow that the *objectives* of those programs are compromised. Rather, the mechanism of wage income insurance may simply shift from public sector redistributive policy to private sector wage equalization through migration.

Suppose now that capital rather than labor is "the" mobile factor of production. The foregoing analysis implies that greater integration of factor markets may increase earnings risk for labor. Greater capital mobility may reduce the riskiness of investment returns at their source. To the extent that capital income streams are tradeable through financial markets, however, the risks to capital income recipients may already be widely shared. Reductions in capital income risk at source may therefore not reduce the income risk of capital owners very substantially. The riskiness of wage income, however, may increase significantly. The analysis presented in Section III suggests that such wage risk can be diminished by reductions in the degree of insurance provided to capital income. One way to do this is by restructing fiscal and other policies. Reductions in effective corporate income tax rates, for example, could reduce the burden of risk shifted from capital income to labor income while simultaneously raising the net return to labor by improving the efficiency of resource allocation.

As a further variation on the model, suppose that there are three factors of production. Suppose that highly-skilled and (generally) high-income workers are treated as a variable input while low-skilled and (generally) low-age workers are relatively immobile. Capital is freely mobile and untaxed and, as indicated in Section II, can be subsumed within the model with no change in the analysis. In this world, greater mobility of high-skilled workers does not raise their average incomes, but it does result in an increase in the average income of *low-skilled* workers, as illustrated in Figure 2. In this respect, greater mobility of high-skilled labor would be inequality-reducing. Nevertheless, low-skilled workers may experience greater income risk as a result of greater mobility of high-skilled workers, while the income risk of the latter may diminish. The allocative losses due to government policies such as personal income taxes, payroll taxes and consumption taxes increase if the market for the high-skilled workers becomes freer. Since these policies also shift income risk to less-skilled workers, scaling back the extent of income-conditioning of tax-transfer policies that apply to high-skilled workers may reduce some of the income shocks to which less-skilled workers might otherwise be exposed.

IV. Conclusion

There are many issues relating to factor market integration and risk that have been ignored here. For this reason, the analysis should be regarded only as suggestive. Important and difficult empirical questions have already been mentioned. In closing, it is useful to highlight some additional topics that warrant further investigation.

Markets for risk. The foregoing analysis applies, in principle, to any situation where there is one potentially mobile variable input that is employed along with a fixed input subject to uncertainty. The focus of the analysis has been on the mean and variance of the income stream at its source. Some income streams, however, notably those accruing to capital investments, can be traded and thus diversified. Increases in capital market integration may not therefore reduce the *cost* of risks that can be pooled by other means, but may instead substitute for some of the functions of financial markets; conversely, development of financial markets may reduce some of the benefits of interjurisdictional capital flows.

Risk-pooling among jurisdictions generally requires cross-ownership of claims on income streams; complete diversification across many jurisdictions implies that the tradeable assets employed in a given jurisdiction will be owned, in equilibrium, by non-residents. This, however, creates an incentive for each local jurisdiction to tax away the income of diversifiable assets, or to seize the assets themselves; see Wildasin and Wilson (1994), Nielsen (1994) and the literature on sovereign debt, e.g. Eaton and Gersovitz (1989). There is therefore a real question about the sustainability of a regime with diversified cross-ownership of assets unless governments can somehow agree, in a *credible* fashion, to restrain themselves from source-based taxation of income or assets owned by non-residents. Liberalization of regulatory constraints on factor movements may provide one means by which such commitments could be made or signalled, perhaps thereby facilitating trading of risky assets.

Localization economies and factor market integration. Urban agglomerations may provide another market mechanism for pooling risk. Krugman (1991, esp. Appendix C) presents a model in which firms with uncorrelated production risks locate together, providing risk-averse workers with protection from wage risk. If firms can bear risk more easily than workers, agglomerations can arise. In its emphasis on pooling of risk through access to dense markets, the present analysis parallels that of Krugman. However, in Krugman's case, dense markets arise through urban agglomerations, whereas in the present analysis it is lower costs of movement to other regions that allow owners of mobile factors to access markets with more stable factor prices. This raises several interesting issues for further analysis, formulated here as conjectures. First, to the extent that agglomerations arise from pooling of labor market risk, greater mobility of labor among regions or countries reduces the benefits of agglomeration and may lead to smaller equilibrium city sizes. By the same token, increases in labor mobility among uncorrelated employers within a metropolitan area due to urban growth or diversification of urban industry reduces the attractiveness of inter-regional migration. Second, although the analysis here has suggested that redistributive policies may reduce interregional factor mobility and the sharing of risks through factor markets, there would seem to be a corollary in the localization-economies context: social insurance reduces the benefits of urban agglomeration and, presumably, leads to smaller equilibrium city size.

Unequal regions and the gains and losses from federation. As noted at the outset, a public policy that provides "insurance" in a long-run sense may be viewed as "redistribution" in the "short run". Incomes *per capita* in different regions of the U.S. have converged substantially over the course of the past century; see e.g. Mills and Hamilton (1984, Figure 2.1). Comparatively free migration of labor and capital within the U.S. has surely assisted that process. For most of the century, however, some regions (notably the South) have been poor relative to other regions. To the extent that labor and capital mobility have contributed to equalization of factor returns, there hve been losers in this process as well as gainers. Within the long-run perspective of the U.S. constitution, such gains and losses may not in themselves be of much concern. For a period of decades, workers or capital owners in one region may suffer reductions in income because of competition from immigrant capital or labor from other regions, but workers and capital owners in each region (locality, etc.) value the option to be able to move elsewhere should economic prospects in their current location take a turn for the worse. Indeed, relative freedom of factor movements within countries is commonplace, and it is clear that restrictions on such freedom (e.g., a prohibition on seeking employment outside of one's city of birth) would result in significant increases in income risk.

Consider, by contrast, the issue of freedom of migration between eastern and western Europe. Rather like the American South, the countries of eastern Europe have incomes much below that of their neighbors to the west. Unrestricted movement of labor and capital among these countries would certainly contribute to "pooling of income risks" or equalization of factor returns. However, it is not clear that this is in the interest of affluent western countries. The analysis in Wildasin (1994) shows that immigration is necessarily harmful to at least some of the initial residents (or, more precisely, the initial owners of the factors of production) of a region if immigrants are net beneficiaries of the fiscal system. (It is even possible that the initial residents may benefit from making transfers to a source jurisdiction if this inhibits immigration.) In the "short run", then, the welfare states of western Europe may be net losers from increased factor mobility. In the "long run", residents in these countries value the option of being able to employ their productive resources outside of their home countries, and might therefore wish to commit to institutional arrangements, such as EU membership, that expand such options. Whether a

78   D. E. Wildasin

country gains or loses from membership in a common market, or from allowing another country to join a common market, is therefore a complex question that depends, in part, on the durability of the institutional arrangements.

References

Atkinson, A. B.: Income maintenance and social insurance. In A. J. Auerbach & M. S. Feldstein (eds.), *Handbook of Public Economics*, North-Holland, Amsterdam, 1987.
Barro, R. J. & Sala-i-Martin, X.: Convergence across states and regions. *Brookings Papers on Economic Activity*, 107–82, 1991.
Boadway, R. W. & Wildasin, D. E.: Optimal tax-subsidy policies for industrial adjustment to uncertain shocks. *Oxford Economic Papers 42*, 105–34, 1990; reprinted in P. J. N. Sinclar & M. D. E. Slater (eds.), *Taxation, Private Information, and Capital*, Clarendon Press, Oxford, 105–34, 1991.
Bureau, D. & Champsaur, P.: Fiscal federalism and European economic unification. *American Economic Review Papers and Proceedings 82*, 88–92, 1992.
Bureau, D. & Richard, C.: Public insurance and mobility: An exploratory analysis in the context of European economic unification. Ministère de l'économie, Direction de la prévision; presented at conference on "Decentralization and the Economic Organization of Space", GREQAM, Marseille, 1994.
De Grauwe, P.: *The Economics of Monetary Integration*. Oxford University Press, Oxford, 1992.
Drèze, J.: Regions of Europe: A feasible status, to be discussed. *Economic Policy 17*, 265–307, 1993.
Eaton, J. & Gersovitz, M.: Country risk and the organization of international capital transfer. In G. Calvo *et al.* (eds.), *Debt, Stabilization, and Development*, Basil Blackwell, Oxford, 1989.
Eichengreen, B.: European monetary integration. *Journal of Economic Literature 31*, 1321–57, 1993.
Krugman, P.: *Geography and Trade*. MIT Press, Cambridge, 1991.
Mills, E. S. & Hamilton, B. W.: *Urban Economics*, third edition. Scott Foresman, Glenview, 1984.
Mundell, R. A.: International trade and factor mobility. *American Economic Review 47*, 321–35, 1957.
Nielsen, S. B.: Withholding taxes and country-specific shocks. Mimeo, Copenhagen Business School, 1994.
Oates, W. E.: *Fiscal Federalism*. Harcourt, Brace, Jovanovich, New York, 1972.
Persson, T. & Tabellini, G.: Federal fiscal constitutions: Part I: Risk sharing and moral hazard. EPRU WP, Copenhagen Business School, 1993.
Sandmo, A. & Wildasin, D. E.: Taxation, migration, and pollution. Norwegian School of Economics and Business Administration, Institute of Economics DP 3/94; Vanderbilt University WP 94-W02, 1994.
Wildasin, D. E.: Income redistribution and migration. *Canadian Journal of Economics 27*, 637–56, 1994.
Wildasin, D. E. & Wilson, J. D.: Risky local tax bases: Risk pooling vs. rent capture. Vanderbilt University WP, 1994.

Public Provision of Private Goods as a Redistributive Device in an Optimum Income Tax Model

Sören Blomquist

Uppsala University, Sweden

Vidar Christiansen

University of Oslo, Norway

Abstract

Public provision of a private good can alleviate the informational problems that restrict redistribution through the tax/transfer system when the identity of high- and low-skill persons is hidden. A Pareto improvement may be achieved by publicly providing a private good, and letting each consumer choose between accepting the provision or buying the good on the market. We characterize goods that are suitable for public provision. Various kinds of social optima, conditional on the nature of preferences and the parameters of the economy, are distinguished and characterized. One or both types of persons may opt for public provision at the social optimum.

I. Introduction

In standard textbooks on public economics, income redistribution and provision of public goods are set forth as the main tasks for the government. In practice, however, a large part — in some countries 30–40 per cent — of government expenditures is on public provision of private goods such as education, health care, day care and care of the elderly. Given its large quantitative importance, it is somewhat surprising that there is no well-established theoretical explanation for public provision of private goods.

*We are grateful for financial support from the Nordic Economic Research Council and the Swedish Council for Social Research, and to Kåre P. Hagen, Victor Norman, Jean-Charles Rochet and two anonymous referees for helpful comments. The first ideas motivating this joint research were conceived in the stimulating academic environment of the 1991 Warwick Summer Research Workshop, which we both attended.

The typical textbook perspective is instead on optimal provision, given the fact that a good is publicly provided. Sometimes it is suggested that *if* a private good is publicly provided, it should be treated in the analysis as if it were a public good. We show that this view is, in general, incorrect.

There have been a few attempts to explain why some private goods are publicly provided. One argument focuses on the connection between some private goods and the tax base. Bergstrom and Blomquist (1993) study how public provision of day care can stimulate the labor force participation of mothers, thereby increasing the tax base and mitigating the adverse effects of the income tax. Others point to externalities from education, health care, etc. as a case for public provision. However, the strongest support for public provision seems to be based on various distributional concerns. The desire to reduce future income inequality is used as an argument for publicly funded schools. A common argument is that there are some goods, like health care and education, for which society's distributional goals are more ambitious than the distributional goals for purchasing power in general. Public provision might be a way to achieve these distributional goals.

Besley and Coate (1991) focus on the general distributional motive, not on specific distributional goals. The important contribution is the observation that different groups of people can value the publicly provided good differently, and that public provision induces self-selection. Blackorby and Donaldson (1988) and Boadway and Marchand (1995) also point to the importance of the self-selection mechanism if we want to understand the role of publicly provided private goods. However, these studies do not give a characterization of goods that might be suitable for public provision.[1]

As assumed by Besley and Coate, publicly provided private goods are characterized by quantity (and/or quality) constraints.[2] In our paper, we assume that the publicly provided quantity cannot be resold or supplemented.[3] An individual can either accept this quantity or buy a quantity of his own choice in the market.

We try to explain *why* public provision of private goods can be beneficial and *what characterizes* goods that are suitable for public provision. We assume distributional concerns to be the driving force

---

[1] Articles by Ireland (1990), Munro (1989, 1991) and Besley (1991) also contain interesting contributions to the literature on publicly provided private goods.

[2] Publicly provided private goods are sometimes such that variations in quality constitute the interesting choice. The model we develop here can be interpreted either as if the quantity of the good can vary or as if the quantity is fixed and quality is the interesting choice dimension.

[3] Sometimes there are possibilities of supplementing a publicly provided good; see Section II.

behind public provision of private goods. However, no specific distributional goals for the publicly provided goods are assumed. Instead we focus on the problem of asymmetric information that limits the income redistribution a government can achieve. Our model synthesizes the ideas in the paper by Besley and Coate and the optimal taxation model with self-selection constraints; see Stiglitz (1987). The publicly provided private good will slacken the self-selection constraint, which restricts the redistribution a nonlinear income tax can achieve.

The problem where the income tax and the publicly provided quantity are determined simultaneously is quite complicated. To get the basic idea across, we therefore give a nontechnical description of the model and the basic results in Sections II and III. The introduction of publicly provided private goods means that we use a particular type of indifference curves. We study individual behavior and these indifference curves in Section II. The optimal taxation problem is described in Section III, where we also present the basic argument as to why and under what conditions public provision of private goods can improve welfare. Section IV gives a more complete description of the possible solutions to the extended optimal taxation problem. In Section V we suggest some applications of our model. Conclusions and a summary are presented in Section VI.

II. Individual Behavior and Indifference Curves

Individuals can sometimes supplement the quantity/quality of a publicly provided private good. However, the possibilities are usually quite limited. For example, if the quality of a publicly funded school is considered too low, it can be supplemented with private tutoring. However, if the quality of the publicly funded school is below a certain level, this is not an attractive solution and the child is placed in a private school. In that case the publicly provided education has to be foregone completely. There are some possibilities of supplementing public health care. However, if a person needs surgery and does not want to remain on the waiting list in the public health care system, he has to forego the publicly provided operation completely and pay the full price of a private operation. It is an empirical fact that when private alternatives are available, many people choose to forego the public provision, rather than accept and attempt to supplement it.[4] To keep the analysis manageable, we study the polar case in which

---

[4] For several decades in the postwar period, state housing banks played a major role in financing housing investments in Norway and Sweden. Loans were offered at a subsidized interest rate, but on the condition that certain cost, size and other maximum standards were observed. No supplementing was allowed. The alternative for those who wanted a larger or more luxurious house was to finance it entirely on normal market terms.

individuals cannot supplement at all.[5]

Let c denote the quantity of a tradeable good, and x the quantity of a good that can be bought on the market but also publicly provided. Throughout the paper we assume that c and x are normal goods. The publicly provided quantity, denoted by $\bar{x}$, can be neither sold nor supplemented. For convenience we normalize the prices of the two goods to one for the time being. Let Y denote before-tax income, B after-tax income, h hours of work and w the wage rate. By definition $h = Y/w$.

We use several types of utility functions. $U(c, x, h)$ denotes the direct utilty function. We assume $U_c > 0$, $U_x > 0$, $U_h < 0$ and that U is strictly quasi-concave. If $\bar{x}$ is foregone and Y/w fixed, an individual's maximization problem can be written as $\text{Max } U(c, x; Y/w)$; s.t. $c + x = B$. The solution yields the demand functions $c(B, Y/w)$, $x(B, Y/w)$ and the conditional indirect utility function $V(B, Y/w) \equiv U(c(B, Y/w), x(B, Y/w); Y/w)$. Hence, $V(B, Y/w)$ shows utility for an individual who buys x on the market instead of accepting $\bar{x}$. If $\bar{x}$ is accepted, utility is given by $U(B, \bar{x}, Y/w)$. The individual is free to accept the publicly provided quantity or forego it and instead buy x on the market. Hence, for given Y and B, the utility is given by the overall optimum utility function: $\Omega(B, \bar{x}, Y/w) = \max\{V(B, Y/w), U(B, \bar{x}, Y/w)\}$.

It is important to know the shape of the indifference curves in the Y, B space that are implied by $\Omega(\cdot)$. If $\bar{x}$ is zero, the individual will buy x on the market and the indifference map is given by $V(B, Y/w)$. For sufficiently high values of $\bar{x}$, the individual will, for all economically interesting values of B and Y, accept the publicly provided quantity so that the indifference map is given by $U(B, \bar{x}, Y/w)$. For an interval of $\bar{x}$, an individual will accept $\bar{x}$ for some values of Y and B and buy x on the market for other values of Y and B. The indifference map will then be a mixture of parts from the $V(\ )$ and $U(\cdot)$ indifference maps. $\bar{x}$ is a shift variable for these indifference curves. Blomquist and Christiansen (1994) provide a detailed exposure of the various types of indifference maps that may arise.

In Figure 1, showing one possible configuration of indifference curves, we have drawn a borderline, $b(Y; \bar{x})$, separating the lower region where the individual will accept the public provision and the upper region where the individual will buy x on the market. In general the borderline is upward or downward sloping as the demand for x is increasing or decreasing in leisure. Below the borderline, the indifference map for $\Omega(\ )$ will consist of $U(\ )$ indifference curves. Above the border it will consist of $V(\ )$ indifference curves. The Ω-indifference curves are shown by the kinked solid curves. The parts of the V- and U-indifference curves which do not form

---

[5] In Blomquist and Christiansen (1995) we study the polar case where individuals can supplement. We also compare the two possible schemes for public provision.

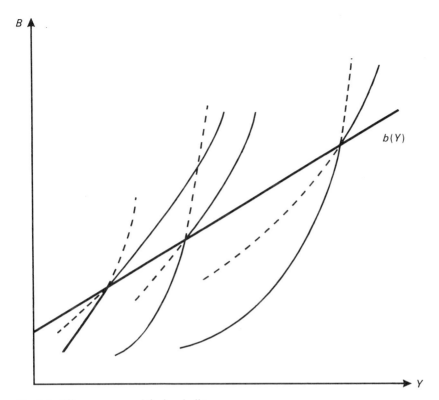

Fig. 1. Indifference map and the borderline.

part of the Ω-indifference map are broken. We note that the upper contour set defined by $\Omega(B, \bar{x}, Y/w) = \tilde{V}$ is nonconvex in B and Y. This nonconvexity has consequences for the optimal taxation-public provision problem studied below. The optimal taxation problem is basically a quasi-concave programming problem. There is a single local maximum which is also the global maximum. The optimal taxation-public provision problem is a nonconcave programming problem with the possibility of several local maxima. Which local maximum that constitutes the global maximum depends on the parameters of the economy and cannot be determined in general. We consider various possibilities in Section IV.

III. The Optimal Taxation Problem and the Self-Selection Constraint

Following Stiglitz (1987) we assume there are two types of persons, of whom one is more able than the other. The wage rate reflects skill. The less and more able persons are indexed by the superscripts 1 and 2, respectively. Ability is private information, so the government cannot impose lump-sum taxes according to ability. We formulate the government's problem as that of maximizing person 1's utility for a given utility level assigned to person 2 and a preset tax revenue requirement. The government specifies an income tax schedule which assigns a net income to each gross income. Since there are only two types of persons, only two points on the income tax schedule need to be specified: one point (Y^2, B^2) that is intended for the high-skill person and another point (Y^1, B^1) that is intended for the low-skill person. The government also has to take into account that each person's income point is chosen by self-selection.

Figure 2 illustrates how the self-selection constraint restricts the utility we can assign to person 1. V^2 is the indifference curve where person 2 obtains the given utility. The tax revenue, T^2, that we can obtain from person 2 is maximized at the point (Y^2, B^2), where the slope of V^2 equals one. Ignoring the self-selection constraint for the moment, the resource constraint implies that we can assign an income point to person 1 along the line $B = Y + T^2$. Given this constraint, person 1's utility is maximized at the point Y^0, B^0. However, if the income tax schedule would consist of the points (Y^0, B^0) and (Y^2, B^2), then person 2 would not choose (Y^2, B^2), but

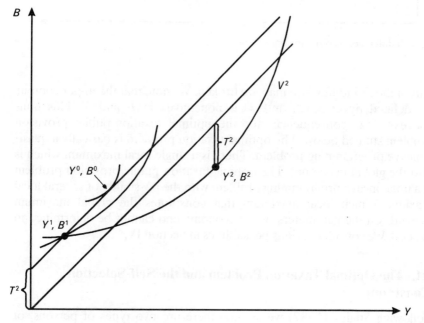

Fig. 2. The optimal taxation problem.

the point (Y^0, B^0). Hence, a tax system consisting of the points (Y^0, B^0) and (Y^2, B^2) is not feasible. In order for person 2 to actually choose (Y^2, B^2), the point intended for person 1 has to be on or below the V^2-curve. This is the so-called self-selection constraint. The point which maximizes person 1's utility and satisfies both the resource constraint and the self-selection constraint is given by (Y^1, B^1) in the figure.

The self-selection constraint restricts the utility we can assign to person 1. The role of public provision of x in our model is to slacken this constraint. If person 2 were to choose (Y^1, B^1), he can use the amount B^1 to buy c and x freely. If we impose constraints on how B^1 must be split between c and x, we can make the point (Y^1, B^1) less attractive to person 2.[6] Thus, by public provision of x we make the income point intended for person 1 less attractive to person 2. Below, we show how public provision can lead to a Pareto improvement and how public provision might accomplish redistribution without any distortions. We then state the problem where the income tax points and the optimal amount of public provision of x are determined simultaneously.

Pareto Improving Public Provision of x

Consider the nonlinear optimum taxation problem described above. We denote the solution as Y_0^1, B_0^1, Y_0^2, B_0^2. Utility for person 2 is given by V^2 and for person 1 by $V(Y_0^1, B_0^1)$. Person 1's demand for good two is given by $x^1 = x(B_0^1, Y_0^1/w^1)$. Let us introduce the publicly provided quantity $\bar{x}$ equal to x^1. Consider the income point $Y^1 = Y_0^1$ and $B^1 = B_0^1 - \bar{x}$. It is obvious that person 1 has the same consumption basket at Y_0^1, B_0^1 with no public provision of x and at Y^1, B^1 with the publicly provided quantity $\bar{x}$. Hence, person 1's utility is the same at Y_0^1, B_0^1 with no public provision of x and the point Y^1, B^1 with $\bar{x}$ publicly provided. Also, the net tax revenue from person 1 including the cost of the publicly provided good, is the same at the two points. We have drawn a U-indifference curve passing through Y^1, B^1 in Figure 3. Utility along this curve is the same as utility along the V-indifference curve passing through Y_0^1, B_0^1. In terms of individual 2's indifference curve V^2, we see that the self-selection constraint does not bind at the point Y^1, B^1. However, we also have to consider person 2's situation if he accepts the publicly provided quantity. In Figure 3 we hypothesize that the U-indifference curve with utility level V^2 is strictly above the point Y^1, B^1. Hence, the self-selection constraint does not bind for the U-indifference curve either. That is, both $V(B^1, Y^1/w^2)$ and $U(B^1, \bar{x}, Y^1/w^2)$

---

[6] If instead of Y^1, B^1 we offer the point Y^1, $B^1 - \bar{x}$, we force person 2 to either consume the point $B^1 - \bar{x}$, $\bar{x}$, or, if he chooses to forego the publicly provided quantity, the point $x(B^1 - \bar{x}, Y^1/w^2)$, $c(B^1 - \bar{x}, Y^1/w^2)$. In either case his utility is less than $V(Y^1, B^1)$.

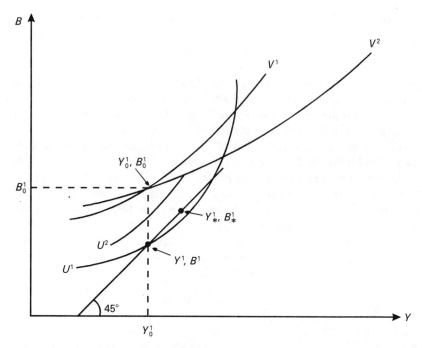

Fig. 3. Pareto improving public provision of x.

are less than V^2. If, instead of Y^1, B^1, we offer the point Y^1_*, B^1_*, this implies a strict increase in person 1's utility. Since $Y^1_* - B^1_* = -T^2 + \bar{x}$, the point also satisfies the government's budget constraint. Hence, we obtain a strict Pareto improvement.

A crucial assumption implicit in Figure 3 is that the U-indifference curve with utility level V^2 is located strictly above the point Y^1, B^1. Figure 4, which illustrates the situation at Y^1_0, B^1_0, can be used to discuss under what conditions this will occur. The indifference curves are drawn conditional on $Y = Y^1_0$ and the budget constraint corresponds to $c + x = B^1_0$. We show an indifference curve $U(c, x; Y^1_0/w^2) = V^2$. Person 2's utility maximizing combination of c and x, if he chooses Y^1_0, B^1_0, is given by c^2, x^2. We do not show the indifference curve $U(c, x; Y^1_0/w^1) = V^1$, but only the utility maximizing point c^1, x^1. The points c^1, x^1 and c^2, x^2 show how persons 1 and 2 spend B^1_0 if they can choose freely and both have labor income Y^1_0. (Without loss of generality we assume that $x^2 > x^1$). Let the public provision $\bar{x}$ be equal to x^1. To keep utility unchanged for person 1, B has to be set so that c^1 can be bought. That is, we have to set $B^1 = B^1_0 - \bar{x}$. This implies that the U-indifference curve for person 1 in Figure 3 is

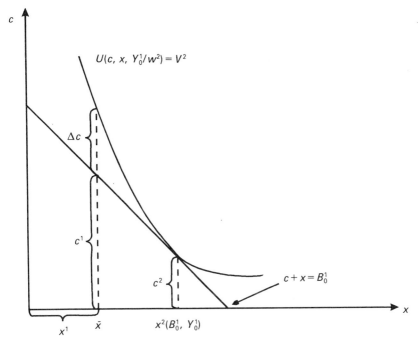

Fig. 4. Conditions for public provision of x to be Pareto improving.

exactly $\bar{x}$ units below the V-indifference curve at $Y = Y_0^1$. For person 2 to achieve utility V^2 if x equals $\bar{x}$, c has to equal $c^1 + \Delta c$. This means that at Y_0^1 in Figure 3, the vertical distance between person 2's U- and V-indifference curves is $\bar{x} - \Delta c$. In order for public provision to be effectual, Δc must be strictly positive. Intuitively, the larger Δc is, the more the self-selection constraint slackens when we introduce public provision of x. The following proposition should be obvious from Figure 4.

Proposition 1. *Public provision of good x cannot improve welfare if any of the conditions i–iii holds: (i) the publicly provided quantity $\bar{x}$ can be resold; (ii) leisure is weakly separable from the two commodities, implying that $x(B, Y/w)$ does not depend on Y; (iii) x and c are perfect substitutes.*[7]

The reverse of proposition 1 implies that public provision is more effectual if the absolute value of $\partial x(B, h)/\partial h$ is large and the indifference

---

[7] For some types of goods we should add that public provision is futile if, contrary to our assumption, it is possible to supplement the good on the market; see Blomquist and Christiansen (1995).

curve $U(c, x; Y/w^2)$ is strongly curved. That is, x and c should be complements.

Nondistortionary redistribution

Consider the optimal taxation problem illustrated in Figure 2. Keeping utility for person 2 at the level V^2, the tax T^2 can be collected from him. This is done in a non-distortionary way. We know that person 1 cannot be offered the point Y^0, B^0, because person 2 would then select that point. Let us for the moment disregard the self-selection constraint and only consider the resource constraint. The utility maximization problem for person 1 is then: Max $U(c, x, h)$; s.t. $c + x = w^1 h + T^2$. We denote the solution by $\hat{c}$, $\hat{x}$, $\hat{h}$, which implies $\hat{Y} = w^1 \hat{h}$. Of course, $\hat{Y}$ is the same as Y^0 in Figure 2 and $\hat{c} + \hat{x} = B^0$. While $V(B^0, Y^0/w^2) > V^2$, it is quite possible that $V(B^0 - \hat{x}, Y^0/w^2) < V^2$ and $U(\hat{c}, \hat{x}, Y^0/w^2) < V^2$. That is, even though we cannot provide the point Y^0, B^0 in cash to person 1, we can provide the consumption point person 1 would choose if he were provided the point Y^0, B^0. Note that the marginal tax is zero for both persons and that we have achieved redistribution without any distortions.

The Optimal Taxation and Public Provision Problem

For sufficiently large redistributions, the self-selection constraint will be binding. Let N^1 and N^2 denote the number of persons of type 1 and 2, respectively. The optimization problem where both the income tax points and the quantity $\bar{x}$ are determined simultaneously can then be formulated as: Max $\Omega(B^1, \bar{x}, Y^1/w^1)$ subject to the utility requirement $\Omega(B^2, \bar{x}, Y^2/w^2) \geq \bar{V}^2$, the self-selection constraint $\Omega(B^2, \bar{x}, Y^2/w^2) \geq \Omega(B^1, \bar{x}, Y^1/w^2)$ and the economy's budget constraint $N^1(Y^1 - B^1) + N^2(Y^2 - B^2) = (M^1(\bar{x}, Y^1, B^1) + M^2(\bar{x}, Y^2, B^2))\bar{x}$. M^i can be either zero or N^i. The government chooses Y^1, Y^2, B^1, B^2 and $\bar{x}$.

IV. Characterization of Social Optima

The description of the optimal taxation-public provision problem in Section III is complete, but misleadingly simple. Since the upper contour set defined by $\Omega(\cdot) = \tilde{V}$ is nonconvex, we have a complicated programming problem with the possibility of several local maxima. A general characterization of the optimum does not convey much insight. We find it more instructive to characterize various types of optima separately. The kind of optimum that will arise depends on the nature of preferences and the specific parameters of the economy. To describe a type of optimum, we apply the term *regime*. A regime is defined by the kind of choices made by the various consumers and by the set of constraints that are binding.

The route we follow is to survey a number of regimes, while only characterizing a few in detail.[7] For simplicity and without loss of generality we assume that there is one individual of each type. Our attention is confined to regimes in which person 1 accepts the fixed, freely provided $\bar{x}$. To describe the conduct of person 2 we have to characterize the consumption point actually assigned to person 2 at the optimum as well as the choice he would make if mimicking person 1's choice. Person 2's actual choice has a bearing on the expenditure side of the government budget constraint. What the mimicker does has a bearing on the self-selection constraint.

Since both persons make a choice with respect to x and with respect to income point (Y, B), there are three ways in which they can be separated, that is, by having completely different vectors (Y, B, x), by only having different income points (Y, B), or by only having different consumption of the x-good. We say that *person 2 is mimicking if he chooses the income point intended for person 1*, irrespective of whether person 2 then makes the same choice of x as person 1.

We see that there are two kinds of self-selection going on concerning person 2. One is the choice between mimicking and not. The other is the choice between accepting $\bar{x}$ or not. The constraint that person 2 should be better off not mimicking is termed the *mimicking constraint*. As discussed below, it may also be socially desirable to induce person 2 not to choose the public provision $\bar{x}$ at the optimum. This means that the gross and net income bundle (Y^2, B^2) assigned to him should not be located below the borderline between regions where $\bar{x}$ is accepted and not. This constraint is termed the *borderline constraint*.

To limit the scope of the analysis we make the following specific assumptions:

A1. The first best social optimum is not attainable.
A2. The mimicking constraint is strictly binding.
A3. Person 1 is assumed to accept the public provision of x.
A4. There is a single crossing point between corresponding V- and U-curves, i.e., curves representing the same utility level.

As shown in Blomquist and Christiansen (1994) a sufficient condition for A4 is that x is monotonically increasing or decreasing along an indifference curve of type $V(B, Y) = \bar{V}$. The former always holds if x is a substitute for leisure in the conditional demand function.

Before proceeding to a more formal analysis, some additional notation will prove useful. Let us write $U^i(c, x, Y)$ for $U(c, x, Y/w^i)$. When public

---

provision is accepted, $c = B$, and we can write $U^i(B, \bar{x}, Y)$. To indicate that person 2 is mimicking, the superscript m is attached to the respective utility functions. This means that $V^m = V(B^1, Y^1/w^2)$ and $U^m = U(c, x, Y^1/w^2)$, where c and x will be specified in each case. Subscripts are used to indicate partial derivatives. Commodity c is used as the numeraire.

To define the various regimes, we need a list of the special cases of the various constraints introduced above. At this stage we find it useful to let p denote the constant marginal cost (and market price) of x. The resource constraint can take the form:

(a) $Y^1 - B^1 + Y^2 - B^2 - p\bar{x} = r$ or   (b) $Y^1 - B^1 + Y^2 - B^2 - 2p\bar{x} = r$,

where r is the net resource requirement of the government.
The minimum utility requirement of person 2 can take the form:

(c) $V^2(B^2, Y^2) = \bar{V}^2$ or   (d) $U^2(B^2, \bar{x}, Y^2) = \bar{V}^2$.

The mimicking constraint can take the form:

(e) $U^m(B^1, \bar{x}, Y^1) \le V^2(B^2, Y^2)$,   (f) $V^m(B^1, Y^1) \le V^2(B^2, Y^2)$,
(g) $U^m(B^1, \bar{x}, Y^1) \le U^2(B^2, \bar{x}, Y^2)$ or   (h) $V^m(B^1, Y^1) \le U^2(B^2, \bar{x}, Y^2)$.

In addition there can be a borderline constraint:

(i) $U^2(B^2, \bar{x}, Y^2) \le V^2(B^2, Y^2)$.

It is obvious that the resource constraint and the minimum utility requirement for person 2 are binding, and the constraints have been formulated as equations from the outset. (a) and (c) apply if person 2 opts for the free choice of x in the market. (b) and (d) apply if person 2 accepts the public provision of x. Which of the mimicking constraints that is relevant depends on the choices of person 1 and of person 2 as a mimicker. Six regimes are displayed in the table below, where the regimes are denoted by roman numerals, and letters in parentheses indicate binding constraints.

Mimicker chooses	Person 2 actually chooses Market x with borderline constraint		Public provision
	Not binding	Binding	
Public provision	I (a),(c),(e)	II (a),(c),(e),(i)	V (b),(d),(g)
Market quantity	III (a),(c),(f)	IV (a),(c),(f),(i)	VI (b),(d),(h)

---

[8] If the scope of the analysis is extended by abandoning assumption A2, we would also have a regime where person 2 does mimic while choosing to buy x on the market, so that separation is solely by choice of x.

We characterize regimes I, II and V in more detail, and comment briefly on the other regimes.[8]

Regimes I & III

The tax design part of this social optimization problem is equivalent to the standard optimum taxation problem; see e.g. Stiglitz (1987). The conventional characterization that $-V_Y^2/V_B^2 = 1$ and $-U_Y^1/U_B^1 < 1$ can easily be derived. We interpret this as person 2 facing a zero marginal tax rate and person 1 facing a positive marginal tax rate. The zero marginal tax rate and the preset utility level of person 2 together determine the income point B^2, Y^2 of person 2 as the point on his V-curve where the slope is unity. Let $T^2 = Y^2 - B^2$ denote the tax collected from person 2, which is also determined when the income point is fixed.

The further optimization is then reduced to maximizing U^1 subject to the mimicking constraint and the resource constraint, and we formulate the Lagrangian

$$\mathcal{L} = U^1(B^1, \bar{x}, Y^1) + \mu(Y^1 - B^1 + T^2 - p\bar{x} - r) - \beta(U^m(B^1, \bar{x}, Y^1) - \bar{V}^2). \quad (1)$$

Deriving first-order conditions and eliminating the Lagrange multipliers, we obtain:

$$\frac{U_x^1}{U_B^1} - p = \frac{1 + U_Y^1/U_B^1}{1 + U_Y^m/U_B^m}\left(\frac{U_x^m}{U_B^m} - p\right) = k\left(\frac{U_x^m}{U_B^m} - p\right), \quad (2)$$

where k is defined by the latter equation. The l.h.s. of (2) is the conventional difference between person 1's marginal benefit from good x and the marginal cost. On the r.h.s. there is a corresponding difference for the mimicker. This difference is multiplied by a term reflecting the effect of the mimicking constraint. It follows from the optimum tax characterization that $0 < k < 1$. The implication is that at the optimum, the consumption of x is distorted in the same direction for person 1 and the mimicker, but the marginal distortion is smaller for person 1. Both distortions are, of course, endogenous. Starting from the mimicker's marginal valuation of good x, we see that if it is greater (less) than the marginal cost, person 1's marginal willingness to pay for good x should deviate positively (negatively) from the marginal cost. In this sense person 1 is underconsuming (overconsuming) good x relative to the first best rule. The intuition is that good x is a more efficient vehicle for transferring resources to person 1, the lower the good is valued by the potential mimicker.

One version of this kind of optimum is illustrated in c, x-space in the Figure 5. F is the production feasibility curve or transformation curve corresponding to Y^1, Y^2 and B^2. That is, it is the graph of the equation $c + px = R$, where R is the residual amount of resources $Y^1 + Y^2 - B^2 - r$.

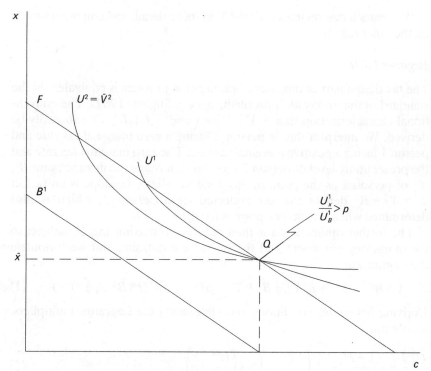

Fig. 5. Regime I, the underconsumption case.

B^1 denotes the budget constraint of person 1 after paying the tax necessary to finance the public provision of x. In Figure 5 we see that given the pure resource constraint, it would be feasible and desirable to offer person 1 a point on the transformation curve to the left of Q. But because of the mimicking constraint this is not possible. Q is the optimum given the mimicking constraint, and this allocation is implemented by offering the budget constraint B^1 and the option to accept $\bar{x}$ free of charge rather than using part of the budget for buying the good x on the market. Since a larger amount of leisure is the only feature that distinguishes the mimicker from person 1, it is easy to see that overconsumption (underconsumption) occurs if the marginal valuation of x in terms of c is decreasing (increasing) in leisure and x is a substitute for (complement to) leisure in the conditional demand function.

Regime III is distinguished from regime I only by the choice of the mimicker who prefers to buy x on the market. The conventional optimum tax results obviously remain valid. By appealing to intuition we can argue that the optimum is characterized by person 1 overconsuming the good x

in the sense that his marginal benefit of x is lower than the marginal cost. The reason is that since the mimicker does not accept the public provision anyway, an increase in $\bar{x}$ is worthless to the mimicker, which means that the public provision is a particularly efficient redistributional tool. Suppose for a moment that $\bar{x}$ is chosen such that person 1's marginal benefit equals marginal cost. Then $\bar{x}$ can be increased and B^1 reduced such that person 1 remains equally well off as person 2, while the mimicker is clearly made worse off. Then the mimicking constraint is relaxed and a Pareto improvement is permitted.

Regimes II & IV

Let us first argue that the income point P_0, where the slope of the V^2-curve is unity, is not optimal in regime II. If the borderline constraint is binding at P_0, it must, by the definition of binding, imply that some otherwise desirable change in B^2, Y^2, $\bar{x}$ is blocked by the constraint. There is no desire to change only the income point B^2, Y^2 since that is the point at which person 2's net tax liability is maximized, and so is the residual amount of resources available for the benefit of person 1 given the utility level of person 2. It is changing $\bar{x}$ that would have to be otherwise desirable. The income point P_0 has the property that to a first-order effect B^2, Y^2 can be changed marginally while keeping tax revenue and person 2's utility unchanged in such a way that the borderline constraint is slightly relaxed, and the desirable change in $\bar{x}$ can take place. This change will tighten the borderline constraint again and move the point at which it is binding away from P_0. Thus deviating from P_0 is Pareto improving.

Since P_0, where the slope of the V^2-curve is unity, is not chosen in regime II, a characteristic of the regime is that the borderline b^2 is located above P_0. (If not, one could let person 2 choose the point P_0, where he pays more tax while retaining his utility level.)

To characterize the optimum, let us start by noting that the utility requirement and the binding borderline constraint implicitly define person 2's gross and net income as functions of $\bar{x}$. By differentiating we can find the effects of changing $\bar{x}$. Inserting the implicit functions into the mimicking constraint and the production feasibility constraint, person 1's gross and net income are also related to $\bar{x}$, and so is the utility of person 1. Differentiating the utility function, and taking account of the implicit functions, we find the effect of a differential change in $\bar{x}$ on person 1's utility. Equating the effect to zero, we get the optimality condition:

$$\frac{\mathrm{d}U^1}{\mathrm{d}\bar{x}}\frac{1}{U_B^1} = \frac{\left[1+\dfrac{U_Y^1}{U_B^1}\right]\left[p+B_x^2-Y_x^2-\dfrac{U_x^m}{U_B^m}\right]}{1+U_Y^m/U_B^m} + \frac{U_x^1}{U_B^1} - p - (B_x^2 - Y_x^2) = 0. \tag{3}$$

This is a straightforward extension of formula (2) in regime I. The only difference is that $B_x^2 - Y_x^2$ is added to the conventional cost p. The additional term is an extra cost of increasing $\bar{x}$ since it is the increase in person 2's net disposable income that is needed to satisfy the borderline constraint. With this qualification, the interpretation of (3) is analogous to that of (2). Condition (3) can be rewritten as

$$\frac{U_x^1}{U_B^1} - p = k\left(\frac{U_x^m}{U_B^m} - p\right) + (1-k)(-T_x^2). \tag{4}$$

The wedge between person 1's marginal benefit and the marginal cost is equal to a weighted average of the corresponding wedge for the mimicker and the loss of tax revenue at the margin. Comparing with (2), there is an extra term which provides an argument for underprovision of x to person 1 relative to the first best rule. The explanation for this effect is that the amount of $\bar{x}$ may have to be limited in order to make it unattractive to person 2. Here, the consumption of good x by person 1 and the mimicker is not necessarily distorted in the same direction.

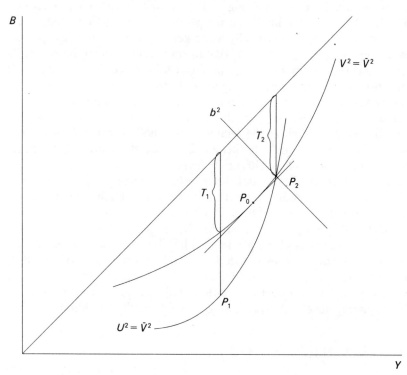

Fig. 6. Regime II.

Let us consider when regime II will occur. At P_0 in Figure 6 the slope of the V^2-curve is one. We already know that in regime II, $\bar{x}$ is assumed to be given such a value that the borderline b^2 is pushed beyond P_0 as shown in the figure. Point P_0 will not be chosen by person 2. But P_1 or P_2 can be assigned to person 2. P_2 is on the borderline when person 2 is just induced to choose x freely. P_1 is the point on the U^2-curve where the gradient is one. At P_1 net tax revenue is less than T_1 since the vertical distance between the two indifference curves is smaller than the cost of the public provision $\bar{x}$. If the tax revenue at P_2, denoted by T_2, is larger than the net tax revenue at P_1, one should select P_2 rather than P_1.

Even though the net tax revenue from person 2 is lower at P_2 than at P_0, it may be that person 1 can be made better off by increasing $\bar{x}$ to the extent that the former point is reached. His marginal valuation of x may be high enough to justify the extra cost in terms of lost tax revenue.

We may note that when the borderline intersects the V^2-curve to the right of P_0, and the optimum is at a point like P_2 in Figure 6, the marginal tax rate of person 2 is negative since $dB^2/dY^2 > 1$. Hence we have a case in which the conventional optimum tax result does not apply.

Regime IV has important features in common with regime II. While the fact that the mimicker does not accept the public provision is an argument in favor of public "overprovision", the quantity $\bar{x}$ may have to be cut back below this level in order to discourage person 2 from accepting it.

Regimes V & VI

If the publicly provided quantity $\bar{x}$ is always accepted by both persons, the good x is analogous to a public good, the price of which is $2p$. The same quantity enters both utility functions, and if this quantity is increased by one unit, the total increase in the amount of the good x is two units, and the additional cost is $2p$. The introduction of a public good into the second best optimum tax model has been studied by Boadway and Keen (1993). By direct analogy we can immediately adopt their main result which states that there is underprovision or overprovision of the public good relative to the Samuelson Rule as the marginal valuation of the public good to the mimicker is greater than or less than that to the low-ability person. "Overprovision" means that the sum of marginal rates of substitution is pushed down to a level below the marginal cost. The intuition for the result is that it is efficient to use the public good as a vehicle for transferring resources to the low-ability person when the mimicker values the good less than the former. By substituting some of the public good for cash, the potential mimicker will have to forfeit more income in order to mimic, and this sacrifice will not be compensated by the public good provision due to his low evaluation of that good.

In our case, providing an amount of x that both persons will accept is like constructing a public good that can be used as a redistributive tool. To discuss the existence of such a regime, let us take as our point of departure the conclusion that *if it is possible to assign to person 2 the income point P_0 where the slope of the V^2-curve is unity, it is always optimal to do so.* Since the vertical distance between the V^2-curve and the U^2-curve is smaller than or at most equal to the cost of the public provision of x, the net tax revenue can always be increased or at least maintained by switching to a point on the V^2-curve. And on the V^2-curve the net tax liability of person 2 is maximized at P_0.

But if assigning P_0 to person 2 is not feasible due to the borderline constraint, it may be that when $\bar{x}$ is increased as far as is welfare improving, a point is reached at which one would rather let person 2 have the public provision as well, because enforcing the borderline constraint becomes too costly. As long as person 2 does not get the public provision, in terms of resources available for person 1, the marginal cost of increasing $\bar{x}$ is $p + B_x^2 - Y_x^2$. At a potential switching point where the borderline constraint is abandoned and person 2 gets the public provision, the marginal cost becomes $p + p\bar{x} - (T_\ast^2 - T_b^2)$, where $(T_\ast^2 - T_b^2)$ is the difference between the tax paid by person 2 when he takes $\bar{x}$ and the tax he pays when induced not to accept $\bar{x}$. It is when this marginal cost is no longer greater than $p + B_x^2 - Y_x^2$ that the switch should take place, e.g. from P_2 to P_1 in Figure 6. If person 1's marginal willingness to pay for $\bar{x}$ is large enough, there is no reason why such a point may not be reached.

Regime VI is distinguished from the preceding one by the mimicker choosing not to accept the public provision. Since an increase in $\bar{x}$ is worthless to the mimicker, it is an efficient tool for increasing the utility of person 1, which explains why overprovision will prevail in this regime.

V. Applications

A private good suitable for the type of public provision scheme studied here should have the following characteristics: (i) the good should be such that it cannot be resold or supplemented, (ii) the demand for the good should vary greatly with leisure for a given consumption expenditure, and (iii) there should be no close market substitutes for the publicly provided good. We now examine how education, health care, day care and care of the elderly, which are four important publicly provided private goods, satisfy these conditions. None of the goods can be resold. The possibilities of supplementing them are also quite limited. (This is partly by construction. For several of the goods it would be easy to construct a voucher system that would make it possible to resell and/or supplement the publicly provided quantity.) None of the goods have close market substitutes. Thus, at least two of the three characteristics are satisfied for these goods. Unfortunately, there are no empirical studies on how the demand for such goods varies with respect to leisure. Below we discuss how the demand varies with respect to leisure for each good.

Education: Education for one's children is a good that can be supplied by both the public sector and private market institutions. Common sense offers no unambiguous guidance as to whether education at school and parents' leisure allocated for the benefit of children are substitutes or complements in the investment in human capital. It may be argued that more leisure makes time available for educating, in a broad sense, one's own children as a substitute for formal teaching. The effect of increased leisure is to reduce the demand for education in the market. High-skill people who work a great deal would then be inclined to demand a large amount of education and be likely to buy private schooling. If mimicking, they would have more leisure and would be more attracted by the public alternative.

Alternatively, it can be argued that efforts by parents to help educate their children are complementary to the teaching they get at school. The implication would be that more leisure stimulates the demand for education. In this case the high-skill person may be inclined to turn to the market for a larger amount of x because he can afford it, while as a mimicker he might prefer to buy a larger quantity of x on the market due to his relatively ample leisure time.

Day care and care of the elderly: We discuss day care, although the same type of argument can also apply to care of the elderly. A child needs care a fixed number of hours per day. Parents usually attend to part of this day care by foregoing leisure time. Basically, one more hour of parental day care is one less hour of leisure time. For a given consumption expenditure, a person with more scarce leisure will want more x than a person with a higher value of leisure. At person 2's actual income point, he may well prefer to buy a quantity of x larger than $\bar{x}$, because he actually has so little leisure time and earns so much money that both needs and means generate a relatively high demand for x. If mimicking, however, he would have considerable leisure and might have a moderate demand for x, implying a modest benefit from $\bar{x}$.

Health care: We assume that individuals can rely on public health care or purchase private health insurance of different quality and coverage. Let x denote the quality of health insurance. A low value of x implies that if a person becomes ill he has to wait for treatment and is less favorably treated. The implication is that it takes people with low-quality insurance longer to get well. Hence, part of the effect of buying high-quality insurance is like buying leisure. If a person has a low value of leisure, *ceteris paribus*, the marginal value of leisure is high and he wants to buy insurance with a high value of x.

VI. Summary and Conclusions

We have shown *why* public provision of a private good can improve welfare and *what characterizes* private goods that are suitable for public provision. Goods suitable for the type of public provision scheme considered are those that cannot be resold or supplemented, that lack close market substitutes, and whose demand varies greatly with leisure. The essence of these requirements is that the provision should not be equivalent to a transfer in cash and should discriminate between different types of persons.

The solution to the optimal taxation and public provision problem can be of several types. We examined solutions or "regimes", where the low-skill person accepts the public provision. It may or may not be in the interest of society to let the high-skill person have an incentive to accept the public provision. In some of the regimes, the high-skill person accepts the public provision, while in others he foregoes it and buys a quantity of his own choice in the market. There is a higher degree of separation when person 2 chooses the market alternative. But in terms of resources available, it may be costly for person 1 to achieve this separation because the disposable income of person 2 may have to be increased in order to induce him not to accept the public provision. Incurring this cost may pay off, or it may be preferable to let both persons accept the public provision. It may be that the total transfer of resources is maximized by choosing a level of x which is also attractive to the high-skill person. The reason is that any attempt to replace some of this amount of x with cash would induce mimicking.

The optimal level of public provision will, in general, be such that the low-skill person either overconsumes or underconsumes x relative to the first best rule that marginal cost equals marginal willingness to pay. Person 2 might be discouraged from choosing the income point of person 1 combined with a high level of x because even a large quantity of x would be of little value to him at this particular income level. Hence the public provision would not offset the disadvantage of having the same low income as person 1. Alternatively, person 2 might be discouraged from choosing the income point of person 1 in combination with a small public provision of x because he would not benefit much from such an ungenerous offer. It might even be worthless to him if he would prefer to forego it anyway. In these cases as well the public provision would not compensate the mimicker for being poor in terms of cash.

It may also be socially desirable that only the low-skill person accepts the public provision. To obtain this outcome through self-selection it may be necessary to reduce the public provision to a level which implies underconsumption for the low-skill person.

References

Bergstrom, T. & Blomquist, S.: The political economy of subsidized day care. WP 1993: 15, Department of Economics, Uppsala University, 1993; forthcoming in *European Journal of Political Economy*.

Besley, T.: Welfare improving user charges for publicly provided private goods. *Scandinavian Journal of Economics 93*, 495–510, 1991.

Besley, T. & Coate, S.: Public provision of private goods and the redistribution of income. *American Economic Review 81*, 979–84, 1991.

Blackorby, C. & Donaldson, D.: Cash versus kind, self-selection and efficient transfers. *American Economic Review 78*, 691–700, 1988.

Blomquist, S. & Christiansen, V.: Public provision of private goods as a redistributive device in an optimal income tax model. WP 1994:26, Department of Economics, Uppsala University, 1994.

Blomquist, S. & Christiansen, V.: Topping up or opting out? The optimal design of public provision schemes. WP 1995:13, Department of Economics, Uppsala University, 1995.

Boadway, R. & Keen, M.: Public goods, self-selection and optimal income taxation. *International Economic Review 34*, 463–78, 1993.

Boadway, R. & Marchand, M.: The use of public expenditures for redistributive purposes. *Oxford Economic Papers 47*, 45–59, 1995.

Christiansen, V.: Which commodity taxes should supplement the income tax? *Journal of Public Economics 24*, 195–220, 1984.

Ireland, N. J.: The mix of social and private provision of goods and services. *Journal of Public Economics 43*, 201–19, 1990.

Munro, A.: In-kind transfers, cash grants and the supply of labour. *European Economic Review 33*, 1597–604, 1989.

Munro, A.: The optimal public provision of private goods. *Journal of Public Economics 44*, 239–61, 1991.

Stiglitz, J. E.: Pareto efficient and optimal taxation and the new new welfare economics. In A. J. Auerbach & M. Feldstein (eds.), *Handbook of Public Economics*, vol. 2, North-Holland, Amsterdam, 1987.

Why are Taxes so High in Egalitarian Societies?

Mats Persson*

University of Stockholm, Sweden

Abstract

In an analysis of the relative income, or relative consumption, hypothesis, it is shown that if the ratio of agent i's consumption to agent j's consumption enters into the utility function, a tax on labor income may increase welfare for all agents. If pre-tax wage inequality is low, all agents will unanimously be in favor of such a tax. Thus there will be a tendency for taxes to be high in societies where pre-tax wage inequality is low.

I. Introduction

At first sight, the above question is deceptively simple: in an egalitarian society there will be a lot of redistribution from the rich to the poor. Thus redistributive taxes will be high. There are, however, two problems with such an answer, indicating that it does not cover the entire truth. First, there seems to be widespread agreement that not only redistributive taxes, but *all* taxes, are high in modern, egalitarian welfare states. A great deal of redistribution is taking place within the middle class, and even over the same individual's life cycle, with no obvious effects in terms of making the poor better off at the expense of the rich.[1] Moreover, the actual incidence of government consumption, which is also high in countries with an even income distribution, is still an unsettled issue.

Second, there is a tendency for taxes to be high in countries where not only *disposable* income, but also *pre-tax* income, is evenly distributed. This is illustrated in Figure 1. In Figure 1a we see the relation between government spending (as a percentage of GDP) and pre-tax income inequality (measured by the Gini coefficient) for those countries for which reasonably comparable data are available. Pre-tax income here is "primary income"

---

*Valuable comments from Jonas Agell, Vidar Christiansen, Thorvaldur Gylfason, and two anonymous referees are gratefully acknowledged.
[1] See for example Lindbeck (1983).

according to the definition of Atkinson *et al.* (1995), i.e., wages, salaries and self-employment income. The regression line for this diagram is:

$$GOVSPEND = 76.21 - 1.00 \cdot GINI + e \qquad R^2 = 0.20$$
$$(1.73)$$

The figure in parentheses is the t statistic; we see that the negative regression coefficient is almost significant at the 5 per cent level and clearly significant at the 10 per cent level. Using another income concept, namely "market income", which includes primary income and various kinds of capital income for which data are notoriously unreliable — for details, see Atkinson *et al.* (1995) — results in the pattern displayed in Figure 1b. Here the regression line reads:

$$GOVSPEND = 78.15 - 0.84 \cdot GINI + e \qquad R^2 = 0.12$$
$$(-1.59)$$

and the t statistic indicates that the coefficient is significantly negative at the 10 per cent level.

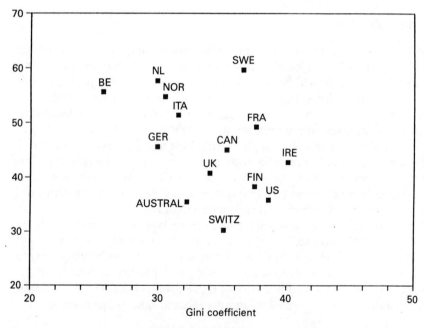

Sources: Atkinson *et al.* (1995, Table 6.4) and OECD Economic Outlook, Dec. 1993.

Fig. 1a. Government spending as a share of GDP and the distribution of pre-tax income (excluding capital gains) in 14 OECD countries.

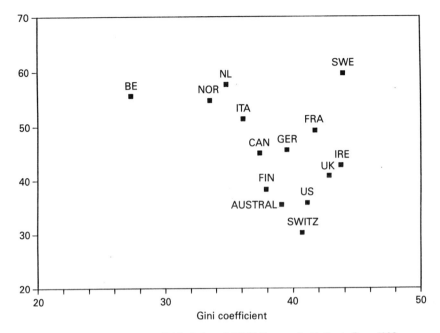

Sources: Atkinson *et al.* (1995, Table 6.7) and OECD Economic Outlook, Dec. 1993.

Fig. 1b. Government spending as a share of GDP and the distribution of pre-tax income (including capital gains) in 14 OECD countries.

Of course, such generalizations should be considered with caution, bearing in mind the overwhelming problems of data quality and data comparability that are involved.[2] Nevertheless, the regression lines indicate that there might be more to the question in the title of this paper than the simple explanation given above. For instance, we have said nothing but causality. Maybe a more even pre-tax income distribution will cause higher government spending — perhaps by public choice arguments, where a more similar electorate could be manipulated more easily by self-interested politicians and bureaucrats? On the other hand, higher taxes

---

[2] A Swedish researcher might, for example, be surprised by the picture conveyed by Figure 1a of Sweden as a country with a fairly large inequality in "primary income". The data are taken from the Luxembourg Income Study, which aims at a high degree of comparability between countries — but *any* researcher can probably find reasons why the data of his or her particular country is not fully comparable to the data of the other countries. The general picture of Figure 1, however, is the same if other data sets are used, for example, that of Freeman and Katz (1994).

might very well lead to a more even distribution of pre-tax income, for example, if the taxes are used to finance a general education program.[3]

Furthermore, although there is a significant covariation, there may not be any causal relationship at all between the income distribution and the size of the public sector. Both of them may be endogenous variables, affected by other, exogenous causes.

There are thus many conceivable ways of linking high taxes to the income distribution. In this paper I discuss one of them which has not, to my knowledge, been analyzed earlier in the literature. It deals with a causation from technology, which determines the pre-tax income distribution, to taxes (saying that a more even distribution will lead to higher taxes) and it builds on the so-called relative consumption, or relative income, hypothesis.

II. The Relative Consumption Hypothesis

The tremendous rate of economic growth during the last hundred years, when real per capita income increased by a factor of maybe 15, raises an intriguing question: why aren't people happier? A sociologist might answer: absolute consumption levels do not matter so much, but relative levels do. If a man's income suddenly increases to make him the richest person in his community, his sense of well-being will increase dramatically. But if everyone else's income also rises in proportion, so that our man retains his initial position in society, his happiness would not increase at all as much as it otherwise would have done.

It is hard to tell whether people actually have such preferences. Some introspection, however, and a few casual observations of human interaction in everyday life, indicate that this seems about as plausible as the standard assumption of microeconomic theory, namely that only absolute consumption matters. The issue is discussed by Esterlin (1974), who also cites a number of studies of what determines people's perception of happiness, and by Layard (1980). Interesting empirical evidence on the relative consumption hypothesis is given in Clark and Oswald (1993). The implications for estimating labor supply if the utility of agents depends on the consumption of other agents are discussed by Blomquist (1993).

The implications for optimal taxation, with an extra term $c_i/\bar{c}$ (where $\bar{c}$ is the average consumption in society) in the utility function of individual i, have been studied by Boskin and Sheshinski (1978). Their study dealt with

---

[3] High taxes might also induce high-income earliers to hide their income to a larger extent than low-income earners. Thus the (pre-tax and post-tax) income distribution, based on officially reported data, may look more egalitarian than it actually is. For an investigation along these lines, see Persson and Wissén (1984).

the case of a linear income tax, while Oswald (1983) analyzed the general, non-linear income tax. A further analysis of the joint problem of optimal (linear) income taxation and the investment in human capital is provided by Lommerud (1989). A common feature of these papers is the purely normative approach; the problem is to find the tax schedule that maximizes a utilitarian social welfare function. Thereby it can be seen how the introduction of a relative consumption term into the utility function affects the standard results of optimal tax theory.

Interesting insights can also be deprived, however, by dropping the utilitarian welfare function and relying on a weaker welfare criterion, namely the Pareto criterion. This in turn makes the positive, rather than the normative, implications of the relative income hypothesis more transparent. Such an approach will give us one possible explanation as to why taxes tend to be high in egalitarian societies. We can begin by spelling out an explicit model. For pedagogical reasons, we confine the analysis to the simplest possible two-person case; the results can easily be generalized to the case of an arbitrary number of persons.

Consider an economy consisting of two (groups of) individuals. For simplicity we assume that they have identical preferences, but this is in no way essential for the argument. The utility of individual i depends on relative consumption c_i/c_j, as well as on absolute consumption c_i, and on labor l_i:

$$u^i = u(c_i/c_j, c_i, l_i) \qquad i, j = 1, 2, \quad i \neq j$$

where $u_1^i > 0$, $u_2^i > 0$, $u_{22}^i \leq 0$, $u_3^i < 0$ and $u_{33}^i \geq 0$. The individual faces a budget constraint in the absence of taxes,

$$c_i = w_i l_i,$$

where w_i is the real wage and where we assume a linear production technology, so wages will be exogenously given in general equilibrium. Here one may wonder why only consumption of the consumption good c_i matters for an individual's relative position, and not *total* consumption of the consumption good *and* leisure $1 - l_i$. Extending that argument, what should matter is perhaps relative indirect utility, v^i/v^j. Without going into this question in detail, it could be said that c_i is more easily observable than leisure (or indirect utility). The driving force behind the relative income term may be a signalling game: what matters for the individual's well-being is access to certain goods outside this model, and the access to those goods is correlated with ability[4] (e.g. with unobservable productivity, w_i). By

---

[4] For an interesting analysis of human behavior in the presence of such non-market goods, see Cole *et al.* (1992).

working hard and displaying a high observable income $l_i w_i$, an individual could thus try to signal a high ability w_i.

Regardless of the more profound reasons for including a c_i/c_j term in the utility function, we know that if such a term is introduced, the agent's optimum is characterized by the first-order condition:

$$\frac{w_i}{w_j l_j} u_1^i + w_i u_2^i + u_3^i = 0 \qquad i, j = 1, 2, \quad i \neq j \tag{1}$$

Agent i takes the labor supply of agent j as given, and (1) thus gives rise to a pair of reaction functions:

$$l_1 = l(w_1, w_2, l_2), \qquad l_2 = l(w_2, w_1, l_1). \tag{2}$$

Solving this system of equations defines a Nash equilibrium

$$l_1^* = l^*(w_1, w_2), \qquad l_2^* = l^*(w_2, w_1) \tag{3}$$

which may, or may not, be unique.

If no relative income effects were present, as in standard microeconomics, we would have $u_1^i = 0$ and consequently the first-order conditions $w_i u_2^i + u_3^i = 0$ would yield ordinary labor supply functions

$$\hat{l}_1 = \hat{l}(w_1), \qquad \hat{l}_2 = \hat{l}(w_2).$$

Since $u_1^i > 0$, equation (1), however, implies that

$$w_i u_2^i + u_3^i < 0,$$

i.e., $l_i^* > \hat{l}_i$. If the agents could somehow be induced to reduce their labor supplies simultaneously by small amounts dl_i^*, such that relative consumption $(l_1^* - dl_1^*) w_1 / (l_2^* - dl_2^*) w_2$ remains unchanged, utility would obviously increase for both of them.

Such a simultaneous reduction in labor supplies does not, however, constitute a Nash equilibrium. It thus cannot be achieved in a noncooperative environment. This is where a collective device, such as an income tax, could play a role. Since the relative consumption term c_i/c_j implies that an individual's labor supply creates a negative externality, the income tax could be regarded as a Pigovian remedy. But the externality is of a rather particular kind, depending on the fact *the ratio c_i/c_j appears as an argument in the utility function*. This issue is discussed further below.

III. Income Taxation

The welfare effects of income taxation depend crucially on whether a society is egalitarian or not, i.e., whether the exogenous wage rates w_1 and w_2 are equal or not. In the following we analyze the possible configurations.

Two Local Results

Assume first that both agents have identical preferences as well as identical wages: $w_1 = w_2 = w$. With a linear tax schedule, the budget constraint reads

$$c_i = k + (1 - t) w l_i,$$

where t is the marginal tax rate and k is a lump-sum transfer. If we impose the restriction that the government's budget must be balanced, i.e., that $tw(l_1 + l_2) = 2k$, a tax increase dt will have no income effect, but only a substitution effect. Thus $dl_i/dt < 0$. Further, since both agents are identical in all respects, $c_1/c_2 = 1$ for all t. This means that the introduction of a linear income tax, such that the government's budget remains balanced, will always increase welfare for both agents.

Let us now assume instead that the innate inequality is at its maximum: $w_1 > 0$ and $w_2 = 0$. Then agent 2 will never find it optimal to work. He will regard his utility as exogenously given and equal to $u^2(c_2/c_1, c_2, 0)$, where c_2 is what he can obtain through the transfer k of the tax system. Thus his utility will be increasing in the tax rate if the economy is on the "left-hand side" of the Laffer curve, i.e., if tax revenue is an increasing function of the tax rate (which we will assume to be the case at least for small values of t). Agent 1, on the other hand, will always lose if the tax rate is increased. Since the behavior of agent 2 is unaffected by the tax rate (i.e., $l_2 \equiv 0$ regardless of the value of t), a tax increase will not alleviate any negative externality harming agent 1.

We can summarize these two results in the following way:

- *If pre-tax wages are equal, a zero tax rate will always be Pareto dominated by a strictly positive tax rate.*
- *If pre-tax wages display a maximum degree of inequality (i.e., $w_i = 0$ for one i), a zero tax rate can never be Pareto dominated by a strictly positive tax rate.*

The Cobb–Douglas Case

The two results above were general in the sense that they did not depend on any assumptions regarding e.g. the utility function. They were local, however, in the sense that they only applied to the polar cases of a minimum ($w_1 = w_2$) or a maximum ($w_1 > 0$, $w_2 = 0$) degree of inequality. For intermediate cases, we have to parameterize the model. Consider the following utility function:[5]

---

[5] This is a formulation which includes $\ln(c_i/c_j)$ as a special case, since

$$\lim_{\gamma \to 1} [1/(1 - \gamma)] x^{1 - \gamma} = \ln x.$$

$$u^i = \frac{\alpha}{1-\gamma} \left[\frac{c_i}{c_j} \right]^{1-\gamma} + \beta \ln(c_i) + (1-\beta) \ln(1 - l_i) \qquad i = 1, 2, \quad i \neq j \qquad (4)$$

Assume first that wages are identical: $w_i = w_j = w$. A linear income tax t yields optimal reaction functions (2) that are rather complicated, but applying the balanced budget condition $2k = t(w_1 l_1 + w_2 l_2)$ and solving yields a fairly simple Nash equilibrium:

$$l_1^* = l_2^* = \frac{(1-t)(\alpha + \beta)}{1 - t\beta + \alpha(1-t)}.$$

Substituting this into the utility function (4) gives us the indirect utility function v^i (where $v^1 = v^2$ for the symmetric case). Differentiating v^i with respect to t (and checking that the second-order conditions are satisfied) yields a surprisingly simple expression for the optimal tax rate:

$$t^* = \frac{\alpha}{\alpha + \beta}. \qquad (5)$$

This function conforms to intuition.[6] A higher value of α means that relative consumption c_i/c_j is more important, and therefore a higher tax rate is required to counterbalance its influence. A lower value of β means that absolute consumption is less important; with $\beta = 0$, only relative consumption matters, and the optimum is attained by letting l_1^* and l_2^* approach zero, which is accomplished by letting $t \to 1$.

If we drop the assumption of equal wage rates, things get more complicated since we also have to take into consideration the redistribution from the high-wage to the low-wage individual. But there is still room for Pareto-efficient income taxation, provided that the wages are not too different.

Using the utility function (4) but assuming that $w_1 = 1$ and $w_2 = w \leq 1$, we can solve the model numerically for various values of w and for various tax rates t. The results of such simulations are reported in Figure 2 for the parameter values $\alpha = 1$, $\beta = 0.5$ and $\gamma = 0$. For each w, the utility-possibility frontier is depicted; as t varies from zero to unity, we move along the frontier and see how the indirect utilities of the two individuals are affected.

Let us look, for example, at the curve associated with $w = 0.90$. The upper left endpoint indicates the indirect utilities[7] when $t = 0$ ($v^1 = 0.306$

---

[6] Substituting (5) into the expression for l_i^*, it is easily shown that $l_i^* \geq 0$ for $1 \geq \beta \geq 0$.

[7] Since the utility function (4) is logarithmic, its numerical value might very well be negative. This is only a matter of choosing the unit of measurement and does not affect the agent's

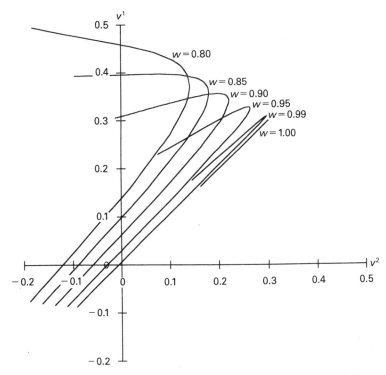

Fig. 2. The utility-possibility frontier for different values of w ($\alpha = 1, \beta = 0.5$).

and $v^2 = -0.011$). Raising t means that we move to the right along the curve. It is obviously possible to increase welfare for both individuals by raising the tax rate — at least for a while. For $t = 0.57$ the value of v^1 attains its maximum ($v^1 = 0.356$ and $v^2 = 0.198$). Thus low values of t are Pareto dominated by $t = 0.57$. Raising t further means that v^2 can be increased only at the expense of v^1, and this goes on until we reach $t = 0.71$ ($v^1 = 0.342$ and $v^2 = 0.222$). A higher t value will cause such large distortions that both agents will suffer; such t values are thus Pareto inferior to

---

preference ordering. Those who do not like negative utility can add an arbitrary positive constant to (4), thereby ensuring that v^i will always be positive. Another way of ensuring non-negative utilities would be to write the utility function of the form

$$u^i = [\alpha/(1 - \gamma)][c_i/c_j]^{1 - \gamma} c_i^\beta (1 - l_i)^{1 - \beta}.$$

Such a function, however, has the disadvantage of yielding optimal reaction functions (2) that are independent of the other person's behavior (i.e., l_j), as in Boskin and Sheshinski (1978). This seems like a rather special case.

Table 1. *Range of Pareto efficient tax rates* $(\alpha = 1, \beta = 0.5)$

w	t_{min}	t_{max}
0.80	0.00	0.75
0.85	0.40	0.73
0.90	0.57	0.71
0.95	0.63	0.69
0.99	0.66	0.67
1.00	0.67	0.67

$t = 0.71$. Thus, for the case of $w = 0.90$, the tax rate should be at least $t_{min} = 0.57$ and at most $t_{min} = 0.71$. Table 1 gives the range of Pareto-efficient tax rates for various values[8] of w.

IV. Conclusions

In the traditional analysis of the optimal linear income tax, originating with Sheshinski (1972), the main purpose of the tax is to accomplish redistribution.[9] The problem is to find tax parameters (k and t in our notation) so as to redistribute income from high-wage individuals, who have a low marginal utility of income, to low-wage individuals, who have a high marginal utility of income, thereby maximizing a social welfare function under a government revenue constraint. In our anlaysis, the reason for introducing an income tax is quite different. Since relative consumption matters, people tend to work too much, and the purpose of the tax is to induce them to consume more leisure. In all of the earlier papers on optimal taxation in a relative-income context, this aspect has been obscured by the approach taken, i.e., of maximizing a utilitarian social welfare function instead of studying Pareto-efficient taxes.

This leads to non-standard conclusions, which might have important implications for our view of the modern welfare state. In the traditional literature on income taxation, a linear income tax with an intercept is distortive, and thus there is always a trade-off between efficiency and equality. The low-wage individual can gain only at the expense of the high-wage individual; we therefore need a social welfare function to be able to determine the "optimal" tax rate, and the tax can be justified only if the two agents are quite different with respect to their innate abilities (the wage rates w_i and w_j in our notation).

---

[8] Note that $w = 1.00$ means that the model has collapsed into the symmetric case $w_1 = w_2 = w$, leading to the optimal tax rate t^* of equation (5).

[9] See e.g. Tuomala (1990).

If relative consumption matters, it is the other way around: even rather high tax rates can increase welfare for both agents, as is shown in Table 1. Moreover, the income tax becomes more justified, *the more similar the agents are*. For a large range of parameter values, we do not even need any social welfare function in order to select the optimal tax rate, but can rely on the weakest criterion of them all — i.e., the Pareto criterion. This aspect has been somewhat obscured in earlier works on the relative consumption hypothesis; those works have been cast in a multi-person framework with individuals of different abilities and where the government has been assumed to maximize a utilitarian social welfare function.[10]

This has an interesting implication for *positive* analysis, and a direct bearing on the question in the title of this paper. If society is egalitarian, in the sense that pre-tax wage rates are equal, it will be more easy to reach unanimity in favor of a high income tax. A maximum value of such a unanimously accepted tax, for the particular Cobb–Douglas example analyzed here, is given in the t_{min} column of Table 1. We see that if the degree of inequality is relatively large (i.e., if $w \leq 0.84$ in our example), the high-income earner will vote against any income tax rate in excess of zero.

References

Atkinson, a. B., Rainwater, L. & Smeeding, T.: Income distribution in OECD countries: Evidence from the Luxembourg Income Study (LIS). OECD, Paris, 1995.
Boskin, M. J. & Sheshinski, E.: Optimal redistributive taxation when individual welfare depends upon relative income. *Quarterly Journal of Economics 92*, 589–601, 1978.
Blomquist, N. S.: Interdependent behavior and the effect of taxes. *Journal of Public Economics 51*, 211–18, 1993.
Clark, A. E. & Oswald, A. J.: Satisfaction and comparison of income. Mimeo, London School of Economics, 1993.
Cole, H. L., Mailath, G. J. & Postlewaite, A.: Social norms, savings behavior, and growth. *Journal of Political Economy 110*, 1092–125, 1992.
Duesenberry, J. S.: *Income, Saving and the Theory of Consumer Behaviour.* Harvard University Press, Cambridge, MA, 1949.
Easterlin, R. A.: Does economic growth improve the human lot? Some empirical evidence. In M. David & M. Reder (eds.), *Nations and Households in Economic Growth*, Academic Press, New York, 1974.
Freeman, R. B. & Katz, L. F.: Rising wage inequality: The United States vs. other advanced countries. In R. B. Freeman (ed.), *Working Under Different Rules*, NBER, New York, 1994.
Layard, R.: Human satisfaction and public policy. *Economic Journal 90*, 737–50, 1980.
Lindbeck, A.: Interpreting income distributions in a welfare state: The case of Sweden. *European Economic Review 21*, 227–56, 1983.

---

[10] Needless to say, our reasoning concerning the existence of Pareto-efficient tax rates also holds in a multi-person framework. In such a case, the term $c_i/\bar{c}$, where $\bar{c}$ is the average consumption in society, enters into the utility function of Agent i.

Lommerud, K. E.: Educational subsidies when relative income matters. *Oxford Economic Papers 41*, 640–50, 1989.

Ng, Y.-K.: Relative-income effects and the appropriate level of public expenditure. *Oxford Economic Papers 39*, 293–300, 1987.

Oswald, A. J.: Altruism, jealousy and the theory of optimal non-linear taxation. *Journal of Public Economic 20*, 77–88, 1983.

Persson, M. & Wissen, P.: Redistributional aspects of tax evasion. *Scandinavian Journal of Economics 86*, 131–49, 1984.

Sheshinski, E.: The optimal linear income tax. *Review of Economic Studies 39*, 297–302, 1972.

Tuomala, M.: *Optimal Income Tax and Redistribution*. Clarendon Press, Oxford, 1990.

Family Policy with Non-cooperative Families*

Kai A. Konrad
Free University of Berlin, Germany

Kjell Erik Lommerud
University of Bergen, Norway

Abstract

We consider a non-cooperative model of a family's time allocation between market work and providing a home-produced family public good (such as child care or care for the elderly). The model predicts underprovision of the public good. Because of crowding out, this does not necessarily warrant public provision. In contrast to other approaches in family economics, we find that attempts to redistribute between spouses may alter the final distribution within the marriage, and that such a policy may be Pareto improving. We also find that some degree of progressivity of the income tax can be welfare improving.

I. Introduction

Much of the public sector activity in European welfare states can be characterized as the public provision of private goods. It is noteworthy that many of these goods are close substitutes for services that could be provided within the boundaries of the family. Examples are upbringing and education of children and care for the sick and elderly. According to a rough estimate, public expenses on child care, education, health and care for the elderly in Sweden and Norway amount to around 20 per cent of GDP.

───────
*This paper was written during visits by Konrad to the University of Bergen and by Lommerud to the Center for Economic Studies in Munich. All stays where financed by NFR-Ruhrgas, for which we are grateful. We also thank our host institutions for their hospitality. An earlier version of this paper has benefited from seminar presentations at the universities of Bergen, Bonn, Mannheim, British Columbia, Simon Fraser University and NHH (Bergen) and at the ESPE 1993 conference in Budapest and the *SJE*'s conference on "The Future of the Welfare State". We thank Douglas Allen, Ted Bergstrom, Ray Rees, Monika Schnitzer, Frances Woolley and an anonymous referee for valuable viewpoints.

Even though the public provision of private goods is such an important real-life phenomenon in many countries, there exists scant economic theoretical work to shed light on the rationale for such policies. Among the relatively few studies at hand, many focus on redistribution issues.[1] A core element in such explanations is that the rich choose private alternatives to the public supply, but still partake in financing the system through the tax bill. This line of argument is unconvincing for countries where private alternatives to the public supply are banned, where the public supply is of a high enough quality so that a private alternative will not be chosen, where even the private alternative is subsidized, or where good alternative instruments for redistribution exist.

As noted, these publicly provided services are often close substitutes for services that could be provided within the family. A natural alternative rationale for their provision might therefore be found in the way subsidized provision of such services alters the time allocation of family members. Subsidized day care, for instance, might increase the labor supply of women and/or enhance the total well-being of children.[2] Such an argument presupposes that there is initially something "wrong" with family time allocation. For one thing, market wages might be distorted signals of family members' labor market productivity, due e.g. to discrimination or taxation.[3] Another possibility is that family decision making is inefficient, for example, because many goods that produced by members of a family are non-rival and non-exclusive among family members, and because binding long-term contracts do not regulate their provision. Underprovision of family public goods may imply that public policy can improve the situation for one family member without hurting the other. It is this possibility that we pursue here.

Family policy is a broad concept, not restricted to such public provision of "family-related" private goods. Many countries undertake cash transfers to families with children, and sometimes this type of transfer is explicitly used in an attempt to tilt the distribution of resources within the family. Moreover, the normal tax system may also be expected to influence the actions and the welfare of family members, and can therefore be viewed as an integral part of family policy. As was the case for in-kind transfers, also for cash transfers and taxes a particular model of how family decisions are reached matters crucially for the evaluation of such policies.

---

[1] See e.g. Blackorby and Donaldson (1988), Ireland (1990) and Besley and Coate (1991).

[2] There exists a substantial empirical literature on the extent to which child care subsidies affect women's labor supply decisions, with Heckman (1974) as a pioneering contribution.

[3] Bergstrom and Blomquist (1993) elaborate on the story that subsidized day care is an indirect way of lowering the income tax rate for women. They give numerical examples where subsidized day care in fact lowers the taxation of those in the population without children.

The economic theory of family time allocation was pioneered by Gronau (1973, 1977) and Becker (1991). They both assumed that family decision making was efficient. The bulk of economic theorizing about the family has since followed this assumption. The efficiency assumption comes in various guises. Becker usually assumes efficiency directly; Gronau and many others achieve efficiency by assuming that the family behaves *as if* it were maximizing a "family utility function" or a utilitarian "welfare function" over the utilities of family members. Nash bargaining models of the family, as first presented by Manser and Brown (1980) and McElroy and Horney (1981), are also efficiency models, even though distribution within the family is regarded as decided by relative bargaining power rather than agreed-on welfare weights.[4]

Efficiency models of the family can be viewed as models of binding contracts, or alternatively, of efficient contracts implicitly enforced through repeated interaction. We find many good reasons for studying family economics with the spectacles of optimal contract theory. After all, family life is usually a long-term affair, so hopefully efficient outcomes are frequently reached, also regarding the production of family public goods. However, as a contrast to these models where efficiency is merely assumed, we find it interesting to experiment with models that allow for inefficient family decision making. One way to introduce inefficiencies in family bargaining is simply to assume that contracting is incomplete. An example of this approach is Lommerud (1989), who assumes that as long as a couple remains married, complete contracts on the allocation of time and the transfer of money are possible, but that the situation after a divorce cannot be fully regulated by contract. Other examples of the transaction costs approach are Pollak (1985), Cohen (1987) and Allen (1990).

If one wants to avoid *ad hoc* assumptions about what contracts are enforceable or not, or bring out the starkest contrast to the complete contracts approach, an alternative modeling strategy for family behavior in the absence of binding contracts is the use of non-cooperative game theory. This is the approach of the present paper. In our view, a non-cooperative approach to family economics is warranted for several rea-

---

[4] Nash bargaining implies that outside options are apt to influence outcomes, which is not the case for welfare maximizing; here lies a possible route for distinguishing empirically between the model types. For an exchange on the issue, see Chiappori (1988, 1991), McElroy and Horney (1990) and McElroy (1990). However, there is some ambiguity as to what should be treated as the threat point in family bargaining. McElroy (1990) takes the threat point to be the utility as single. Modern bargaining theory, notably Binmore, Rubinstein and Wolinsky (1986), emphasizes that "utilities during conflict" should be treated as the threat point. And, of course, if a couple cannot agree on what sofa to buy, divorce does not automatically result.

sons. Perhaps the most forceful argument for considering non-cooperative families comes from one of the efficiency models of family time allocation itself. In bargaining models, the status quo point is arguably better described by the non-cooperative equilibrium in a family game than by the utilities as single. This means that a thorough understanding of non-cooperative family models is a prerequisite for understanding cooperative bargaining models of the family.[5] Non-cooperation can also be a realistic account of life in some families. A couple at or beyond the brink of divorce, tied together by mutual concern for their children, is also a family, as is a lone mother who constantly quarrels with her teenage daughter, or a brother and sister both trying to shift the responsibility for elderly parents onto the other. Moreover, many important family decisions — such as choice of education, career path, the number of children — are rather irreversible choices, so repeated interaction cannot be used to argue that they are taken in an efficient way.

A few previous papers apply non-cooperative game theory in a family setting. One seminal paper is Leuthold (1968). The intent of her model is to study how income transfers influence the work decisions of the poor. Other contributions include Kooreman and Kapteyn (1990), Ulph (1988) and Wooley (1988). The literature on the "rotten-kid" model, initiated by Becker (1974, 1981) and elaborated by, among others, Bergstrom (1989a) and Bruce and Waldman (1990), also considers non-cooperative family behavior. Household production is a neglected issue in these papers on non-cooperative families, but it is nevertheless a standard question in family economics.[6] Apart from our study, non-cooperative family models with household production can be found in Bragstad (1991) and Lundberg and Pollak (1993, 1994).

Our model is one where two family members can choose whether to use their time in a way that is only beneficial to themselves (earning private money) or to use time to produce a family public good. Child care is one example of such a good, care of elderly parents another. The only interdependency between the family members is through their mutual concern for the public good. There is no love or altruism. The game played between the two is a fully non-cooperative, one-shot game. Even in such a setting there will be a tendency towards specialization between spouses in

[5] Both Ulph (1988) and Woolley (1988) have expressed exactly this point, and it is endorsed by Lundberg and Pollak (1993). Using the non-cooperative outcome as a fallback in bargaining also seems consistent with the Binmore–Rubinstein–Wolinsky argument that the fallback should reflect utility during conflict (see footnote 4).
[6] We think labor supply choices can be an example of decisions made early in a marriage, later proving to be rather irreversible, for many reasons. And as argued, perhaps a non-cooperative framework is especially fitting for this type of decisions.

market work and the provision of child care according to comparative advantages in market work and household production. There is less specialization, however, than in a cooperative efficiency model. Absolute advantages also turn out to be important in determining who provides the family public good.

In this framework we investigate the effects of different types of family policy. First, we ask whether the non-cooperative family model can provide a rationale for public provision of goods such as child care and care for the elderly. The answer is not straightforward. Even though there is underprovision, public provision of e.g. child care tends to crowd out the provision by family members, perhaps even by more than 100 per cent, so total provision tends not to increase. It is not until family contributions are driven down to zero or some minimum level that public provision actually increases the total provision of the good in question. The public should therefore either provide a great deal of the good — or nothing. However, we find that publicly provided day care can have distribution effects that benefit women.

We also evaluate other family policy measures within the non-cooperative model. Many policy measures in many countries seek to tilt the distribution of resources within a family from the male towards the female. We look at a lump-sum redistribution from the male to the female. In other economic family models this typically has no effect, as the family itself can undo the redistribution. In our paper, such a redistribution can actually bring about a Pareto improvement. But it is more doubtful that such a policy instrument can actually influence the distribution of resources within the family.

In addition, we look at how the normal system of income taxation influences the sexual division of labor and the welfare of the family. One result is that a wage tax financed by lump-sum taxes within our framework is Pareto improving. We also study a situation where the male initially pays a higher marginal tax rate than the female. Increasing progressivity in the sense of increasing the tax rate of the male can in this case lead to an efficiency improvement, as it discourages him from using his time in the labor market, and hence, drives him into contributing to the family public good.

The models of Bragstad (1991) and Lundberg and Pollak (1993) lie closest to our work. Bragstad looks at how differences in preferences (rather than productivities) determine the sexual division of labor in a non-cooperative model. The focus is not on family policy. From a model perspective, the main difference between our paper and Lundberg and Pollak (1993) is that we do not start with an assumption of exogenous "separate spheres", where each person specializes in particular tasks, so that any equilibrium is a corner solution — where redistribution is known to matter.

Instead, we show that the well-known neutrality of redistribution policy in private provision of public goods games breaks down *even* in an interior equilibrium, when both spouses contribute to the family public good and earn labor market income, but have differing comparative advantages in these skills. Hence, transfers and other redistributional policies are not neutral as regards the non-cooperative Nash equilibrium (and, in turn, affect the threat point of cooperative bargaining in the family or the punishment outcome of any infinitely repeated game). Apart from this, we extend the government's set of policy variables. In particular, in addition to transfers between spouses, we consider symmetric and gender specific income taxes, and public provision of the family public good.[7]

The remainder of this paper is organized as follows. In Section II the basic model framework is presented along with the comparative statics of income and of comparative advantages in market or household work. The non-cooperative framework is used in Section III to evaluate the effects of public provision of a perfect substitute for the family public good, of income redistribution between spouses, and of symmetric and asymmetric wage taxes. Section IV summarizes the paper.

II. A Model Framework for Non-cooperative Family Economics

Consider a family consisting of two decision units, a (he) and b (she). Throughout we use subscripts and superscripts $i = a, b$ to refer to either one of the two. Both persons get utility from consuming amounts of a purely private good, x_i, and of a family public good, G.[8] Examples of the

---

[7] Some readers may find that models with a sexual division of labor, i.e., breadwinning fathers and housekeeping mothers, might sound hopelessly dated in view of the gender revolution from the 1960s and onwards. But e.g. Joshi (1988), in describing the British experience, writes of women's "changed dependency" rather than of economic liberalization. True, there has been an enormous increase in women's labor market participation over the last twenty years, but women have for the most part gone into a limited number of female occupations, and they have to a large extent chosen part-time work. Joshi's conclusion is that women still choose labor market adaptions that are compatible with having the main responsibility for children. Fuchs (1989) reports a similar pattern of occupational segregation and part-time work for the U.S., and the experiences of most Western economies seem to be parallel. This suggests that it still is relevant to study models where specialization within the family is important for labor supply. However, such specialization no longer finds its expression in women not working, but in the more subtle way that both men and women work, but that women unlike men tend to sacrifice career development for their children's needs.

[8] But as hinted at in the introduction, the time allocation problem in families would be described more precisely as choosing between work that is compatible with having the main responsibility for children and work with good career opportunities. Our model could be reformulated in this direction.

public good could be happy and well-educated children, the well-being of elderly parents, a clean house or a beautiful garden. The utility functions of a and b are

$$u^i(x_i, G). \tag{1}$$

Preferences may be asymmetric. We make the following assumptions about utilities in (1):

(Q) The utility functions are twice differentiable and strictly quasi-concave.

(E) Both goods are essential; $\dfrac{\partial}{\partial x_i} u^i(0, G) = \infty$, and $\dfrac{\partial}{\partial G} u^i(x_i, 0) = \infty$.

A person allocates his or her working time m between working in the outside labor market, $m - c_i$, and working at home and thereby contributing to the public good, c_i. Spouses may be differently productive in the two tasks. Let h_i be the productivity in household production (providing the public good); one unit of i's labor generates h_i units of the public good. The productivity in the labor market is described by the hourly market wage, w_i. The amount of the public good i provides is denoted by $g_i = h_i c_i$. Aggregate provision is $G = g_a + g_b$.[9]

The decision problem of a, who optimizes his choice of c_a under the Nash conjecture about his wife's choice of c_b, can be described as follows:

$$\max_{x_a, G} u^a(x_a, G) \tag{2}$$

s.t.

$$\omega_a \equiv w_a m + v_a + (w_a/h_a) h_b c_b \geq x_a + (w_a/h_a) G, \tag{3}$$

$$G - h_b c_b \geq 0, \tag{4}$$

$$x_a \geq v_a. \tag{5}$$

The inequalities (4) and (5) are simply non-negativity constraints for a's allocation choice of his time between the different types of labor. To explain (3), we note first that a's maximum market income $w_a m$, plus

---

[9] It is, of course, an exaggeration that market work only produces a pure private good for an agent, whereas time spent at home only produces a pure public good. First, spending money might have positive effects for one's spouse. Also, taking care of children might produce more value for the person who is actually with the children than for a non-present spouse; not only the total amount of child care, but also one's own contribution *per se* are important. In the literature on charity a parallel phenomenon is referred to as the "warm glow" of giving; see Andreoni (1989). We still find it plausible that securing one's own labor market career is more of a private good than child rearing, and as a benchmark case we have chosen the pure private good–pure public good formulation.

monetary wealth v_a must be larger than or equal to his private consumption plus the cost of his contribution to the public good. After deciding how to divide his time between market work and homeproduction, a consumes all of his own income. In particular, because the model is fully non-cooperative and one-shot, there are no monetary transfers between spouses. Person b contributes $h_b c_b$ to the public good. For a this has an income equivalent of $(w_a/h_a) h_b c_b$. This income is added to both sides of the budget constraint, and the relation $G = h_a c_a + h_b c_b$ is used. This yields a's *imputed income* $\omega_a = w_a m + v_a + (w_a/h_a) h_b c_a$ on the l.h.s. and his *imputed expenditure* for the private and the public good on the r.h.s. of (3). Hence, (3) is a's budget restriction, stated in this rather awkward way to facilitate formal analysis. The decision problem for b is of the equivalent type and is arrived at by substituting all a by b, and vice versa.

Except for the inequality constraints (4) and (5), these maximization problems for given contributions of the other person do not differ from an ordinary two-good maximization problem of a household with income ω_i and prices of 1 for the private good and (w_i/h_i) for the public good, and define a's and b's demands $f^i(\omega_i)$ for the public good. A Nash equilibrium is defined as a pair of contributions (c_a^*, c_b^*) such that they are mutually optimal responses, and yield quantities (x_a^*, x_b^*, G^*) of private and public good consumption.

Throughout the paper we make the following further assumption:

(N) The income consumption curves $x^i(G)$ that solve the maximization problem (2) subject to (3) for different given levels, ω_i, of imputed income, and given productivity ratios w_i/h_i, have strictly positive finite slope everywhere.

This is a standard assumption and is usually referred to as the "normality assumption", since it is equivalent to assuming that x_i and G are superior goods everywhere — implying that the Engel curves $f^i(\omega_i)$ for the public good have a slope $\partial f^i/\partial \omega_i \in (0, h_i/w_i)$.

Let $x^i(G)$ be i's income consumption curve that belongs to the productivity ratio w_i/h_i. Assumptions (N) and (Q) imply that

(P1) $u_G^i(x_i, G) < (>)(w_i/h_i) u_x^i(x_i, G)$ for all points (x_i, G) with $x_i < (>) x^i(G)$.

This property is used to prove:

Proposition 1. *Under (N) and (Q), the Nash equilibrium exists and is unique for given monetary wealth and given productivities.*

The proof of existence is straightforward and follows the line of argument in Bergstrom, Blume and Varian (1986). The uniqueness result is somewhat different from the standard results in the literature on private provision of a public good in that productivities influence both the endowments and the relative price of the private and the public good (see Appendix).

An interior private provision equilibrium can be characterized as follows. Both individuals consume the same quantity of the public good, G^*. Further, $G^* = h_a c_a^* + h_b c_b^*$ and $x_i^* = w_i(m - c_i^*) + v_i$, fulfill

$$(w_i/h_i) u_x^i(x_i^*, G^*) = u_G^i(x_i^*, G^*) \qquad \text{for } i = a, b, \tag{6}$$

that is, both individuals end up on their income consumption curves $x^a(G)$ and $x^b(G)$. Along these curves the slope of indifference curves equals $-(w_i/h_i)$ for $i = a, b$.[10]

To get some idea of how the family allocation of time depends on productivities and productivity differences, we briefly review some comparative statics. Consider an interior equilibrium with $(x_a^*, x_b^*, g_a^*, g_b^*)$ for given productivity parameters (w_a, w_b, h_a, h_b) and initial monetary wealth v_a and v_b. Consider a small increase in v_a. Since the new interior equilibrium fulfills (6), making use of property (P1) and the budget constraints, this implies $dx_a^* > 0$, $dx_b^* > 0$, $dG^* > 0$, $dg_b^* > 0$ and $dg_a^* < 0$. Hence, an increase in income by one spouse benefits both; it has a positive spillover.

A change in productivities typically involves income effects and substitution effects. To describe the pure substitution effect we devise the following comparative statics experiment. Consider an interior equilibrium $(x_a^*, x_b^*, g_a^*, g_b^*)$ for given values w_a, w_b, h_a, h_b. Suppose a's wage increases marginally to $\hat{w}_a$ and h_a drops to $\hat{h}_a$, such that if he still chooses to buy x_a^*, his remaining time is just sufficient to provide g_a^*, i.e., there exists a $c_a^0 \in [0, m]$ with $\hat{w}_a(m - c_a^0) = w_a(m - c_a^*)$ and $\hat{h}_a c_a^0 = h_a c_a^*$. Then for the new equilibrium $(\hat{x}_a, \hat{x}_b, \hat{g}_a, \hat{g}_b)$, $\hat{x}_a > x_a^*$, $\hat{x}_b < x_b^*$, $\hat{G} < G^*$.

This can be shown by contradiction. Suppose $\hat{x}_a \le x_a^*$. Then, by a's budget restriction, $\hat{g}_a \ge g_a^*$. Further, the increase in w_a/h_a leads to a new income-consumption curve $\hat{x}^a(G)$ with $\hat{x}^a(G) \ge x^a(G)$ for all G. Therefore, $\hat{x}_a \le x_a^*$ requires $\hat{G} < G^*$. Otherwise $(\hat{x}_a, \hat{G})$ is not on a's new income-consumption curve. Now consider the effect on b. As a (weakly) increases his contribution to the public good, this means that b's imputed income (weakly) increases, which implies that she will choose a point further

---

[10] The intuitive reason for uniqueness is seen by considering an increase in G^*. For given transfers, each G goes together with amounts of consumption of the private good, where each individual contributes to the public good what he or she does not consume in units of the private good. Both $x^a(G)$ and $x^b(G)$ are increasing in G. Hence, there can be only one amount of G where $(\omega_a - x^a(G))$ and $(\omega_b - x^b(G))$ just suffice to generate G.

[11] Suppose the per-child cost of care is U-shaped with respect to the number of children. Then there is an optimum employees-children ratio. Minimum average cost of producing public day care defines π.

outwards on her income consumption curve, i.e., she will choose $\hat{x}_b \geq x_b^*$ and $\hat{G} \geq G^*$. But this contradicts $\hat{G} < G^*$. Therefore, $\hat{x}_a \leq x_a^*$ cannot be an equilibrium. Since the equilibrium exists and is unique, $\hat{x}_a > x_a^*$ must hold. But $\hat{x}_a > x_a^*$ implies $\hat{g}_a < g_a^*$, which in turn implies that b chooses a point inwards on her income-consumption curve with $\hat{x}_b < x_b^*$ and $\hat{G} < G^*$.

These results show that the substitution effect of an increase in a's labor market productivity hurts his spouse. Her utility is reduced. Whether a's utility increases or decreases cannot be determined without further assumptions about his utility. In a perfectly symmetric initial situation, it hurts the spouse more than it can possibly hurt him; since both suffer the same drop in G, he gains some amount of private consumption and she loses some.

In a non-cooperative model, there are tendencies whereby the person with a comparative advantage in the production of the family good contributes more towards its provision, that the person with the stronger preference for the public good contributes more to it, and that the "richer" spouse contributes more. One way to be "rich" is to be able in both lines of work, which means that absolute, not only comparative advantages matter for the family allocation of time. In efficiency models of the family, typically only comparative advantages matter. It can also be shown that there is underprovision of the public good in the non-cooperative model in the sense that there is a feasible allocation with more public good that makes both better off. Intuitively, when one of the spouses works at home he or she does not take into account that his or her work benefits the other spouse. This leads to underprovision. Differing preferences of the spouses generally rule out interpersonal utility comparisons. Suppose for illustration, however, that spouses are identical with respect to preferences, endowments and market wages and differ only with respect to productivity at home: let the female have an advantage in household production. The female will then be the one who contributes more towards the family public good. In such a situation the male is better off than the female, as both spouses (by necessity) enjoy the same amount of the public good, whereas the female gets less of the private good since she has less time to work in the labor market. Some may choose to interpret this as women being oppressed.

III. Fiscal Policy and the Family Allocation of Time

We now investigate how different policies affect the time use and welfare of a family in the non-cooperative Nash equilibrium. We consider governmentally supplied in-kind contributions to the public good, lump-sum redistributions among family members, and proportional wage taxes.

Public Provision of the Family Public Good

Let π be the governmental cost (in monetary units) for contributing a unit of child care, while costs within the family are w_a/h_a and w_b/h_b, respectively. Generally, π may be higher or lower than the unit cost for any one of the family members.[11] Arguments suggesting that public day care has a cost advantage over family care are that there might be substantial increasing returns and that the professionalism of day care workers can add elements to a child's upbringing that parents perhaps cannot. An argument in the opposite direction is that high quality day care, of the type found in many Scandinavian day care centers, is only achieved at the expense of not utilizing increasing returns to any substantial degree. Moreover, even if care within the family means one adult looking after fewer children, that adult is free to perform many other household tasks. Care within the family also means that specialized buildings and equipment are not needed, and the lack of professionalism is perhaps compensated by parental love. We will not try to settle the discussion as to whether the government produces day care with a cost advantage or disadvantage relative to the family itself, but pursue both possibilities in what follows.[12]

We assume that the government's cost is either higher than that of the family member with the highest cost, or lower than that of the family member with the lowest cost. This means that either condition (7) or condition (8) characterizes governmental cost:

$$\pi > \max\{(w_a/h_a), (w_b/h_b)\}, \text{ or} \tag{7}$$

$$\pi < \min\{(w_a/h_a), (w_b/h_b)\}. \tag{8}$$

For brevity, we omit the case where the government's cost lies between those of the two spouses. The following result holds.

Proposition 2. *Consider an interior private provision equilibrium that fulfills* (Q), (E) *and* (N). *A small governmental contribution* $dg_s > 0$ *that is financed by lump-sum taxation of one of the family members is more than*

---

[12] For simplicity, our model assumes that day care services cannot be bought in the market. But it is quite unnatural to assume that the government has access to a production technology for day care that private organizations do not have. If the government produces a perfect substitute for child care within the family at a cost disadvantage, this is fully compatible with an absence of private market alternatives. Things are more difficult when the government has a cost advantage. We then rely on the argument that in spite of the cost advantage, professional care becomes more expensive in the end because it uses taxed labor, which the family does not. Whether or not production costs for professional day care should be corrected for such tax wedges is a fundamental question, depending on whether or not the tax system was optimally designed to begin with, and we will not delve fully into this matter here.

100 percent crowded out if (7) holds, whereas crowding out is less than 100 percent if (8) holds.

Proof: Suppose (7) holds. The lump-sum tax that is collected from, say individual a, is $dS = \pi\, dg_s$. Aggregate contributions $G = g_a + g_b + g_s$ go down as can be shown by contradiction. Suppose they go up. Then $d(g_a + g_b) \geq -dg_s$. But, as

$$dS = \pi\, dg_s > \max\{(w_a/h_a)\, dg_s, (w_b/h_b)\, dg_s\},$$

this implies that x_i has to drop for at least one family member. For this individual the condition $u_x^i(x_i, G + dG) = u_G^i(x_i, G + dG)$ is violated for $dG \geq 0$. This is a contradiction. The proof for incomplete crowding out when (8) holds proceeds along analogous lines.∎

If the government tries to compensate for the family's own under-provision of day care by providing free public care, it faces a serious crowding-out problem. This crowding-out problem in the private provision of a public good is aggravated if the government is less efficient in providing the family public good. If the government wants to increase the aggregate amount of provision, and finances its contributions by taxation of contributors, it first must crowd out private contributions completely. Only then will additional spending increase total provision. A government that wants to increase the total amount of resources spent on child care faces an all-or-nothing option. Totally taking over responsibility for day care is a very expensive policy; leaving children with too little care is a rather undesirable alternative.

If the basis for family policy is that absent such policy measures the level of child care will be inefficiently low, it is hard to argue that such inefficiencies arise to an equal extent for all children. Many families have to be expected to overcome the problems of non-cooperation. Speculatively, rather than subsidizing all families, an alternative policy could be to single out "problem families" where the parents provide little or next-to-nothing of child care — and use available resources to better the situation for the children in these families, in various ways. The mere fact that these parents contribute little towards the upbringing and education of their children makes the crowding-out problem relatively cheap to overcome.

But even if one meets with difficulties when trying to use public provision of day care to overcome the underprovision of child care, such provision can in fact alter the intrafamily distribution of resources. For illustration, focus on the case where public provision exactly crowds out family provisions. Assume again that spouses have identical preferences and monetary wealth, let them have the same ability for market work, but let females be more productive in providing the family public good. We have argued above that in this case — absent any public policy — the female's private good consumption will be lower than that of the male in spite of her being at least as able in any line of work. When private contributions are fully crowded out and only the government provides the public good, both spouses will then have identical consumption bundles if taxes to pay for public day care are split evenly between the two. Intra-family distribution has become more even, but if public provision is produced at a cost disadvantage, the increase in equity must be weighed against decreased efficiency.

Our discussion of public provision of day care should not necessarily be taken to refer to publicly produced day care; only that a *specified amount* of day care is subsidized 100 percent. Of course, hardly any country sub-sidizes day care to that extent, but results of the same flavor would obtain if we studied the public provision of a specified amount of day care at a rate below 100 percent.

The basic problem behind the crowding-out problem is non-observ-ability of family members' own contributions to the public good. Given that it is difficult to increase the provision of goods such as child care by subsidizing them, a second-best strategy could be to tax time uses that are alternative to child care, such as market work. We pursue this possibility later on. First, however, we examine whether or not lump-sum redistribu-tions between spouses can be used to alter intrafamily distribution in the non-cooperative model.

Lump-Sum Redistributions between Spouses

Lump-sum redistributions between spouses are certainly neutral in a family situation where a family welfare function is maximized, and also in the other efficiency model of family, the efficient Nash bargaining model. In a truly non-cooperative family, income redistribution can be expected to matter. Lundberg and Pollak (1993) claim that intrafamily distribution will vary systematically with the control of resources, and, hence, transfers can be expected to be non-neutral. They explore the non-neutrality of voluntary income transfers between spouses when spouses have fully specialized in tasks, due to traditional gender roles and governmental sup-plementary benefits. We think there is a major problem with respect to voluntary transfers: timing. In a one-shot game, taking things literally, individuals have earned their money only after they have made their allocation decision about time. Hence, it is impossible to make uncondi-tional money transfers in order to affect the time allocation of the spouse in a one-period model. Once a person has earned the money and can give it to the spouse, it is too late to affect his or her time allocation decision. In order to bring strategic transfers into play, it has to be assumed that it is possible to make a binding contract on transfers, but at the same time, to rule out binding contracts on time allocation. This timing problem does not arise with governmental lump-sum redistribution.

Here we consider such governmental redistribution in an interior equilibrium without any *a priori* assumption about traditional gender roles. From results in Warr (1982) and Bergstrom, Blume and Varian (1986), it is known that lump-sum redistributions between participants in a Nash game of private provision of a public good are allocatively neutral in a situation where all participants make positive contributions and have the same productivities in contributing to the public good. In this context, productivities are measured as individuals' opportunity cost in units of the private consumption good for contributing an additional unit to the public good. Warr's (1982) famous neutrality result fails to hold when $(w_a/h_a) \neq (w_b/h_b)$.

Proposition 3. *Consider an interior private contribution equilibrium of a family in which* (Q), (E) *and* (N) *hold. Suppose that* $w_a/h_a > w_b/h_b$. *Then a small redistribution* T *from individual* a *to individual* b *leads to a Pareto superior equilibrium.*

Proof: Let the equilibrium without redistribution be (x_a^*, x_b^*, G^*). Consider a small transfer that leads to a new equilibrium $(x_a^{**}, x_b^{**}, G^{**})$. Since the new equilibrium is an interior equilibrium it suffices to show that $G^{**} > G^*$, since this implies $x_i^{**} > x_i^*$ for $i = a, b$ by (P1), which, in turn, implies that both a and b are better off in the new equilibrium. In an equilibrium we have $h_a m + (h_a/w_a)v_a = (h_a/w_a)x_a + g_a$, and $h_b m + (h_b/w_b)v_b = (h_b/w_b)x_b + g_b$, and, hence,

$$G + (h_a/w_a)x_a + (h_b/w_b)x_b = (h_a/w_a)v_a + (h_b/w_b)v_b + (h_a + h_b)m. \tag{9}$$

In an interior equilibrium, both individuals are on their income consumption curves. Let $x^a(G, h_a/w_a)$ and $x^b(G, h_b/w_b)$ denote these income consumption curves for given productivity values. By (N), these curves are strictly increasing in G. We can substitute them in (9) and obtain

$$G + (h_a/w_a)x^a(G, h_a/w_a) + (h_b/w_b)x^b(G, h_b/w_b)$$
$$= v_a h_a/w_a + v_b h_b/w_b + (h_a + h_b)m. \tag{10}$$

A redistribution T from a to b increases the r.h.s. of (10) by $T(h_b/w_b - h_a/w_a)$ which is positive by the assumptions made in Proposition 3. Therefore, for (10) to hold after the transfer, the l.h.s. must increase. This is possible only for an increase in G, since the l.h.s. consists of a sum of three functions each of which is strictly increasing in G. ■

Proposition 3 shows that an *a priori* assumption about specialization according to separate spheres is *not* required for having non-neutral income redistribution policies in non-cooperative families. Income distribution can be non-neutral also in interior equilibria, if relative productivities differ. Of course, differing productivities need some explanation, too, and socialization according to traditional gender norms may well contribute to a fuller explanation. Note that the proposition holds for any interior equilibrium, regardless of which income distribution prevails before the small change is made. The policy conclusions depend on whether the time allocation in the family is described by the non-cooperative equilibrium, or whether this only serves as a threat point. If the non-cooperative equilibrium only serves as a threat point for cooperative bargaining outcomes, it matters for the impact of redistributional policy who would gain *more* in the non-cooperative equilibrium from the shift in the threat point due to governmental transfers, which would require a cardinal concept of utility as, for instance, in Nash bargaining. If the non-cooperative equilibrium describes the actual family allocation of time, *government should extend the amount of redistribution at least up to the point where the equilibrium after redistribution is no longer an interior equilibrium.* As long as perfect specialization (abstinence from contributions to the public good by one of the spouses) is not accomplished, a further increase in the amount redistributed to the person with the comparative advantage in public good provision makes both of them better off.

It should be noted that even though lump-sum redistributions from the male to the female can actually lead to a Pareto improvement, this type of policy is quite problematic if the aim is to change intrafamily distribution. In voluntary contribution games without comparative advantages there is a tendency for the "richer" person to contribute the most. If one unit of income is transferred from person *a* to person *b*, *a* contributes one unit of income less to the public good, *b* one unit more. From a distributional viewpoint, the redistributional effect of the transfer is undone by changes in private contributions. In our model, the wife may have a comparative advantage in household production — meaning that she can provide the public good at a lower "cost". A transfer that induces the female to work more at home and the husband less can therefore improve efficiency. However, if the female, when getting a transfer paid by the male, reduces her labor market income correspondingly in order to provide more of the public good, intrafamily distribution has not necessarily become more favorable for the female.

Wage Taxes

Consider an initial equilibrium of family child care that is characterized by an interior equilibrium. Both individuals contribute positive amounts. Suppose that government imposes a small proportional income tax with tax rate τ on labor income (or increases a given tax marginally). The tax proceeds are assumed to be used for purposes that do not interfere with the time allocation problem of the family. Hence, from the individuals' perspective, with respect to their labor decision, the tax is equivalent to a reduction in productivity in the labor market from w_i to $(1-\tau)\,w_i$, for $i = a, b$. As described in Section II, such productivity decreases have income effects and substitution effects, and the total effects on labor allocation and even on individuals' utility in the Nash contribution equilibrium are ambiguous.[13]

Note that the potentially Pareto-improving effect of wage taxation appears only in an interior equilibrium, i.e., if both individuals contribute to the public good. If the initial equilibrium has zero contributions by one of the spouses, say $g_a = 0$, then a small increase in the wage tax certainly makes b, the contributor, worse off. She may increase or decrease her contribution to the public good (due to the different strengths of the income effect and the substitution effect). If she decreases her contribution, the non-contributor also ends up worse off. If she increases her contribution, the non-contributor may end up better off or worse off, depending on whether her additional provision of the public good overcompensates his income loss from his decreased net wage.

A sharper result can be obtained for the case of lump-sum redistributed tax proceeds.

Proposition 4. *Consider an initial non-cooperative symmetric interior equilibrium. A small proportional income tax with lump-sum redistributions to each individual that are equal to his or her labor income taxes in the equilibrium is strictly welfare increasing.*

Proof: Let $x^i(G, \tau)$ be the income consumption curves for $i = a, b$ for a given wage tax rate τ.

By (Q) and (N),

$$\partial x^i(G, \tau)/\partial \tau < 0. \tag{11}$$

The tax proceeds are $\tau w_a(m - c_a^*) - S_a = \tau w_b(m - c_b^*) - S_b = 0$ in the equilibrium, where the asterisk denotes equilibrium values, and S_a and S_b are lump-sum redistributions to a and b, respectively. The aggregate resource constraint that has to be fulfilled in any equilibrium is (9). Substituting the income consumption curves into (9) yields

$$G^* + (h_a/w_a)x^a(G^*, \tau) + (h_b/w_b)x^b(G^*, \tau)$$
$$= h_a m + (h_a/w_a)v_a + h_b m + (h_b/w_b)v_b. \tag{12}$$

---

[13] See Cornes and Sandler (1989) for the case with strict symmetry.

A small increase in τ changes $x^a(G^*, \tau)$ and $x^b(G^*, \tau)$ in (12). If G^* were to stay constant or even to decrease by an introduction of a small income tax, then the r.h.s. of (12) would be unchanged, but, due to (11), the l.h.s. would strictly decrease. Therefore, an increase in the income tax rate τ increases the equilibrium value of public good provision. Since G^* is underprovided for $\tau = 0$, the introduction of a small redistributed proportional income tax is welfare increasing. ∎

The result is structurally equivalent to Boadway, Pestieau and Wildasin (1989) who argue that lump-sum tax financed subsidies for the public good reduce the underprovision problem by increasing the incentives for private provision of the public good.[14] A lump-sum redistributed tax on labor market income, which is the private good here, has the same effect, provided that there is no third activity for which time can be used. Of course, there is: leisure. It would therefore be superior if government could choose lump-sum financed subsidies for child care. But, as mentioned, it may be difficult for the government to measure child care activities. This lack of observability rules out such a subsidy policy. Taxing labor market income may be a second-best policy. Considering the effect of recent tax policy, tax reforms of the tax-cut-cum-based-broadening type in recent years started from a positive tax rate level. Therefore, it cannot be answered on purely theoretical grounds whether, in this situation, the family public good was in fact undersupplied; hence, the reforms may or may not have aggravated an existing underprovision problem.

Proposition 4 considers a situation where both individuals are affected by the tax reform. Suppose that the tax is not strictly proportional but has a deductible, y: $T_i = \tau[\max(w_i(m - c_i) - y, 0)] - S_i$. Then one of the individuals may be unaffected by a revenue neutral reduction in τ. Recent reductions in marginal taxes in many countries have typically reduced the marginal tax rate of many men more than that of their wives. A deductible allows for the possibility that spouses initially face different marginal tax rates and that a reform affects only one of them.

Proposition 5. *Consider a tax system with* $T_i = \tau[\max(w_i(m - c_i) - y, 0)] - S_i$ *with individual lump-sum redistributions* S_i *that are equal to* $\tau[\max(w_i(m - c_i^*) - y, 0)]$ *in the equilibrium for both* $i = a, b$. *Suppose the initial equilibrium is an interior equilibrium with* $\tau[\max(w_b(m - c_b^*) - y, 0)] = S_b = 0$.

(i) A small increase in the marginal tax rate that is compensated by an increase in lump-sum redistributions to a increases G^* and x_b^* and decreases x_a^*.

(ii) *A small increase in the marginal tax rate with additional tax proceeds lump-sum redistributed to b increases G^* and x_b^* if $(h_a/w_a) \leq (h_b/w_b)$.*

Proof: (i) Similar to the proof of Proposition 4, the aggregate resource constraint can be written as (12). The r.h.s. stays invariant, and so does $x^b(G^*, \tau)$. However, $x^a(G^*, \tau)$ becomes flatter. Hence, the new equilibrium is incompatible with the same or a lower G^*. Moreover, an increase in G^* necessitates an increase in x_b^*, since $\partial x^b(G^*, \tau)/\partial G^* > 0$. Moreover, someone has to pay for these increases. Hence, x_a^* has to go down. (ii) The comparative static experiment in (ii) can be decomposed into the comparative static experiment in (i) plus a lump-sum redistribution from a to b. By Proposition 3, this redistribution increases G^* if income is redistributed from the individual with smaller (h_i/w_i) to the other. ∎

The point in part (i) of Proposition 5 is similar to Bergstrom's (1989b) analysis of the disadvantage of being subsidized when making contributions to the public good. Lowering (increasing) the marginal tax of the husband increases (decreases) the wife's comparative advantage in household production. If the wife is the one with a comparative advantage for producing the family public good, in efficiency models this directly leads to increased specialization in the family (abstracting from the possibility of corner solutions). In the non-cooperative model we would expect things to be more complicated; a reduction in one person's marginal tax has an impact both on comparative advantages and on who is the "richer" in the relationship. We know that both of these matters influence the allocation of time within the family. If the person that faces an increase in marginal tax also gets the proceeds from the income tax back as a lump-sum transfer, he has not become "poorer" in the process. We are left with the effect through comparative advantages — and naturally get a result that mirrors what we would get in an efficiency model.

IV. Conclusions

The bulk of economic family models assumes that family decisions are efficient, meaning that implicit optimal contracts between family members can be enforced. As a contrast, we think there are good reasons to develop non-cooperative family models, where family members act strategically. The basic framework of this paper is that people use their time either to earn market income, which is a private good, or to provide a family public good. In Nash equilibrium there is underprovision of the family public good (child care being an important example). As in efficiency models, there is a tendency for the task to be performed mostly by the person with a comparative advantage in household production. However, in a strategic model we expect less drastic specialization between the spouses, since the one specializing in household production is not adequately compensated by the other. In the strategic model, contrary to the efficiency model, there is also a tendency for absolute advantages to matter, in the sense that the "richer" spouse provides more of the public good.

Especially if the underprovided family-specific public good is child care, a government might want to interfere. The problem is that public provision of a perfect substitute for the family public good is likely to be crowded out by reductions in contributions from family members. Under natural assumptions, crowding out will be more than 100 pecent. This leaves the government with an "all-or-nothing" choice; it should either provide child care massively or not at all. A possible policy suggestion is to single out problem families where children receive very little care, and use available resources to improve the situation of these children. We do argue, however, that publicly provided day care can help to redistribute resources from men towards women.

We also investigated the effects of other types of family policies. Unlike the outcome in many other economic family models, here it *is* possible to influence the equilibrium outcome for the family by lump-sum redistribution from one spouse to the other. Moreover, such redistribution might in fact lead to a Pareto improvement. On the other hand, such a "redistribution" policy may have counterintuitive and undesirable effects on the distribution of resource within the family.

Further, we examined how the normal income tax system influences the family in the non-cooperative framework. Moving towards a more progressive tax system may in fact improve the family's situation. A key point is that a wage tax discourages market work and, in doing so, drives the taxpayer towards alternative time uses, such as contributing to the family public good.

Appendix. Proof of Proposition 1

Existence: Analogous to Bergstrom, Blume and Varian (1986) and therefore omitted.

Uniqueness: Consider the aggregate budget constraint, expressed in units of the public good that must hold in any equilibrium (x_a^*, x_b^*, G^*),

$$G^* + (h_a/w_a) x_a^* + (h_b/w_b) x_b^* = (h_a/w_a) v_a + (h_b/w_b) v_b + (h_a + h_b) m. \tag{A1}$$

The equilibrium values for private consumption are

$$x^{a*}(G^*) = \max(w_a m + v_a, x^a(G^*)) \tag{A2}$$

and

$$x^{b*}(G^*) = \max(w_b m + v_b, x^b(G^*)). \tag{A3}$$

Note that $\max(w_a m + v_a, x^a(G^*))$ and $\max(w_b m + v_b, x^b(G^*))$ are increasing in G^* by (N). Inserting (A2) and (A3) into (A1) yields

$$G^* + (h_a/w_a)x^{a*}(G^*) + (h_b/w_b)x^{b*}(G^*) = (h_a/w_a)v_a + (h_b/w_b)v_b + (h_a + h_b)m. \quad (A4)$$

The r.h.s. of (A4) is independent of G, and the l.h.s. of (A4) is strictly increasing in G^*. Hence, (A4) has at most one solution for G^*. But this unique G^* determines unique amounts of private consumption in (A2) and (A3). ■

References

Allen, Douglas: An inquiry into the state's role in marriage. *Journal of Economic Behavior and Organization 13*, 171–91, 1990.

Andreoni, James: Giving with impure altruism: Applications to charity and Ricardian equivalence. *Journal of Political Economy 97*, 1447–58, 1989.

Andreoni, James & Bergstrom, Theodore C.: Do government subsidies increase the private supply of public goods? CREST WP 92-11, Department of Economics, University of Michigan.

Becker, Gary S.: A theory of social interactions. *Journal of Political Economy 82*, 1063–93, 1974.

Becker, Gary S.: Altruism in the family and selfishness in the market place. *Economica 48*, 1–15, 1981.

Becker, Gary S.: A Treatise on the Family. Enlarged edition, Harvard University Press, Cambridge, MA, 1991.

Bergstrom, Theodore C.: A fresh look at the rotten kid theorem — and other household mysteries. *Journal of Political Economy 97*, 1138–59, 1989a.

Bergstrom, Theodore C.: Puzzles: Love and spaghetti, the opportunity cost of virtue. *Journal of Economic Perspectives 3*, 165–73, 1989b.

Bergstrom, Theodore & Blomquist, Sören: The political economy of subsidized day care. WP 1993:15, Department of Economics, Uppsala University.

Bergstrom, Theodore, Blume, Lawrence & Varian, Hal: On the private provision of public goods. *Journal of Public Economics 29*, 25–49, 1986.

Besley, Timothy & Coate, Steven: Public provision of public goods and the redistribution of income. *American Economic Review 81*, 979–84, 1991.

Binmore, Ken, Rubinstein, Ariel & Wolinsky, Asher: The Nash bargaining solution in economic modelling. *Rand Journal of Economics 17*, 176–88, 1986.

Blackorby, Charles & Donaldson, David: Cash versus kind, self-selection and efficient transfers. *American Economic Review 78*, 691–700, 1988.

Boadway, Robin, Pestieau, Pierre & Wildasin, David: Tax-transfer policies and the voluntary provision of public goods. *Journal of Public Economics 39*, 157–76, 1989.

Bragstad, Torunn: Private provision of a public good — The significance of thresholds. Mimeo, University of Oslo, 1991.

Bruce, Neil & Waldman, Michael: The rotten kid theorem meets the Samaritan's dilemma. *Quarterly Journal of Economics 105*, 155–65, 1990.

Chiappori, Pierre-André: Nash-bargained households decisions: A comment. *International Economic Review 29*, 791–6, 1988.

Chiappori, Pierre-André: Nash-bargained household decisions: A rejoinder. *International Economic Review 32*, 761–2, 1991.

Cohen, Lloyd: Marriage, divorce and quasi-rents; Or "I gave him the best years of my life". *Journal of Legal Studies 16*, 267–303, 1987.

Cornes, Richard & Sandler, Todd: Public goods, growth, and welfare. *Social Choice and Welfare 6*, 243–51, 1989.

Fuchs, Victor R.: Women's quest for economic equality. *Journal of Economic Perspectives 3*, 25–41, 1989.

Gronau, Reuben: The intrafamily allocation of time: The value of housewives' time. *American Economic Review 63*, 634–51, 1973.

Gronau, Reuben: Leisure, home production and work — The theory of the allocation of time revisited. *Journal of Political Economy 85*, 1099–123, 1977.

Heckman, James: Effects of child care programs on women's work effort. *Journal of Political Economy 82*, 136–63, 1974.

Ireland, Norman: The mix of social and private provision of goods and services. *Journal of Public Econmics 43*, 201–19, 1990.

Joshi, Heather: Changing roles of women in the British labour market and the family. DP in Economics 88/13, Birkbeck College.

Kooreman, Peter & Kapteyn, Arie: On the empirical implementation of some game theoretic models of household labor supply. *Journal of Human Resources 25*, 584–98, 1990.

Leuthold, Jane: An empirical study of formula income transfers and the work decisions of the poor. *Journal of Human Resources 3*, 312–23, 1968.

Lommerud, Kjell Erik: Marital division of labor with risk of divorce: The role of "voice" enforcement of contracts. *Journal of Labor Economics 7*, 113–27, 1989.

Lundberg, Shelly & Pollak, Robert: Separate spheres bargaining and the marriage market. *Journal of Political Economy 101*, 988–1010, 1993.

Lundberg, Shelly & Pollak, Robert: Noncooperative bargaining models of marriage. *American Economic Review, Papers and Proceedings 84*, 132–7, 1994.

Manser, Marilyn & Brown, Murray: Marriage and household decision making: A bargaining analysis. *International Economic Review 21*, 31–44, 1980.

McElroy, Marjorie B.: The empirical content of Nash-bargained household behavior. *Journal of Human Resources 25*, 559–83, 1990.

McElroy, Marjorie B. & Horney, Mary Jean: Nash-bargained household decisions: Towards a generalization of the theory of demand. *International Economic Review 22*, 333–49, 1981.

McElroy, Marjorie B. & Horney, Mary Jean: Nash-bargained household decisions: Reply. *International Economic Review 31*, 237–42, 1990.

Pollak, Robert: A transaction cost approach to families and households. *Journal of Economic Literature 23*, 581–608, 1985.

Ulph, David: A general noncooperative Nash model of household behaviour. Mimeo, University of Bristol, 1988.

Warr, Peter: Pareto optimal redistribution and private charity. *Journal of Public Economics 19*, 131–8, 1982.

Weiss, Yoram & Willis, Robert J.: Children as collective goods and divorce settlements. *Journal of Labor Economics 3*, 268–92, 1985.

Woolley, Frances: A non-cooperative model of family decision making. DP TIDI 125, London School of Economics, 1988.

Socio-Economic Status and Child Health: Does Public Health Insurance Narrow the Gap?

*Janet Currie**

University of California, Los Angeles CA, USA

Abstract

Drawing on evidence from the U.S., this paper examines the effects of public health insurance on children. Recent expansions of American public health insurance programs to previously ineligible children have created a great deal of variation that can be used to identify their effects. Results indicate that providing public insurance to poor children narrows socio-economic gaps in utilization and health among children. However, inefficiencies and inequities in the allocation of health care remain, which suggests that universality and outreach programs are also important components of the public health systems common in Europe.

I. Introduction

Universal eligibility for health care is one of the pillars of the welfare state. Yet there is little hard evidence that programs designed to guarantee access to all have succeeded in narrowing gaps in health associated with socio-economic status (SES). For example, the influential Black report in Great Britain concluded that class-based disparities in mortality actually increased following the introduction of national health insurance and that other policies might be more effective in promoting equality in health outcomes; see Townsend, Davidson and Whitehead (1988). Continuing disparities in the utilization of care and in health among children are particularly troubling since many view equal access to health care for

---

*I would like to thank Jon Gruber, Peder Pedersen, Duncan Thomas, two anonymous referees, participants in the *SJE*'s conference on "The Future of the Welfare state" and seminar participants at Uppsala University for helpful comments. Financial support from the Alfred P. Sloan Foundation and from UCLA's Center for American Politics and Public Policy is gratefully acknowledged. All opinions are my own and should not be attributed to these organizations.

children as a basic human right; cf. U.S. National Commission on the International Year of the Child (1980). Moreover, ill health in children has been shown to contribute to sickness and early mortality among adults; cf. Barker and Osmond (1986), Forsdahl (1977) and Wadsworth (1986).

The disturbing findings of the Black report suggest that lack of health insurance may not be the only barrier to the effective utilization of care. Many European countries have acted to remove other potential barriers by sending public health nurses directly to children's homes (Denmark), requiring parents to bring children to designated centers for care (Sweden), or rewarding parents who bring children in for care (Austria). However, even if all parents were equally likely to seek care for their children, there may be disparities in the quality of care received. A recent U.S. study by Pui *et al.* (1995) suggests that higher mortality rates among black pediatric cancer patients reflect inferior care for black children.

More broadly, it has been argued that improvements in the standard of living and public health measures (environment) have done more to improve health in the past 150 years than advances in personal medical care; see Preston (1977). In a recent study, Kunst and Mackenbach (1994) examined socio-economic differences in mortality rates in the Netherlands, Sweden, Denmark, Norway, the U.S., France, Italy, Finland, and England and Wales. They found that the biggest differentials were in the U.S., France and Italy, the countries that have the most overall inequality in incomes and education. Conversely, the Netherlands, Sweden, Denmark and Norway had the smallest differentials. Similarly, Antonovsky (1967) found that American SES differentials in mortality narrowed through the 1940s, and then remained constant, a pattern that is similar to trends in income inequality in the U.S. More recently, Waldman (1992) found a relationship between income inequality and infant mortality rates. These patterns suggest that inequalities in health mirror overall inequality, and that they cannot be entirely eliminated by changes to the health care system.

These observations raise several questions. First, can it be shown that public insurance has a positive effect on child health? Second, how efficiently is care provided under public health insurance? Do the additional public health programs that many European countries have in place mean that health care is utilized more efficiently than it would be under an insurance-only system? Third, is there any evidence that low SES children with the same insurance coverage as other children receive inferior care? These questions are becoming increasingly pressing as governments struggle to bring health care costs under control without irreparably damaging social safety nets.

Europeans may feel that there is little to be gained from study of the American health care system. After all, at 9 per 1,000, Americans have the highest rate of infant mortality in the developed world. However, because universal health insurance coverage for low income children has been phased in gradually in the U.S., it is possible to use differences in the insurance programs adopted by states to isolate the effects of health insurance. In contrast, most European countries offer the analyst a single before/after comparison so that it is difficult to control for other potentially confounding factors. In addition, the U.S. is relatively homogeneous. Previous attempts to examine cross-country variation in the relationship between SES and health indicate that the cross-country differences are at least as great as the within-country ones; cf. Valkonen (1989).

An additional advantage is that most U.S. states have not adopted aggressive outreach programs of the type described above. Hence, it is possible to isolate the pure effect of health insurance in a way that would be difficult using European data. And while evidence regarding factors associated with the inferior medical treatment of minority children in the U.S. is not directly transferable to the European context, the growing importance of immigrants and ethnic minorities in many European countries suggest that inequality of treatment may be a problem there too.

The paper is laid out as follows. Section II provides a bare-bones overview of the institutional background. Section III gives an overview of the evidence, and Section IV concludes. The evidence presented here suggests that contrary to the findings of the Black report, public health insurance does reduce SES-related health differentials, at least among children. However, in the absence of universality and aggressive outreach, the usage of preventive care may be inefficiently low, while the utilization of palliative care may be inefficiently high. Moreover, there is evidence that minority children receive less care, conditional on their insurance coverage.

II. Institutional Background

The United States does not have universal coverage, but has public insurance programs that cover the elderly, the disabled, and some of the women and children in poor families. The Medicaid program provides comprehensive health insurance to women and children in low-income families, and is the program focused on here. Medicaid was implemented in the late 1960s and early 1970s, and was phased in at different rates across the states. From the inception of the Medicaid program until the mid-1980s, Medicaid coverage was tied to the receipt of cash welfare. Income thresholds for welfare varied widely across states, but were almost always below the poverty line. In general only female-headed households were eligible to receive benefits. Hence, as many as 30 percent of poor children lacked health insurance coverage; cf. Bloom (1990).[1]

In response to this lack of coverage, and to high rates of mortality and morbidity among U.S. children,[2] the past decade has seen an expansion of Medicaid eligibility first to pregnant women and children in two-parent families with incomes below welfare cutoffs, and then to women and children in families with higher incomes. By July 1, 1991, states were required to cover all children born after September 30, 1983 whose family incomes were below the poverty line. In addition, states can receive federal matching funds in order to cover children in families with incomes less than 185 percent of the poverty line; cf. U.S. House of Representatives (1993). Currie and Gruber (1994) estimate that these Medicaid expansions roughly doubled eligibility for Medicaid coverage among pregnant women from 15 to 35 percent, while Currie and Gruber (1996) find that eligibility among children increased from 15 to 30 percent.

Typically, states were first given the option of extending coverage to specific groups, and then required to do so. The important point is that since states took up these options at different rates, and programs varied tremendously in terms of generosity to begin with, there has been a great deal of variation across states in both the income thresholds and the age limits governing Medicaid eligibility. Table 1 illustrates this point using information from 11 of the largest states. As of January 1988, eight of these states had taken advantage of the option to extend Medicaid coverage to previously ineligible children. By December 1989, all 11 of them had done so. However, there was still a great deal of variation across states in the generosity of the program. For example, Pennsylvania had extended coverage to children up to 6 years old in families with incomes below 100 percent of the poverty line, while New York only covered children up to one-year old, but extended coverage to infants in families with incomes up to 185 percent of the poverty line.[3] This variation in eligibility across states, years and child age groups can be used to identify the effects of eligibility for public insurance.[4]

---

[1] Stigma associated with the receipt of cash welfare benefits may also have prevented some families from seeking coverage.

[2] Compared to Canadian children, U.S. children under 1 year of age have a 14 percent higher mortality rate. The differential for 1–4 year olds is 8 percent; cf. Kozak and McCarthy (1984).

[3] Overall, only 26 states had taken advantage of the option to extend Medicaid coverage to previously ineligible children by January 1988. By December 1989, all 50 states had expanded Medicaid coverage to at least some additional children.

[4] Other studies have examined the relationship between insurance coverage and child health, but have had difficulty isolating its effects. For example, the RAND health insurance study randomly assigned patients to various insurance treatments, but the number of

Table 1. *Age and income eligibility thresholds for expanded Medicaid coverage*

State	Age 1/88	Income 1/88*	Age 12/89	Income 12/89
California			5	100
Connecticut	1	100	1	185
Florida	2	100	6	100
Illinois			1	100
Massachusetts	2	100	5	100
Michigan	2	100	3	100
New Jersey	2	100	2	100
New York			1	185
Ohio	1	100	1	100
Pennsylvania	2	100	6	100
Texas			4	100

Source: Yelowitz (1994). * = Income is given as a percent of the federal poverty line.
** = Vermont obtained a waiver in order to set the income limit at 225 percent.

III. The Evidence

Insurance and Children's Health

The least controversial measure of health is mortality. Although many analyses of SES-related differentials focus on mortality, mortality is affected by both underlying health status and medical care received, and these factors cannot be separated out using mortality data alone. In the case of infants, it is possible to proxy underlying health status using birth-weight. For example, Horbar *et al.* (1993) found that in a sample of very low birthweight children weighing between 601 and 1,300 grams at birth, each increase in birthweight of 100 grams was associated with a decrease of approximately 10 percent in the probability of death, other things being equal. In contrast, infant mortality rates reflect not only the health of the fetus but also the effect of any interventions that occur during or after birth. New technologies have had dramatic effects on the survival rate of low birthweight infants. Buehler *et al.* (1985) report that improvements in birthweight-specific mortality rates accounted for 91 percent of the overall decline in neonatal mortality in the U.S. between 1960 and 1980.

---

children involved in the study was too small to allow any definitive conclusions; cf. Valdez (1985). Using hospital discharge data, Braveman (1989) found that infants without health insurance were more likely to suffer adverse health outcomes, but she was unable to control for the selection issues involved.

High-tech neonatal care is very expensive[5] and surviving low birth-weight babies are at increased risk of handicaps such as cerebral palsy of significant degree, major seizure disorders, blindness, deafness and learning disabilities; see McCormick *et al.* (1992). Hence, for both humanitarian and economic reasons, the best way to reduce infant mortality is to reduce the incidence of low birthweight through appropriate use of preventive prenatal care.

Accordingly, Currie and Gruber (1994) focus on the recent extensions of Medicaid eligibility in the U.S. to pregnant women and infants and ask whether these extensions reduced the incidence of low birthweight in addition to reducing the infant mortality rate. They used a detailed simulation model of state rules, combined with the individual-level socio-economic and demographic information available in the annual March Current Population Survey (CPS),[6] to calculate the fraction of 15–44 year-old women who would be eligible for Medicaid coverage in the event of pregnancy in each state and year from 1979 to 1990. They then estimated models in which the fraction of low birthweight infants in the state and the state infant mortality rates are functions of the fraction of women eligible. State and year dummies were included in the models in order to control for any state or year specific determinants of mortality.

A possible drawback is that the since Medicaid is means tested, the actual fraction eligible for Medicaid may depend on business cycle effects or omitted variables specific to states and years. Similarly, the fact that in 1990 the state of Mississippi had the highest fraction eligible of any state reflects both the generosity of the state program and the relative poverty of Mississippians. It is possible to construct an eligibility measure that reflects only variations in state rules as follows: (a) draw a sample of women from a nationally representative survey (the CPS) and (b) calculate the fraction of women in this sample who would be eligible for Medicaid in each state and year. This "simulated eligibility" measure will be exogenous as long as state rules can themselves be treated as exogenous variables. An additional advantage of this procedure is that sampling variation due to the fact that there are small cell sizes in some states and years is eliminated.

The first panel of Table 2 shows the estimated effects of Medicaid eligibility estimated using both the actual and simulated eligibility

---

[5] For example, in 1984, the cost of caring for a surviving baby weighing less than 2,500 grams in the U.S. was $9,712, compared to $678 for a heavier infant; see U.S. Office of Technology Assessment (1987).

[6] The CPS is run by the U.S. Census bureau and is used to generate unemployment rate figures and many other government statistics. About 100,000 individuals are surveyed each month, but the nature of the questionnaire changes from month to month and the most detailed demographic information is asked in March.

Table 2. *Effects of Medicaid expansions on infant mortality and low birth-weight, 1979–90*

	Low birthweight		Infant mortality	
	Actual eligibility	Simulated eligibility	Actual eligibility	Simulated eligibility
Panel 1: Models using fraction eligible under any expansion				
Fraction eligible	−4.211	−7.431	−2.093	−3.458
	(2.886)	(3.848)	(0.819)	(1.090)
Intercept	74.29	75.25	9.162	9.571
	(1.145)	(1.371)	(0.325)	(0.388)
Adjusted R^2	0.969	0.969	0.906	0.906
Panel 2: Models using fraction eligible under "targeted" expansions				
Fraction eligible	−7.749	−15.37	−1.752	−3.989
	(4.123)	(5.920)	(1.176)	(1.689)
Intercept	74.13	75.49	8.814	9.201
	(0.983)	(1.226)	(0.280)	(0.350)
Adjusted R^2	0.969	0.969	0.905	0.906
Panel 3: Models using fraction eligible under "broad" expansions				
Fraction eligible	−0.565	−1.451	−0.108	−0.336
	(2.458)	(6.178)	(0.699)	(1.757)
Intercept	74.35	74.35	8.440	8.447
	(1.406)	(1.397)	(0.400)	(0.397)
Adjusted R^2	0.981	0.981	0.910	0.910

Source: Currie and Gruber (1994). All regressions also include state and year dummies.

measures. Table 2 shows that the estimated effect of Medicaid eligibility is biased towards zero when actual eligibility is used. This finding suggests that the fraction eligible is positively correlated with omitted characteristics of states (such as poverty) that are themselves correlated with poor birth outcomes. Estimates using the simulated eligibility measure suggest that the observed 20 percentage point increase in eligibility over the 1980s reduced the incidence of low birthweight by 2 percent and the incidence of infant mortality by 7 percent. This result suggests that at least some babies were being saved through effective utilization of parental care rather than through expensive interventions during or after birth.[7] Cole (1994) reports similar results regarding the incidence of low birthweight using county-level data.

---

[7] Since about 8 percent of children are of low birth weight and only 0.9 percent of children die, it is possible that the 2 percent reduction in low birth weight could account for all of the reduction in infant mortality.

This finding supports an earlier study by Hanratty (1992) which showed that the introduction of universal health insurance in Canada was associated with a decrease in the infant mortality rate.[8] As in the U.S., health insurance was adopted by the Canadian provinces at different rates. She also asked whether the introduction of national health insurance increased birthweights, with ambiguous results.

The discussion above indicates that increasing eligibility for public insurance among poor children narrows gaps in infant health between high and low SES groups. It is more difficult to document a relationship between public insurance coverage and health among older children. Currie and Gruber (1996) explore this issue using data from the U.S. National Health Interview Surveys (NHIS). The NHIS interviews a large, nationally representative cross section of American families each year. While some information, such as income, is collected only at the household level, a great deal of information is collected about each person in the household. The sample used here is based on the pooled 1984–92 waves of the NHIS. It is limited to children less than 15 years of age to avoid complications due to "children having children" — under the Medicaid expansions teenage girls could become eligible for Medicaid coverage in the event of pregnancy, even if they were not previously eligible.

By combining household information with information about state laws and the child's age, it is possible to determine whether or not each child in the household was eligible for Medicaid. Table 3 indicates that over the entire 1984–92 period, 22 percent of the sample children were eligible.[9] Table 3 also shows the subset of indicators of utilization and health discussed by Currie and Gruber (1996) that I focus on in this section. The measure of utilization is whether or not the child has been to the doctor in the past 12 months. Since every child should receive at least one visit a year, this measure is a relatively clean measure of utilization that is not confounded by morbidity.[10] The health outcome examined is whether or not the child is reported by the responding parent to be in fair or poor health (henceforth, poor health), rather than in excellent or good health. Although this measure is inherently subjective, self-ratings of health status

---

[8] In 1966, the federal government passed the Medical Care Act which offered federal funding to all provinces that introduced comprehensive universal coverage. Between July 1, 1968 and April 1, 1972, all the Canadian provinces took up this offer.

[9] If household income was missing, it was imputed using the household's demographic and other socio-economic characteristics, in conjunction with coefficients from income regressions estimated using each year's March CPS.

[10] On the other hand, number of doctor visits would not be a good measure of health, since conditional on measures of medical need, lower SES individuals get fewer visits; cf. Aday (1975).

Table 3. *Selected NHIS sample means by Medicaid eligibility*

	All	Medicaid eligibles
% Eligible	0.22 (0.0001)	—
# Observations	226,819	49,654
% No doctor's visit last 12 months	0.20 (0.001)	0.20 (0.002)
In fair or poor health	0.03 (0.0003)	0.05 (0.001)
Family and Child Characteristics		
Black	0.18 (0.001)	0.35 (0.002)
Hispanic	0.12 (0.001)	0.22 (0.002)
Highest grade of female head	12.39 (0.006)	10.58 (0.014)
No male head	0.22 (0.001)	0.51 (0.002)
Family income < 2*Poverty	0.12 (0.001)	0.97 (0.0001)
Central city	0.32 (0.001)	0.48 (0.002)

Source: Currie and Gruber (1996). Standard errors in parentheses.

have been shown to be predictive of mortality differentials among adults; cf. Idler and Angel (1990). A possible problem with this measure, however, is that parental perceptions about child health may be influenced by contacts with the medical system.

Table 4 shows that, perhaps surprisingly, Medicaid-eligible children are as likely to have at least some visits in the year as other children. However, they are much more likely to be reported to be in poor health. Hence, conditional on need, it appears that Medicaid eligible children may be less likely to receive care. The Medicaid children are also younger on average, which is to be expected given the way the expansions have been phased in — and one might expect younger children to have more doctor visits, other things being equal.

The remainder of Table 4 compares the characteristics of selected Medicaid-eligible children to those of the full sample and shows that Medicaid-eligible children are disadvantaged in most observable respects: they are more likely to belong to minority groups, have less educated parents, and are more likely to live in poor, inner-city, female-headed households. It is also likely that they differ in ways that are not observed, which may be correlated with utilization of care and health status. Hence,

Table 4. *Medicaid eligibility, utilization and child health*
(Data from the U.S. NHIS)

	No visit last 12 months	Health fair or poor
Medicaid eligibility	−0.077	—
	(0.031)	
No visit last 12 months	—	−0.117
		(0.161)
Income bracket		
Income < 10,000	0.017	0.016
	(0.016)	(0.004)
10,000 < income < 20,000	−0.005	0.002
	(0.003)	(0.002)
20,000 < income < 30,000	−0.036	−0.006
	(0.006)	(0.004)
30,000 < income < 40,000	−0.058	−0.010
	(0.007)	(0.007)
40,000 < income < 50,000	−0.074	−0.013
	(0.007)	(0.009)
Family income > 50,000	−0.082	−0.014
	(0.007)	(0.011)
R-squared	0.099	0.017
Number of observations	226,604	227,093

Notes: Standard errors in parentheses. The regressions also covered child characteristics including gender, race, hispanic ethnicity; family characteristics including parents education, absence of male head, number of siblings, whether the mother or father responded, whether there were other male or female relatives in the household, central city, and rural location; dummy variables for each year of age, interactions between age and mother's educational attainment (less than 12, greater than 12 years), dummies for each year, interactions between year dummies and mother's educational attainment, and dummy variables for each state. The left out income category is "missing". If there is no male head of household, the male head's education is set to zero.

OLS estimates of the effects of medicaid eligibility on the variables of interest are likely to be subject to omitted variable bias.

In order to address this problem, Currie and Gruber (1996) instrumented individual eligibility using the simulated fraction of children in the same state, year and age group who were eligible for Medicaid. Using the March CPS, 1,000 children of each age were drawn for each year. Then, the fraction of each of these groups of children who would have been eligible for Medicaid under each state's rules was calculated for every year. This "simulated instrument" is purged of any variation stemming from variations in characteristics of children and their families across states. It is a valid instrument as long as dummy variables for each state/year/age group can be legitimately excluded from the models of utilization and health outcomes. Note that dummy variables for state, year and each year of age, as well as interactions between age and state and age and year are included in both the first and second stage regressions.[11] These variables control for characteristics of states, years and ages that could be correlated with the outcome variables, as well as for omitted variables such as nationwide technology changes or state programs affecting specific age groups.

The results of this instrumental variables procedure are shown in Table 4. The first column shows that Medicaid eligibility does increase utilization of care — the probability that a child did not receive a doctor's visit in the past year falls by 8 percent. The estimated effect is comparable to the effect of raising income from the lowest category, to between $40,000 and $50,000. Currie and Gruber (1996) found that in contrast, OLS estimates are biased towards zero by omitted variables — the OLS estimate is only 2 percent. Note that the probability that there are no visits falls with income. Since the poor are sicker, this result suggests that the "no visits" measure really captures utilization rather than morbidity. The probability of no visits also falls with parents' education, as one would expect.

The second column shows a model in which parent-reported health status is regressed on "no visits". Since whether or not there is a visit is a choice, it is instrumented using the simulated eligibility measure discussed above. The assumption underlying this specification is that "no visits" is an adequate marker for changes in utilization that are affected by eligibility. But the point estimate on "no visits" is wrong signed and not statistically significant. Self-reported health status does, however, move in the expected way with education and with income — relative to other children, children whose mothers lack a secondary diploma are about 2 percent more likely to be in poor health, and the poorest children are 1–2 percent more likely to be in poor health. However, the effects are nonlinear. Having a college-educated mother or raising income above $10,000 has no significant effect on the probability that poor health is reported.

The insignificant effect of utilization on parental reports of health status is disappointing given the large sample size, and the fact that if the marginal product of visits diminishes with the number of visits, then one would expect the move from "no visits" to "at least one visit" to have the greatest marginal impact on health. Part of the problem is that as discussed above, parental reports of children's health status are not objective measures of underlying health.

In order to confront this problem, Currie and Gruber (1996) estimated models in which aggregate child mortality rates depend on the fraction of

---

[11] The results are similar if interactions between states and years, age and years, age and state, and maternal education and state are included in the model, or if we include state specific trends instead of state*year interactions.

children eligible in each state, year and age group.[12] Using this objective measure of child health they found that the 15 percent increase in the fraction of children eligible for public insurance between 1984 and 1992 was associated with a 4.5 percent decline in child mortality. In summary, this evidence suggests that extending public insurance to pregnant women and children is associated with significant decreases in infant and child mortality. Since these improvements are concentrated among the poorest, they necessarily reflect lower SES-related health differentials.

The Efficiency of Utilization of Care

A second set of questions that can be posed is whether these improvements in health were "purchased" in the most efficient way possible? If it is true that " an ounce of prevention is worth a pound of cure" then we would hope that public insurance increased the use of preventive care as well as care for sick children.

Cole (1994) tackled this efficiency question directly by examining the effect of the expansions on the use of prenatal care. She followed a two-step procedure. First, she regressed individual-level information about birthweight and parental care from American *Vital Statistics* records (1983–90) on maternal characteristics. Then, she aggregated the residuals up to the county level, and regressed these measures on the fraction of Medicaid eligibles in the county and on other county characteristics. This procedure "nets out" variations between counties in the characteristics of their residents. In a sample of high poverty counties, she found that an increase in the fraction eligible increased the use of prenatal care: the 20 percent increase in eligibility that took place over the 1980s is estimated to have reduced the fraction of women who delayed obtaining prenatal care beyond the first trimester by 5 percent, to 17 percent.

She also aggregated the individual-level data by state, race, age group, and marital status, and alternatively by state, race, age group and education group. These regressions show that among teenaged mothers and unmarried mothers, the Medicaid expansions significantly increased the utilization of prenatal care and reduced the incidence of low birthweight and preterm births. Among these "at-risk" populations, a 20 percentage point increase in Medicaid eligibility was associated with a 25 percent decline in the number of women delaying prenatal care, and decreases in the incidence of low birthweight and preterm births of approximately 4 percent and 8 percent, respectively.

On the other hand, Currie and Gruber (1994) found evidence that some groups of newly eligible pregnant women were not drawn into prenatal

---

[12] Data are available for two age groups: children 1–4 and children 5–14.

care. In particular, they distinguished between expansions that were targeted to very low income women who had been ineligible for Medicaid because of family structure (e.g. because they were married), and broader expansions that made women eligible by raising income thresholds. Panels 2 and 3 of Table 2 indicate that only the more narrowly targeted expansions improved child outcomes.

Why were the broader expansions to women of higher income ineffective and what conclusions can be drawn from this about the efficacy of public health insurance programs? Currie and Gruber (1994) used individual-level data from the CPS to show that the reason why the broader expansions were ineffective is that they did not increase Medicaid *coverage*.[13] That is, women who became eligible for Medicaid as a result of higher income thresholds did not take up their new benefits. On the other hand, poorer women did take up their benefits at about the expected rate.[14] These results hold even when the sample is restricted to women without private insurance coverage.

The problem may be due to the fact that women who became eligible as a result of higher income thresholds were unfamiliar with the social insurance system, and did not realize that they were eligible for Medicaid coverge. This interpretation is supported by case studies. For example, Piper *et al.* (1990) found that a 1985 expansion of eligibility in Tennessee increased Medicaid enrollments, but that most of the increase took place within thirty days prior to delivery. Clearly, this represents a very inefficient pattern of usage. The women did not take advantage of the insurance to obtain prenatal care, but appear to have been enrolled when they arrived at the hospital to deliver. The fact that coverage of pregnant women went up at all probably reflects the incentives that hospitals have to recoup the costs of treating these women from the government.[15]

These findings suggest that while the expansions did improve infant health, they may not have done so in the most efficient way possible. They

---

[13] Individuals were asked whether they were covered by Medicaid at any point in the past year. Currie and Gruber use each woman's socio-economic characteristics to calculate whether or not she would have been eligible for Medicaid in the event of pregnancy, under either the targeted or the broad expansions. Coverage is then regressed on eligibility. The models control for demographic characteristics and income as well as for state and year. There are approximately 456,000 observations. Their results regarding low take-up of means-tested social insurance programs are consistent with those of Blank and Ruggles (1993) and Blank and Card (1991).

[14] They estimate that for every 100 women made potentially eligible under the targeted expansions, 9.6 took up their benefits, which represents almost full take-up given current fertility rates.

[15] Hospitals that accept any federal funds are not permitted to turn away a woman who is already in labor and maternity care is the single largest component of uncompensated care for U.S. hospitals.

point to an important benefit of universal programs — if everyone is covered, people will not fail to seek care solely because they are unaware of their entitlements. To the extent that people are aware of their eligibility but still fail to seek care, outreach may also be important. Several states have accompanied changes to their Medicaid programs with such programs. Evaluations of these programs may shed more light on the importance of outreach.

Insurance Coverage and Inequities in Children's Utilization of Care

The third question posed above was whether children with the same insurance coverage received the same care. Currie and Thomas (1995) compared the effects of Medicaid coverage and of private health insurance coverage on children's utilization of medical care. In order for Medicaid coverage of poor children to eliminate socio-economic gaps in health, it would have to be the case that gaps in health stemmed mainly from differential utilization of care, and that the main reason that poor children were less likely to receive care was because they lacked health insurance coverage. It is possible that insured children from low SES families will receive less care than other children because their parents are not informed about the value of medical care, or because they face other barriers such as transportation or child care costs.

In addition, children insured by the Medicaid program may lack access to care because many providers do not accept Medicaid payments, or limit the amount of time that they spend with Medicaid patients; cf. Sloan, Mitchell and Cromwell (1978) and Decker (1993).[16] The latter problem is one that could arise even with universal health insurance. It has been argued that in the U.S., problems of access are particularly acute among black children because of residential segregation; cf. Fossett and Peterson (1989). On the other hand, urban teaching hospitals tend to be located in inner-city areas with high concentrations of Afro-American residents — hence children in these locations have access to the best quality hospital care. Currie and Thomas focused on racial differences and asked whether Medicaid coverage has differential effects on whites and blacks.

They used data from the National Longitudinal Survey of Youth (NLSY), which began in 1979 with 6,283 young women (and an equal number of young men). These respondents have been followed in every year since. Beginning in 1986, the children of the NLSY mothers have been surveyed at two year intervals. For each child, the survey asks

---

[16] Doctors have many reasons for refusing to participate in the Medicaid program, ranging from low reimbursement rates, cf. Currie, Gruber and Fischer (1995), to red tape, to fears that high-risk patients may sue.

whether the child was covered by Medicaid or private insurance; when the child last had a preventive care visit, and the number of illnesses requiring medical attention in the past year. Clearly, the latter measure is an indicator of both morbidity and the propensity to utilize care, as discussed above. The longitudinal nature of the data allows inclusion of a fixed effect for each child which controls for any unobserved, constant, characteristics of the home environment and of the child that might be correlated with Medicaid status. Thus, the identification of the effect of Medicaid comes from within family variation in eligibility rather than from inter-state

Table 5. *Effect of Medicaid and private insurance on utilization of medical care; fixed effects estimates*

	Routine checkup conditional logit		Visits for illness OLS first differences	
	(1)	(2)	(3)	(4)
Insurance				
(1) if on Medicaid	0.727	0.656	0.515	0.570
	(0.253)	(0.257)	(0.150)	(0.154)
*Black	−0.334	−0.321	−0.703	−0.863
	(0.365)	(0.373)	(0.220)	(0.225)
(1) if on private insurance	0.073	0.088	0.392	0.377
	(0.181)	(0.182)	(0.111)	(0.112)
*Black	0.005	−0.001	−0.571	−0.520
	(0.315)	(0.317)	(0.194)	(0.194)
Child characteristics				
Age (in months)	−0.002	−0.002	−0.011	−0.011
	(0.003)	(0.003)	(0.002)	(0.002)
*Black	0.003	0.002	0.007	0.008
	(0.005)	(0.005)	(0.003)	(0.003)
Mother characteristics				
(1) if spouse present	−	−0.199	−	0.071
		(0.202)		(0.117)
*Black	−	−0.319	−	−0.427
		(0.354)		(0.200)
(1) if mother employed	−	−0.210	−	0.153
		(0.148)		(0.091)
*Black	−	0.219	−	−0.437
		(0.269)		(0.172)
Current income (1,000's)	−	0.001	−	0.001
		(0.002)		(0.002)
*Black	−	−0.002	−	−0.003
		(0.006)		(0.003)
Log likelihood	−681.4	−677.8	−	−
R-squared	−	−	0.023	0.027

Source: Currie and Thomas (1995). Standard errors in parentheses. 2,560 children in sample.

variation in Medicaid rules. Results estimated using the 1986 and 1988 waves of the survey are shown in Table 5. Models of whether or not the child had a routine checkup in the past 6 months are shown in columns 1 and 2 and are estimated using Chamberlain's conditional logit. Models of the number of visits for illness appear in columns 3 and 4 and are estimated using OLS in first differences. The first and third columns include changes in Medicaid and private insurance status along with changes in the child's age. However, due to the nature of the program, many mothers exit Medicaid via marriage or employment. Therefore, in the second and fourth columns, controls are added for these changes. In all the models, each covariate is interacted with an indicator equal to one if the child is black — hence the effects of insurance coverage are allowed to differ with the race of the child.

These estimates indicate that while private insurance has no significant impact on the probability of a routine checkup, Medicaid has a statistically significant effect: white children are 15 percent more likely to receive a checkup if they have Medicaid coverage, while black children are 10 percent more likely (although the difference between white and black children is not statistically significant). This result may reflect the fact that in the U.S., many private insurance plans do not cover preventive pediatric care. In contrast, both private insurance coverage and Medicaid coverage are associated with a higher number of visits for illness among white children, while for black children, insurance coverage has no significant effect on the number of visits. Hence, although extending insurance coverage to poor children does narrow the gap in utilization of care, it does not do so equally for all children.

A question that is not resolved by this study is whether these racial disparities can be attributed to a shortage of providers, other barriers to care, or differing attitudes towards care? It would be interesting to see whether differences in care by SES or minority group status existed in European countries in which all patients were entitled to care and aggressive outreach programs minimized the role of attitudes. A recent U.S. study of elderly patients who all had the same type of health insurance coverage found that even within the same hospital, patients from poor neighborhoods received worse treatment; see Kahn (1994). Hence, it is possible that differences in care continue to exist partly because of discrimination against low SES persons on the part of medical personnel.

IV. Discussion and Conclusions

The evidence presented in this paper demonstrates that public insurance coverage narrows socio-economic gaps in the utilization of health care and in health outcomes. However, the American example suggests that means-

tested public insurance programs may not result in a very efficient allocation of medical resources. In particular, there is some evidence that the
eligible underutilize preventive care and hence may end up overutilizing
sick care. To the extent that universal eligibility and aggressive health programs address this problem, they may result in a more efficient allocation
of resources. The third conclusion is that minority children appear to benefit less from public coverage than other children. Research in Europe
could shed light on whether this finding reflects inadequacies in the American system or a more widespread form of discrimination against lower
SES individuals.

References

Aday, Lu Ann: Economic and noneconomic barriers to the use of needed medical services.
Medical Care 18 (6), 447–56, 1975.
Antonovsky, Aaron: Social class, life expectancy and overall mortality. *Milbank Memorial
Fund Quarterly 45*, 31–73, 1967.
Barker, D. J. & Osmond, C.: Infant mortality, childhood nutrition, and ischemic heart
disease in England and Wales. *Lancet 1*, 1077–81, 1986.
Blank, Rebecca & Card, David: Recent trends in insured and uninsured unemployment: Is
there an explanation? *Quarterly Journal of Economics 106*, 1157–90, Nov. 1991.
Blank, Rebecca & Ruggles, Patricia: When do women use AFDC & food stamps? The
dynamics of eligibility vs. participation. NBER WP 4429, Cambridge, MA, Aug. 1993.
Bloom, Barbara: Health insurance and medical care. *Advance Data from Vital and Health
Statistics of the National Center for Health Statistics.* no. 188, NCHS Public Health
Service, Washington DC, Oct. 1, 1990.
Braveman, Paula, Oliva, G., Miller, M. G., Reiter, R. & Egerter, S., Adverse outcomes and
lack of health insurance among newborns in an eight-county area of California, 1982 to
1986. *New England Journal of Medicine 321* (6), 508–13, 1989.
Buehler, J. W., Kleinman, J. & Hogue, C., Birth weight-specific infant mortality, U.S., 1960
and 1980. *Public Health Reports 102* (2), 3564–7, 1985.
Cole, Nancy: Increasing access to health care: The effects of Medicaid expansions for
pregnant women. Mimeo, Abt Associates, Cambridge, MA, June 1994.
Currie, Janet & Gruber, Jonathan: Saving babies: The efficacy and cost of recent expansions
of Medicaid eligibility for pregnant women. NBER WP 4644, Cambridge, MA, Feb.
1994.
Currie, Janet & Gruber, Jonathan: Health insurance eligibility, utilization of medical care,
and child health. Forthcoming in *Quarterly Journal of Economics*, 1996.
Currie, Janet, Gruber, Jonathan & Fischer, Michael: Physician payments and infant health:
Effects of increases in Medicaid reimbursements. *American Economic Review 85*, May
1995.
Currie, Janet & Thomas, Duncan: Medical care for children: Public insurance, private
insurance and racial differnces in utilization. *Journal of Human Resources 30* (1), Winter
1995.
Decker, Sandra: The effect of physician reimbursement levels on the primary care of
Medicaid patients. Mimeo, Harvard University, 1993.
Forsdahl, A.: Are poor living conditions in childhood and adolescence an important risk
factor for arteriosclerotic heart disease? *British Journal of Preventive and Social Medicine
31*, 91–5, 1977.

152   J. Currie

Fossett, James & Peterson, John: Physician supply and Medicaid participation: The causes of market failure. *Medical Care 27*, 386-96, 1989.

Hanratty, Maria: Canadian national health insurance and infant health. Mimeo, Cornell University, 1992.

Horbar, Jeffrey, Wright, Elizabeth, Onstad, Lynn *et al.*: Decreasing mortality associated with the introduction of surfactant therapy: An observational study of neonates weighing 601 to 1,300 grams at birth. *Pediatrics 92* (2), 191-6, Aug. 1993.

Idler, E. L. & Angel, R. J.: Self-rated health and mortality in the NHANES-I Epidemiologic Follow-Up study. *American Journal of Public Health 80*, 446-52, 1990.

Kahn, Katherine *et al.*: Health care for black and poor hospitalized Medicare patients. *Journal of the American Medical Association 271* (15), 1169-74, Apr. 20, 1994.

Kozak, L. J. & McCarthy, E.: Hospital use by children in the United States and Canada. *Vital and Health Statistics*, Series 5, no. (PHS) 84-1477, U.S. Public Health Service, Washington DC, Aug. 1984.

Kunst, Anton & Mackenback, Johan: The size of mortality differences associated with educational level in nine industrialized countries. *American Journal of Public Health 84* (6), 932-7, June 1994.

Marmot, M. G. & McDowall, M. E.: Mortality decline and widening social inequalities. *Lancet 2*, 274, 1986.

McCormick, Barbara *et al.*: The health and developmental status of very-low-birthweight children at school age. *Journal of the American Medical Association 267*, 1992.

Piper, J. M., Ray, W. & Griffin, M.: Effects of Medicaid eligiblity expansion on prenatal care and pregnancy outcomes in Tennessee. *Journal of the American Medical Association 264* (17), 2219-23.

Preston, Samuel: Mortality trends. *Annual Review of Sociology 3*, 163-78, 1977.

Pui, C. H. *et al.*: Outcome of treatment for childhood cancer in black as compared with white children. *Journal of the American Medical Association*, 633-7, Feb. 22, 1995.

Sloan, Frank, Mitchell, Janet & Cromwell, Jerry: Physician participation in state Medicaid programs. *Journal of Human Resources 13*, 211-45, 1978.

Starfield, Barbara: *Effectiveness of Medical Care: Validating Clinical Wisdom*. Johns Hopkins University Press, Baltimore, 1985.

Townsend, Peter, Davidson, Nick & Whitehead, Margaret: *Inequalities in Health*. Penguin, London, 1988.

U.S. House of Representatives: *Green Book 1993: Background Material on Programs Under the Jurisdiction of the Committee on Ways and Means*. GPO, Washington DC, 1993.

U.S. National Commission on the International year of the Child: *Report to the President*, GPO, Washington DC, 1980.

U.S. Office of Technology Assessment: *Neonatal Intensive Care for Low Birthweight Infants: Costs and Effectiveness*. OTA-HCS-38, GPO, Washington DC, 1987.

Valdez, Burciega *et al.*: The consequences of cost sharing for children's health. *Pediatrics 75*, 957-61, 1985.

Valkonen, Tapani: Adult mortality and level of education: A comparison of six countries. In J. Fox (ed.), *Health Inequalities in European Countries*, Gower, Brookfield, 1989.

Wadsworth, M. E.: Serious illness in childhood and its association with later-life achievement. In Richard Wilkinson (ed.), *Class and Health*, Tavistock, London, 1986.

Waldman, Robert: Income distribution and infant mortality. *Quarterly Journal of Economics 152* (4), 1283-302, Nov. 1992.

Yelowitz, Aaron: The Medicaid notch, labor supply and welfare participation: Evidence from eligibility expansions. Mimeo, MIT, 1994.

Is it Legitimate to Encourage Work Sharing?*

Nina Maderner
University of Vienna, Austria

Jean-Charles Rochet
University of Toulouse, France

Abstract

A generalization of Mirrlees' income taxation model is formulated in which qualifications of workers are both endogenous and observable by the government. Individuals differ by their unobservable abilities, which simultaneously affect their disutility of labor and their cost of training. In general the optimal tax schedule depends not only on income but also on its "components", i.e., wage rate (or qualification) and labor supply. We find conditions under which it is optimal to subsidize lower qualifications or to encourage work sharing.

I. Introduction

There is a fundamental inconsistency in the classical income taxation model initiated by Mirrlees (1971) and further developed by e.g. Atkinson (1973), Atkinson and Stiglitz (1980) and Sheshinski (1972). Indeed, in this model, the incentive problem associated with income taxation is captured by the assumption that individual wages and labor supplies are not separately observable by the government, which can only use wage income (that is, the product of these two quantities) as a basis for taxation. Therefore, redistribution is limited by the fact that those who are more productive will have less incentives to work (as soon as the marginal tax rate is positive) than in the case of lump-sum taxation. However, it is also

*This is a revised version of the paper, originally entitled "Redistributing Income Through Inefficient Employment", which we presented at the *SJE*'s conference on "The Future of the Welfare State". We are grateful to Thomas Piketty and to the participants of this conference for their comments, and in particular to Sören Blomquist, Vidar Christiansen, Assar Lindbeck and Kjell Erik Lommerud. The ideas of this paper emanated from discussions with Paul Seabright. We also thank Helmuth Cremer and Pierre Pestieau for helpful discussions at an early stage, and two anonymous referees and the editors for their constructive criticisms. The usual disclaimer applies.

assumed in this model that the labor market is competitive and efficient, and that individual wages equal individual productivities, which are perfectly observed by firms. It is difficult to understand why the government cannot observe individual productivities, whereas firms observe them perfectly.

For the same reason, this model is not appropriate for the study of important questions such as minimum wage legislation; see e.g. Guesnerie and Roberts (1987) and Marceau and Boadway (1994). Nor can it be applied to other measures which have been discussed for decreasing the unemployment burden: work sharing schemes and subsidies to low qualified jobs. Work sharing has been criticized on the grounds that it is inefficient from a technological viewpoint. Another argument is that as the productivity of the more qualified workers increases rapidly, and provided that disutility of labor is bounded from below, it may become useless or socially wasteful to employ workers with low qualifications. The standard critique regarding subsidies to low qualifications is that redistribution should be carried out only through the tax system and that such subsidies would only distort the allocation of labor in the economy. We prove here that these arguments are not correct when the imperfections of the redistribution system are introduced. In order to focus on this aspect, we abstract from the difficulties associated with frictions on the labor market that generate unemployment: we assume that the labor market is perfect and therefore that unemployment is *voluntary*. In this paper we concentrate on the individuals' decisions regarding whether or not to participate in the labor force and how much to invest in human capital. We want to determine how these decisions are affected by income taxation (including income maintenance schemes) and government subsidies to low qualifications.

In Section II we define an extension of the Mirrlees model in which qualifications of workers are both endogenous and observable by the government. Individuals differ by their inobservable abilities, which simultaneously affect their disutility of labor and their cost of training. The redistributive objectives of the government are represented by the maximization of a utilitarian welfare function, under a revenue requirement and incentive compatibility (or self-selection) constraints.

In Section III we consider the characteristics of the second-best optimum in the simple case where there are only two types of individuals. Then we show that this optimum can be decentralized by a generalized tax function which depends not only on wage income but separately on its "components", i.e., wage rate and labor supply. We give conditions under which this optimal tax schedule has the property that for the same income level, individuals who work less pay less taxes. We interpret this as encouraging work sharing. Under an alternative condition on preferences, we obtain the opposite property that for the same income level, individuals with lower qualifications pay less taxes.

In Section IV we study a general equilibrium version of our model in which wages depend on total labor supply, and also on average qualifications. This (positive) externality in the production process provides a further argument in favor of work sharing, since it indirectly encourages workers to acquire higher qualifications.

II. A Model of Income Taxation with Endogenous Qualifications

Our main objective in this paper is to analyze the possible justifications of policy measures such as encouragement of work sharing or subsidies to low qualified jobs. As we have already remarked, the standard income tax model is inadequate for this purpose since, in that model, individual qualifications and labor supplies are not (separately) observable by the government. We therefore start by building a more complex (and we hope, more realistic[1]) model in which the government is able to observe both the number L of hours worked, and the worker's qualification q (which we identify for the moment with his or her competitive wage).

In our model, individuals differ by a parameter θ (measuring their "ability" or their "taste") which is not observable by the government. Together with the tax schedule, this parameter θ determines their investment in human capital (materialized by the qualification q they choose to obtain) and their labor supply L.

For simplicity, we consider a static model, in which these training and labor supply decisions are taken simultaneously. Although these assumptions are obviously unrealistic, they will allow us to obtain, in the simplest possible way, an analysis of policy measures which could not be performed using the standard income taxation model. In particular, we study generalized tax schedules $T(q, L)$ in which income tax T depends not only on income $Z = qL$ but also on its "components" q and L.

For a particular combination (q, L), we say that work sharing is encouraged if individuals who work less pay less taxes, their total income being kept constant:

$$\left(\frac{\partial T}{\partial L}\right)_{qL} = \frac{\partial T}{\partial L} - \frac{q}{L}\frac{\partial T}{\partial q} > 0. \tag{1}$$

---

[1] The simple fact that such policy measures may exist (as well as others like minimum wage legislation) indicates that individual wage rates and number of hours worked are, to some extent, observable. However, the realism of our assumptions is clearly limited by the possibilities of manipulation open to firms. For instance, they can collude with workers and offer to understate the wage rate (and overstate the number of hours worked to keep the wage bill constant) in order for the workers to receive subsidies.

Similarly, we say that lower qualifications are subsidized if individuals who choose lower qualifications pay less taxes, their income being kept constant:

$$\left(\frac{\partial T}{\partial q}\right)_{qL} = \frac{\partial T}{\partial L} - \frac{L}{q}\frac{\partial T}{\partial q} > 0. \tag{2}$$

It is interesting to note that these two conditions are mutually exclusive. Indeed, let us denote:

$$\Delta(q, L) = \left(q\frac{\partial T}{\partial q} - L\frac{\partial T}{\partial L}\right)(q, L). \tag{3}$$

If $\Delta(q, L) > 0$, then lower qualifications are subsidized (in the neighborhood of (q, L)), whereas work sharing is encouraged if and only if $\Delta(q, L) < 0$. The limiting case $(\Delta = 0)$ corresponds to a situation where the optimal tax depends only on income $Z = qL$.

Individual preferences are represented by a general utility function:

$$U = u(C, L, q, \theta), \tag{4}$$

where $C = qL - T(q, L)$ denotes consumption (that is, net income), and θ is a "taste" or "ability" parameter (private information of each individual). We assume that u is concave[2] in (C, L, q) with $u_C > 0$, $u_q < 0$ and $u_\theta > 0$. Note that the choice variables (C, L, q) are all observable by the government; this is the main departure from the standard model. For simplicity we assume that θ can only take two values $(\theta \in \{\theta_1, \theta_2\}$ with proportions π_1 and π_2). The objective of the government is to maximize a utilitarian welfare function:

$$W = \sum_{k=1}^{2} \pi_k u(C_k, L_k, q_k, \theta_k), \tag{5}$$

under a revenue requirement constraint:

$$\sum_{k=1}^{2} \pi_k(q_k L_k - C_k) \geq D, \tag{6}$$

where D is interpreted as the overall tax revenue required by the government in per capita terms, or equivalently we assume that the size of the population is normalized to one. We also have to take into account incentive compatibility (or self-selection) constraints:

$$u(C_1, L_1, q_1, \theta_1) \geq u(C_2, L_2, q_2, \theta_1), \tag{7}$$

---

[2] Concavity is required because we use a utilitarian welfare function.

and:

$$u(C_2, L_2, q_2, \theta_2) \geq u(C_1, L_1, q_1, \theta_2). \tag{8}$$

Since only one of these constraints will be binding at the optimum, we can assume without loss of generality (after a possible redefinition of θ) that it is constraint (8). Types θ_1 then have to be interpreted as the less "favored" agents, towards whom the government would like to redistribute income. This redistributive objective will be limited by the incentive compatibility constraint (8), which states that types θ_2 must not have a (strict) interest in pretending they are of type θ_1 (or "mimic" types θ_1 in the terminology of adverse selection models). Later we give conditions under which types θ_1 indeed correspond to the less "qualified" workers (i.e., $q_1 < q_2$). It is more convenient to rewrite (8) as follows:

$$u(C_2, L_2, q_2, \theta_2) - u(C_1, L_1, q_1, \theta_1) \geq R(C_1, L_1, q_1), \tag{9}$$

where:

$$R(C_1, L_1, q_1) = u(C_1, L_1, q_1, \theta_2) - u(C_1, L_1, q_1, \theta_1) \tag{10}$$

represents the *informational rent* of types θ_2.

We are now in a position to state the optimization program that defines the second-best optimum:

$$(\mathscr{P}) \begin{cases} \max \sum_{k=1}^{2} \pi_k u(C_k, L_k, q_k, \theta_k) \\[2mm] \text{for } (C_k, L_k, q_k) \, k = 1, 2 \text{ such that:} \\[2mm] \sum_{k=1}^{2} \pi_k(q_k L_k - C_k) \geq D, \quad (6) \\[2mm] u(C_2, L_2, q_2, \theta_2) - u(C_1, L_1, q_1, \theta_1) \geq R(C_1, L_1, q_1). \quad (9) \end{cases}$$

III. Characterization and Implementation of the Second-Best Optimum

Characterization

Denoting by μ and ν the multipliers associated with constraints (6) and (9), the Lagrangian of problem $\mathscr{P}$ can be written:

$$\mathscr{L} = \sum_{k=1}^{2} (\pi_k + \nu_k)(u(C_k, L_k, q_k, \theta_k) + \mu_k(q_k L_k - C_k - D)) - \nu R(C_1, L_1, q_1)$$

where by definition $\nu_2 = -\nu_1 = \nu$ and $\mu_k = \mu \pi_k / (\pi_k + \nu_k) \, (k = 1, 2)$.

The first-order conditions give

$$\mu_2 = \frac{\partial u}{\partial C}(x_2) = -\frac{1}{L_2}\frac{\partial u}{\partial q}(x_2) = -\frac{1}{q_2}\frac{\partial u}{\partial L}(x_2) \tag{11}$$

with $x_2 = (C_2, L_2, q_2, \theta_2)$, and:

$$\mu_1 = \frac{\partial u}{\partial C}(x_1) - \frac{v}{\pi_1 - v}\frac{\partial R}{\partial C} = -\frac{1}{L_1}\left[\frac{\partial u}{\partial q}(x_1) - \frac{v}{\pi_1 - v}\frac{\partial R}{\partial q}\right]$$

$$= -\frac{1}{q_1}\left[\frac{\partial u}{\partial L}(x_1) - \frac{v}{\pi_1 - v}\frac{\partial R}{\partial L}\right] \tag{12}$$

with $x_1 = (C_1, L_1, q_1, \theta_1)$.

How to Implement the Second-Best Optimum

Let $T(q, L)$ represent the generalized tax schedule designed to implement the second-best optimum characterized above. An individual of type θ will choose q and L so as to maximize $u[qL - T(q, L), L, q, \theta]$. Assuming an *interior solution* (and differentiability of the tax schedule at the maximum)[3] the first-order conditions give:

$$\left(q - \frac{\partial T}{\partial L}\right)\frac{\partial u}{\partial C} + \frac{\partial u}{\partial L} = 0, \qquad \left(L - \frac{\partial T}{\partial q}\right)\frac{\partial u}{\partial C} + \frac{\partial u}{\partial q} = 0$$

or:

$$\frac{\partial T}{\partial L} = q + \frac{\partial u}{\partial L}\bigg/\frac{\partial u}{\partial C}, \quad \frac{\partial T}{\partial q} = L + \frac{\partial u}{\partial q}\bigg/\frac{\partial u}{\partial C}.$$

Using (11) and (12), which characterize the second-best optimum, we immediately obtain the usual property that marginal tax rates are zero at the top (i.e., for types θ_2):

$$\frac{\partial T}{\partial L}(q_2, L_2) = \frac{\partial T}{\partial q}(q_2, L_2) = 0.$$

---

[3] As remarked by Stiglitz (1982), the optimal tax schedule in a discrete model is not differentiable everywhere. However, it is typically differentiable at the points chosen by agents.

At the bottom of the distribution we have:

$$\frac{\partial T}{\partial L}(q_1, L_1) = \frac{v}{(\pi_1 - v)(\partial u/\partial C)(x_1)} \left[\frac{\partial R}{\partial L} + q_1 \frac{\partial R}{\partial C} \right] \tag{13}$$

and

$$\frac{\partial T}{\partial q}(q_1, L_1) = \frac{v}{(\pi_1 - v)(\partial u/\partial C)(x_1)} \left[\frac{\partial R}{\partial q} + L_1 \frac{\partial R}{\partial C} \right] \tag{14}$$

The expressions between brackets can be interpreted by using the fact that R can also be written:

$$R(C_1, L_1, q_1) = \int_{\theta_1}^{\theta_2} \frac{\partial u}{\partial \theta}(C_1, L_1, q_1, \theta) \, d\theta.$$

Recall that we have to compute:

$$\Delta(q_1, L_1) = q_1 \frac{\partial T}{\partial q}(q_1, L_1) - L_1 \frac{\partial T}{\partial L}(q_1, L_1).$$

Using the above formulas, this can be written:

$$\Delta(q_1, L_1) = \frac{v}{(\pi_1 - v)\partial u/\partial C(x_1)}$$

$$\times \left[\int_{\theta_1}^{\theta_2} \left(q_1 \frac{\partial^2 u}{\partial \theta \, \partial q} - L_1 \frac{\partial^2 u}{\partial \theta \, \partial L} \right)(C_1, L_1, q_1, \theta) \, d\theta \right]. \tag{15}$$

Therefore, if $(q_1(\partial^2 u/\partial \theta \, \partial q - L_1(\partial^2 u/\partial \theta \, \partial L))$ always has the same sign, it is also the sign of $\Delta(q_1, L_1)$. It turns out that this condition is related to the properties of the constrained labor supply function $\hat{L}(\theta)$, defined by $\hat{L}(\theta) = \arg\max_L u(C, Z/L, L, \theta)$, where the income levels C and Z (net and gross) are given. In words, $\hat{L}(\theta)$ represents the labor supplied by an individual of type θ, when his or her gross $(Z = qL)$ and net (C) income levels are fixed. It is easy to see that:

$$\forall (C, Z), \, \theta \rightarrow \hat{L}(\theta) \text{ increasing} \Leftrightarrow \forall (C, L, q, \theta) \quad q \frac{\partial^2 u}{\partial \theta \, \partial q} - L \frac{\partial^2 u}{\partial \theta \, \partial L} < 0. \tag{16}$$

$$\forall (C, Z), \, \theta \rightarrow \hat{L}(\theta) \text{ decreasing} \Leftrightarrow \forall (C, L, q, \theta) \quad q \frac{\partial^2 u}{\partial \theta \, \partial q} - L \frac{\partial^2 u}{\partial \theta \, \partial L} > 0. \tag{17}$$

Proposition 1. (*a*) *If condition* (*16*) *is satisfied* (*labor supply always increases with* θ *when income is fixed*), *then* $\Delta(q_1, L_1) < 0$ *and work sharing is encouraged for types* θ_1.
(*b*) *If condition* (*17*) *is satisfied* (*labor supply always decreases with* θ *when income is fixed*), *then* $\Delta(q_1, L_1) > 0$ *and lower qualifications are subsidized for types* θ_1.

The Case of Separable Preferences

In order to gain a better understanding of conditions (16) and (17), let us examine the particular case in which preferences are separable with respect to consumption:

$$U = u(C) - \psi(L, q, \theta).$$

In this specification, ψ is interpreted as the total cost of labor and investment in human capital, for an individual of type θ. Our assumptions on U translate into $u' > 0$, $\psi_L > 0$, $\psi_q > 0$, $\psi_\theta < 0$. Condition (16) is then equivalent to:

$$\frac{q\psi_{\theta q}}{\psi_\theta} < \frac{L\psi_{\theta L}}{\psi_\theta}, \tag{18}$$

which means that the marginal cost ψ_θ is less elastic to changes in qualification q than to changes in labor supply L.

Under this specification we can also analyze in more detail the individual choices in terms of qualification and labor supply. Indeed, separability of consumption allows us to define an auxiliary function $v(Z, \theta)$, interpreted as the cost of obtaining gross income Z for an individual of type θ:

$$v(Z, \theta) = \begin{cases} \min \psi(L, q, \theta) \\ qL = Z \end{cases}$$

where the minimum is obtained for $L = L(Z, \theta)$ and $q = q(Z, \theta)$. By construction, we have:

$$q(Z, \theta)\, L(Z, \theta) = Z \qquad \text{for all } Z, \theta.$$

Therefore by differentiating this equality with respect to Z and θ, we obtain, respectively:

$$q_Z L + q L_Z = 1,$$

and:

$$q_\theta L + q L_\theta = 0. \tag{19}$$

When taxation depends only on income, the optimization program of an individual of type θ can be written:

$$\max_{Z}\{u(Z - T(Z)) - v(Z, \theta)\}.$$

In particular, the single-crossing property (which guarantees that more able people get higher incomes) is equivalent to the familiar condition $v_{\theta Z} < 0$ (the marginal cost of income decreases with θ). Although most of our analysis does not depend on this condition (this is why we have adopted general preferences), the interpretation of our results will be easier if we assume:

(A1) $L_Z > 0$, $\qquad q_Z > 0$,

and

(A2) $\psi_{\theta L} < 0$, $\qquad \psi_{\theta q} < 0$.

(A1) means that when individuals of a given ability want higher incomes (which is the case, for instance, when marginal tax rates decrease), they both work more $(L_Z > 0)$ and choose higher qualifications $(q_Z > 0)$. This is analogous to the classical assumption that substitution effects dominate income effects. (A2) means that more able individuals simultaneously have a lower marginal cost of labor and of qualification. These two properties imply the single-crossing condition. Indeed, by the envelope principle:

$$v_\theta(Z, \theta) = \psi_\theta(L(Z, \theta), q(Z, \theta), \theta),$$

and therefore:

$$v_{\theta Z}(Z, \theta) = \psi_{\theta L} L_Z + \psi_{\theta q} q_Z < 0.$$

However, equation (19) shows (as we already remarked) that q_θ and L_θ have opposite signs. When condition (16) is satisfied, $L_\theta > 0$ and work sharing has to be encouraged (cf. proposition 1). When condition (17) is satisfied, $q_\theta > 0$ and lower qualifications have to be subsidized.

IV. A General Equilibrium Formulation

So far, we have studied a partial equilibrium model, where (as in most of the literature on income taxation) competitive wages are independent of labor supply and total output is just the sum of individual productions. Stiglitz (1982) has shown that such a formulation could be misleading. For instance, when the different qualities of labor are not perfect substitutes, the general equilibrium effects dominate at the top of the distribution of types, and the marginal tax rate is negative.

Unlike the Stiglitz model, in our formulation individual qualifications are both endogenous and observable. Therefore individuals of different

abilities have possibilities of obtaining the same qualifications, and therefore the same jobs, albeit at different training costs. This allows us to insist
on another type of general equilibrium effects, associated with positive
externalities in the training process. This is why we have chosen to assume
perfect substitutability between the different qualifications. On the other
hand, total output per worker depends positively on average qualification:

$$Q = f(N, \bar{q}), \tag{20}$$

where $N = \pi_1 q_1 L_1 + \pi_2 q_2 L_2$, and $\bar{q} = \pi_1 q_1 + \pi_2 q_2$.

f is supposed to be increasing and concave in both variables. Since we
assume that the labor market is competitive, wages are proportional to
qualifications:

$$W_i = \frac{\partial Q}{\partial(\pi_i L_i)} = q_i \frac{\partial f}{\partial N}. \tag{21}$$

Capital is supposed to be fixed, and profits $(Q - \Sigma_{i=1}^2 \pi_i W_i L_i)$ are
distributed according to some prespecified rules. As usual, individuals
behave competitively: when they choose q_i and L_i they take $\bar{q}$ and N as
given.

Given these assumptions, the second-best optimum is now determined
by:

$$\mathscr{P}' \begin{cases} \displaystyle\max_{C_k, L_k, q_k} \sum_{k=1,2} \pi_k u(C_k, L_k, \theta_k) & \text{under the constraints} \\[2mm] \displaystyle f(N, \bar{q}) - \sum_{k=1,2} \pi_k C_k \geq D & (22) \\[2mm] u(C_2, L_2, q_2, \theta_2) - u(C_1, L_1, q_1, \theta_1) \geq R(C_1, L_1, q_1). & (23) \end{cases}$$

Using the same notations as before, the Lagrangian of this maximization
problem can be written:

$$\mathscr{L}' = \sum_{k=1,2} (\pi_k + \nu_k)(u(C_k, L_k, q_k, \theta_k) - \mu_k C_k)$$

$$+ \mu[f(N, \bar{q}) - D] - \nu R(C_1, L_1, q_1).$$

The first-order condition for an *interior* solution give:

$$\mu_2 = \frac{\mu}{1 - (\nu/\pi_2)} = \frac{\partial u}{\partial C}(x_2)$$

$$= -\frac{1}{q_2(\partial f/\partial N)} \frac{\partial u}{\partial L}(x_2) = -\frac{1}{(\partial f/\partial N)L_2 + (\partial f/\partial q)} \frac{\partial u}{\partial q}(x_2)$$

and:

$$\mu_1 = \frac{\mu}{1 - (v/\pi_1)} = \frac{\partial u}{\partial C}(x_1) - \frac{v}{\pi_1 - v}\frac{\partial R}{\partial C}(x_1)$$

$$= -\frac{1}{q_1(\partial f/\partial N)}\left[\frac{\partial u}{\partial L}(x_1) - \frac{v}{\pi_1 - v}\frac{\partial R}{\partial L}(x_1)\right]$$

$$= -\frac{1}{L_1(\partial f/\partial N) + (\partial f/\partial \bar{q})}\left[\frac{\partial u}{\partial q}(x_1) - \frac{v}{\pi_1 - v}\frac{\partial R}{\partial q}(x_1)\right]$$

On the other hand, the individual optimization problem is now given by:

$$\mathscr{P}' \begin{cases} \max_{C_i, L_i, q_i} u(C_i, L_i, q_i, \theta_i) \\ \text{under the constraint} \\ C_i = q_i \dfrac{\partial f}{\partial N} L_i - T(q_i, L_i) + B_i \end{cases}$$

where B_i represents the share of total profits received by i.
The first-order conditions give:

$$\frac{\partial u}{\partial C}\left(q_i \frac{\partial f}{\partial N} - \frac{\partial T}{\partial L}(q_i, L_i)\right) + \frac{\partial u}{\partial L}(x_i) = 0$$

$$\frac{\partial u}{\partial C}\left(L_i \frac{\partial f}{\partial N} - \frac{\partial T}{\partial q}(q_i, L_i)\right) + \frac{\partial u}{\partial q}(x_i) = 0$$

and therefore

$$\frac{\partial T}{\partial L}(q_i, L_i) = \frac{(\partial u/\partial L)(x_i)}{(\partial u/\partial C)(x_i)} + q_i \frac{\partial f}{\partial N}$$

$$\frac{\partial T}{\partial q}(q_i, L_i) = \frac{(\partial u/\partial q)(x_i)}{(\partial u/\partial C)(x_i)} + L_i \frac{\partial f}{\partial N}.$$

Recall the expression of Δ:

$$\Delta(q, L) = q\frac{\partial T}{\partial q} - L\frac{\partial T}{\partial L}$$

$$= q\frac{(\partial u/\partial q)}{(\partial u/\partial C)} - L\frac{(\partial u/\partial L)}{(\partial u/\partial C)}.$$

Therefore:

$$\Delta(q_2, L_2) = -\frac{\mu_2}{(\partial u/\partial C)(x_2)} q_2 \cdot \frac{\partial f}{\partial q} < 0 \tag{24}$$

and

$$\Delta(q_1, L_1) = \frac{1}{(\partial u/\partial C)(x_1)} \cdot \left\{ \frac{\nu}{\pi_1 - \nu} \left(q_1 \frac{\partial R}{\partial q_1} - L_1 \frac{\partial R}{\partial L_1} \right) - \mu_1 q_1 \frac{\partial f}{\partial \bar{q}} \right\}. \tag{25}$$

As in the Stiglitz model (but for different reasons), $\Delta(q_2, L_2)$ is now smaller than 0; this means that work sharing has to be encouraged at the top of the distribution. The interpretation is that if work sharing is encouraged, this provides incentives for individuals to acquire higher qualifications. This in turn is beneficial if there are positive externalities in the training process.

Considering $\Delta(q_1, L_1)$, we now have the weighted sum of two terms: an "incentive" term $(q_1(\partial R/\partial q_1) - L_1(\partial R/\partial L_1))$ as before, and an "efficiency" term $- q_1(\partial f/\partial \bar{q})$ which is always negative. Thus, work sharing becomes more likely than in our partial equilibrium formulation because even if the incentive term is positive (which implies that low qualifications would have to be subsidized in the partial equilibrium model), this may be counterbalanced by the efficiency term, which is always negative.

V. Conclusion

The objective of this paper is twofold. First, we formulated an extension of the standard income taxation model, in which individual qualifications and labor supplies are separately observable by the government. Such a model is needed if we want to understand the impact of income taxation on human capital investments by workers. It could also be applied to the analysis of policy measures such as minimum wage legislation or workfare programs. Second, we focused on the choices of qualifications and studied how they are affected by the redistributive objectives of the government, represented by the maximization of a utilitarian welfare function under a revenue requirement and incentive compatibility constraints.

We examined the implementation of this second-best optimum through a generalized tax function $T(q, L)$ which depends on qualification q and labor supply L. The usual case is when T depends only on income $Z = qL$, which means that $(q(\partial T/\partial q) - L(\partial T/\partial L) = 0)$. We show that this property will only be satisfied at the top of the distribution of types, that is (typically) for high wages and high labor supplies. At the bottom of the distribution, we find a condition (condition (16)) under which $q(\partial T/\partial q) - L(\partial T/$

∂L) < 0, which means that (for the same income) individuals who work less will pay less taxes. We interpret this as work sharing encouragement. We then extended our analysis to a general equilibrium formulation, in which wages depend on total labor supply (measured in units of "elementary" labor) and also on average qualification, in order to capture a positive externality in the production process. This provides a second motivation for encouraging work sharing, i.e., to encourage choices of higher qualifications, and therefore internalizing the externality of the production process. It is clear that this externality can be internalized by other means (like direct subsidization of education by the government). However, we regard our analysis as shedding light on a novel argument for subsidizing work sharing.

References

Atkinson, A. B.: How progressive should income tax be? In M. Parkin & A. R. Nobay (eds.), *Essays in Modern Economics*, Longman, London, 1973.
Atkinson, A. B. & Stiglitz, J. E.: *Lectures on Public Economics.* McGraw Hill, London, 1980.
Guesnerie, R. & Roberts, K.: Minimum wage legislation as a second best policy. *European Economic Review 31*, 491–8, 1987.
Marceau, N. & Boadway, R.: Minimum wage legislation and unemployment insurance as instruments for redistribution. *Scandinavian Journal of Economics 96*, 67–81, 1994.
Mirrlees, J. A.: An exploration of the theory of optimum income taxation. *Review of Economic Studies 38*, 175–208, 1971.
Sheshinski, E.: The optimal linear income tax. *Review of Economic Studies 39*, 297–302, 1972.
Stiglitz, J. E.: Self-selection and Pareto efficient taxation. *Journal of Public Economics 17*, 213–40, 1982.

Labor Supply Responses and Welfare Effects of Tax Reforms*

Rolf Aaberge

Statistics Norway, Oslo, Norway

John K. Dagsvik

Statistics Norway, Oslo, Norway

Steinar Strøm

University of Oslo, Norway

Abstract

During the late 1980s and early 1990s, taxation of wage income has undergone a change towards a proportional tax regime in many countries. Our analysis shows that gradual tax reforms in Norway may have removed some of the distortions on worker behavior. Moreover, we find that proportional taxes may reduce the inequality in the distribution of disposable household income. Yet, when the distributional consequences are related to changes in individual welfare, we find that rich households may benefit far more than households at the other tail of the income distribution, because they earn more without any significant increase in effort.

I. Introduction

A common feature of the Scandinavian welfare states, in particular in the first three decades of the postwar period, has been strong political support for a redistributive policy that narrowed income differentials through a progressive income tax. For instance, in 1979 the Norwegian marginal tax rate on incomes in the top decile of the income distribution was at an all-time high and equal to 74 percent. By contrast, the marginal tax rate on incomes in the bottom decile was 32 percent.

The prevailing view among economists in the 1960s and early 1970s was that the distortions on worker behavior caused by a progressive income tax were rather modest. Since the late 1970s there has been a

*We thank Tom Wennemo for programming assistance, Anne Skoglund for editing the paper, and the editors and anonymous referees for helpful comments.

growing concern among economists regarding the extent to which high and progressive taxes are eroding the efficiency of the market economy through the disincentives and distortions created by the tax system; see Sandmo (1991) for a historical review of the changing attitudes among economists in the postwar period. Today, public finance scholars, in particular, believe that taxes on labor income cause major distortions on worker behaviour.

In recent years we have witnessed a similar shift in attitudes among leading politicians. Consequently, during the 1980s and early 1990s the marginal tax rates on high labor incomes in Norway were gradually reduced, with the most substantial reduction taking place from 1991 to 1992. The marginal tax rates on incomes in the bottom decile of the income distribution have been changed moderately. As a result, the progressive income tax of today is much less steep than in the late 1970s.[1]

One objective of this paper is to examine the distortion on worker behavior caused by the progressive income tax of 1979, that is before the gradual reduction in (formal) marginal tax rates took place. Another objective is to examine the distributional consequences of two tax reforms, one hypothetical and one real. The tax system of 1979 is evaluated against a proportional tax regime and against the tax rules of 1992.

Our analysis shows that when the tax system of 1979 was replaced by the rules of 1992, mean welfare (defined as the mean of households utility levels) increased. However, the order of magnitude of this increase in mean welfare was less than the mean welfare gain obtained by introducing proportional taxation of wage income. The large difference in mean welfare gains is mainly due to the labor supply responses in the lower tail of the household income distribution. The labor supply incentives, in particular for married females, in the lower tail of the income distribution were much less improved by the 1992 reform than by the hypothetical proportional tax reform. Consequently, further reforms of the present tax system towards proportional taxation of wage income may give a substantial increase in mean welfare and thus a substantial reduction in the cost of taxation. Moreover, our analysis shows that such further reforms of the tax system may reduce the inequality in the distribution of after-tax household income. This surprising result is driven by the labor supply

---

[1] It should be emphasized, however, that there could be a considerable difference between the effective and formal marginal tax rates. In 1979 all interest payments were deductible against a maximal marginal tax rate of 74 percent, while in 1992 deductions were only allowed against a marginal tax rate of 28 percent (equal to the marginal tax rate on capital income). These changes in deduction rules implied that although the differences between the formal tax rates of the 1970s and early 1990s were large, the differences between the effective rates were much smaller, in particular for net borrowers in the high income brackets.

responses caused by a proportional tax reform, since we find that this reform induces the "poor" to work much harder than before. For these poor households, the decrease in the value of leisure nearly outweighs the welfare gain related to increased consumption. For the "rich" households, the impact of the proportional tax reform on leisure is rather modest, while consumption increases considerably. Thus, when the distributional consequences are judged in terms of the changes in individual welfare in a heterogeneous population, the rich may benefit far more from further reforms towards proportional taxation of wage income than the poor.

The paper is organized as follows. In the analysis of tax reforms we apply a microeconometric labor supply model. Since microeconometric studies of tax reforms, in which observed as well as unobserved heterogeneity are accounted for, are rather novel, we focus on some methodological issues in Section II. Section III gives a brief outline of the labor supply model. In Section IV we present the empirical specification of the model and the estimation results. The model is estimated on Norwegian labor market and tax return data from 1979 for married couples. Section V gives the policy simulation results, and Section VI summarizes the main findings.

II. Methodological Issues

Our point of departure, on which the policy evaluation methodology is based, is a particular framework of modeling labor supply behavior developed in Dagsvik (1994) and adopted by Dagsvik and Strøm (1995) for the purpose of analyzing labor supply. The modeling approach differs from the conventional empirical models of labor supply, in which labor supply is derived from utility maximization where only consumption and leisure are the choice variables of the household. In these conventional models, agents are supposed to have no preferences over other important job characteristics, such as the nature of the tasks to be performed, location of workplace, social environment and working conditions. The framework proposed in Dagsvik and Strøm (1995) acknowledges these qualitative aspects of jobs by modelling labor supply behavior as a discrete choice problem, where the alternatives are "job packages". These job packages are characterized by specific attributes such as hours of work, wage rates and other non-pecuniary variables. In addition, this framework is able to take into account that there are important quantity constraints in the market, in the sense that different types of jobs are not equally available to every agent. Agents differ by qualification, and jobs differ with respect to qualification required.

A labor supply model can be used to identify the gains and losses from tax reforms by applying different Hicks-compensating measures; see

Auerbach (1985), Hausman (1984) and King (1987) for a discussion of alternative money metrics of welfare change, and Kay (1980) for arguments in favor of using equivalent variation (EV). In this study we apply EV. Loosely speaking, EV is measured as the amount of money that has to be added to the household's disposable income under the initial tax rules in order to make the household indifferent between the initial and the alternative tax system. Note that EV is measured at the household level. EV sums up the household net welfare gain/loss associated with behavioral responses induced by tax reforms, say, increased consumption and reduced leisure.

In the empirical measurement of the cost of taxation — or of the gain/loss of tax reforms — several approaches have been pursued in the literature. One common approach is to analyze tax reforms on the basis of a computable general equilibrium model with one — or a limited number of — representative household(s) representing labor supply and commodity demand in the economy. A standard reference by now is Ballard *et al.* (1985), and for an application to the Norwegian economy, see Vennemo (1992). The advantage of a general equilibrium approach is that it allows for wage rates and prices to respond to changes in tax rates. One serious objection to the standard approach is that it ignores all — or a substantial part — of the heterogeneity in the economy. Heterogeneous preferences are important not only for estimation, but also for simulation and welfare analysis. This latter aspect has been neglected relative to the attention that heterogeneity has received in the literature on estimation and testing.

Some of the problems that arise in the empirical analysis of tax reforms stem from the existence of non-linearities in the agents' budget constraints. In the representative agent setting in general equilibrium models, important non-linearities in the budget constraints are not accounted for. From a theoretical point of view the presence of non-linearities in the budget constraints implies that there is no representative consumer; see King (1987).

An alternative approach pursued in the literature is to estimate the overall gain from tax reforms as the area under the Hicks-compensated aggregated labor supply curve. In this approach the wage rate is exogenously given, which implies a partial equilibrium setting. As with the general equilibrium modeling strategy, heterogeneity is ignored and no distributional consequences can be traced. A standard reference on this topic is . Browning (1987). It should be noted that evaluating tax reforms by aggregating — explicitly or implicitly — welfare gains and losses across households is critical, since it assumes a utilitarian welfare function for society.

In most of the previous microeconomic analyses of labor supply responses and welfare effects of tax reforms, rather simple functional forms (typically linear and loglinear) were chosen, which tend to make the analysis unconvincing, since the results often do not seem to be robust as regards the choice of functional form; see e.g. Hausman (1985), Blomquist (1983) and Blundell *et al.* (1988).

An empirical micro-model — such as the one we apply here — is designed to account for observed as well as unobserved heterogeneity. Unobserved heterogeneity arises from the fact that as econometricians we are unable to observe all factors that affect individual tastes and opportunities. These unobservables are modeled as random variables, i.e., money metrics of welfare change, say EV, at the household level becomes a random variable; see King (1987) and Atkinson (1990). In other words, micro-econometric models allow the analyst to study the distribution of EV which accounts for observed and unobserved heterogeneity in tastes and choice constraints. There has not been a strong tradition in applied welfare analysis to include stochastic terms when a model is applied in policy assessments, as is evident from the prominent works of Hausman (1985), Hausman and Poterba (1987) and Blomquist (1983).

There is no general agreement on how the information captured by EV should be summarized when EV is random. Haneman (1982) discusses two alternative approaches. The first is to use the mean of the distribution as a measure of the overall gain. The second is to apply the median of the distribution. Here, we follow the former approach. In addition, we provide information about other parameters of the distribution of welfare gains and losses across households.

III. A Brief Outline of the Labor Supply Model

For expository simplicity, we begin by focusing on single-person households which, to the analyst, have observationally identical characteristics and constraints.

In our setting each agent faces a different set of non-market and market opportunities (jobs). It is understood that "jobs" may be specified in such detail that there exists a wide range of hours-wage combinations in the market. Let $B_i(h, w)$ denote the set of jobs with hours $h > 0$, and wage rate $w > 0$, that are feasible to agent i. $B_i(0,0)$ is the set of non-market opportunities. Let $U_i(C, h, j,)$ denote the utility for agent i of consumption C, hours h and opportunity j, where $j \in B_i(h, w)$, $h \geq 0$, $w \geq 0$.

The economic budget constraint is given by

$$C = f(wh, I), \tag{1}$$

where I is non-labor income and f is a function that transforms gross income into after-tax income. The price index of the composite good (called consumption) is equal to one. When inserting the budget constraint into the utility function we get $U_i(f(wh, I), h, j)$.

Assume furthermore that

$$U_i(f(wh, I), h, j) = v(f(wh, I), h) \, \varepsilon_{ij}(h, w), \tag{2}$$

where $v(C, h)$ is a positive, deterministic function which is quasi-concave in (C, h), increasing in the first argument and decreasing in the second. The term $\varepsilon_{ij}(h, w)$ is a random taste shifter that is supposed to capture the effect of unobservable attributes associated with opportunity j. Note that this term is viewed as random only from the econometrician's point of view, while it is assumed known to the agent. Specifically, $\{\varepsilon_{ij}(h, w)\}$ accounts for the fact that for a given agent, tastes may vary over opportunities, hours and wages, and for a given opportunity, tastes may vary across agents. We now define

$$V_i(h, w) = \max_{j \in B_i(h, w)} U_i(f(wh, I), h, j). \tag{3}$$

$V_i(h, w)$ is the conditional indirect utility function, given hours of work and the wage rate. In other words, for agent i, $V_i(h, w)$ is the utility of the most preferred opportunity among the feasible opportunities with hours h and wage rate w.

From (2) and (3) we get

$$V_i(h, w) = \psi(h, w) \, e_i(h, w) \tag{4}$$

where

$$e_i(h, w) = \max_{j \in B_i(h, w)} \varepsilon_{ij}(h, w) \tag{5}$$

and

$$\psi(h, w) = v(f(wh, I), h). \tag{6}$$

Recall that hours and wage rates are fixed for each job so that when a job has been chosen, then hours and wage rate follow. The individual agent is assumed to choose the job that maximizes utility. The corresponding hours and wage rate, (h, w), therefore follow from maximizing $V_i(h, w)$.

Next we briefly consider the structure of the choice probabilities of realized hours and wage rates, i.e., the hours and wage rate that correspond to the agent's choice. These probabilities enter the likelihood function which is used when estimating the unknown parameters of the model.

Let $n_i(h, w)$ be the number of jobs in $B_i(h, w)$ and let $\tilde{g}(h, w)$ be the mean of

$$\frac{n_i(h, w)}{\sum_{x>0} \sum_{y>0} n_i(x, y) + n_i(0, 0)}$$

across agents. Assume that the taste shifters are i.i.d. with distribution

$$P(\varepsilon_{ij}(h, w) \leq y) = \exp\left(-\frac{1}{y}\right). \tag{7}$$

Equation (7) follows from the assumption that agents have preferences over job types that satisfy the "independence from irrelevant alternatives" property. The taste shifters are also assumed to be stochastically independent of the choice sets $\{B_i(h, w)\}$.

Let $\varphi(h, w)$ be the probability that agent i will choose a job with hours and wage rate (h, w). If the mean of $\Sigma_{x, y} \, n_i(x, y)$ is large, the assumptions introduced above imply that

$$\varphi(h, w) \equiv P[V_i(h, w) = \max_{x, y} V_i(x, y)]$$

$$= \frac{\psi(h, w)\, \tilde{g}(h, w)}{\psi(0, 0)\, \tilde{g}(0, 0) + \sum_{x>0} \sum_{y>0} \psi(x, y)\, \tilde{g}(x, y)}, \tag{8}$$

for $h > 0$, $w > 0$. For the sake of interpretation it is convenient to express (8) as

$$\varphi(h, w) = \frac{\psi(h, w)\, g_0 g(h, w)}{\psi(0, 0) + g_0 \sum_{x>0} \sum_{y>0} \psi(x, y)\, g(x, y)} \tag{9}$$

where

$$g(h, w) = \frac{\tilde{g}(h, w)}{\sum_{x>0} \sum_{y>0} \tilde{g}(x, y)} \tag{10}$$

and

$$g_0 = \frac{\sum_{x>0} \sum_{y>0} \tilde{g}(x, y)}{\tilde{g}(0, 0)}. \tag{11}$$

The function $g(h, w)$ is denoted the conditional opportunity density of hours and wage rates, and it can be interpreted as the mean of the fraction of feasible jobs with hours h and wage rate w. Similarly, g_0 is the mean of the fraction of feasible opportunities that are job opportunities. Note that

g_0 is not necessarily less than one. The probability of not working equals

$$\varphi(0,0) = \frac{\psi(0,0)g_0}{\psi(0,0) + g_0 \sum_{x>0} \sum_{y>0} \psi(x,y)g(x,y)}. \tag{12}$$

The functional form of (9) and (12) is particularly attractive. The labor supply density $\varphi(h, w)$ is expressed as a simple function of the structural term of the utility function, $\psi(\cdot)$, and of $g_0g(\cdot)$, which is an aggregate representation of the set of feasible job opportunities.

The identification of $g_0g(\cdot)$ and $\psi(\cdot)$ and their inter-relationship are discussed in Dagsvik and Strøm (1995); it is found that the identification problem can only be fully solved when additional assumptions about the distribution of offered hours are made. The model discussed here is related to models developed in the travel demand literature; see Ben-Akiva and Lerman (1985).

The extension of the model outlined above to deal with the joint decisions of husband and wife is straightforward. The household utility function is now assumed to have the structure:

$$U_i(C, h_F, h_M, j_F, j_M) = v(C, h_F, h_M) \varepsilon_{ij_Fj_M}(h_F, w_F, h_M, w_F), \tag{13}$$

where F, M index female and male, respectively. Apart from the bivariate indexation of job opportunities, the probabilities of realized hours and wage rates are completely similar to (9) and (12). Below we only show the probability of realized hours and wage rates when both spouses work:

$$\varphi(h_F, h_M, w_F, w_M) = \frac{\psi(h_F, h_M, w_F, w_M)g_{0FM}g_F(h_F, w_F)g_M(h_M, w_M)}{D} \tag{14}$$

where

$$D = g_{0FM} \sum_{x_1>0} \sum_{x_2>0} \sum_{y_1>0} \sum_{y_2>0} \psi(x_1, x_2, y_1, y_2)g_F(x_1, y_1)g_M(x_2, y_2)$$

$$+ g_{0M} \sum_{x_2>0} \sum_{y_2>0} \psi(0, x_2, 0, y_2)g_M(x_2, y_2)$$

$$+ g_{0F} \sum_{x_1>0} \sum_{y_1>0} \psi(x_1, 0, y_1, 0)g_F(x_1, y_1) + \psi(0,0,0,0), \tag{15}$$

and where $\psi(h_F, h_M, w_F, w_M) = v(f(h_F w_F + h_M w_M, I), h_F, h_M)$, and $f(\cdot)$ represents the budget constraint. The different terms of the opportunity density may be interpreted as follows: $g_k(h_k, w_k)$ is the mean fraction of jobs with hours and wage rate (h_k, w_k) that are feasible to gender $k, k = F, M$; g_{0FM} is the mean fraction of opportunities that are feasible job opportunities to the couple; g_{0k} is the mean fraction of opportunities that are feasible job opportunities to gender k. Note that the structure of g_{0FM} allows opportunity sets for husband and wife to be correlated. The wife's and the husband's opportunity sets may be correlated because they both live in the same place and consequently operate on the same local labor market.[2]

IV. Empirical Specification and Estimation Results

In order to estimate an empirical model it remains to specify the structural part of the utility function and the opportunity densities. Let A_k, $k = M, F$ denote the age of spouse k, and let $CU6$ and $CO6$ denote the number of children less than and above six years of age. The deterministic part of the utility function is assumed to have the following functional form:

$$\log v(C, h_M, h_F) = \alpha_2 \frac{(10^{-4}C)^{\alpha_1} - 1}{\alpha_1}$$

$$+ \left(\frac{L_M^{\alpha_3} - 1}{\alpha_3}\right)(\alpha_4 + \alpha_5 \log A_M + \alpha_6(\log A_M)^2)$$

$$+ \left(\frac{L_F^{\alpha_7} - 1}{\alpha_7}\right)(\alpha_8 + \alpha_9 \log A_F + \alpha_{10}(\log A_F)^2$$

$$+ \alpha_{11} CU6 + \alpha_{12} CO6) + \alpha_{13} L_F L_M \tag{16}$$

where $L_k = 1 - h_k/8760$, $k = M, F$. $\alpha_1, \alpha_2, \ldots, \alpha_{13}$, are unknown parameters. Note that since 8760 is the total number of annual hours, L_k is equal to normalized annual leisure for gender k. If $\alpha_1 = \alpha_3 = \alpha_7 = 0$, then the utility function is loglinear in consumption and leisure, and if they are equal to one it is linear; for a recent use of this functional form in econometric work, see McFadden and Leonard (1993). If $\alpha_1 < 1$, $\alpha_3 < 1$, $\alpha_7 < 1$, $\alpha_2 > 0$,

$$\alpha_4 + \alpha_5 \log A_M + \alpha_6(\log A_M)^2 > 0$$

---

[2] This model is formulated in a discrete choice setting. In Dagsvik (1994) a pure-choice-of-attribute modeling framework with continuous attributes was developed, from which an empirical labor supply model for married couples was specified and estimated by Dagsvik and Strøm (1995). Thus the model given by (14) and (15) is the discrete version of this model.

and

$$\alpha_8 + \alpha_9 \log A_F + \alpha_{10}(\log A_F)^2 + \alpha_{11} CU6 + \alpha_{12} CO6 > 0,$$

then $v(C, h_M, h_F)$ is increasing in C, decreasing in (h_M, h_F), and quasi-concave in (C, h_M, h_F). Note that the marginal utility of income only depends on household consumption and that it is declining with household consumption.

Household consumption is assumed to be equal to disposable income. The f-function that represents the budget constraint follows from the tax and benefit rules. Claimed deductions are also accounted for, but these are suppressed in the notation here. A non-convex budget set may follow when effective marginal taxes are not uniformly increasing with income and/or when spouses are jointly taxed for incomes in certain income brackets. Certain benefit rules may add to this non-convexity of the budget set. Taxable income is equal to gross income minus deductions, which may vary across households. In 1979 parts of the taxes were levied on gross income and other parts on taxable income (description of the tax rules as of 1979 and 1992 are available on request).

We assume that offered hours and wages are independently distributed. It is important to note that this assumption does not exclude that realized hours and wages are dependent. Realized hours and wages follow from the optimal job chosen and this choice depends on preferences. The justification for the assumption that offered hours of work and wages are independent is that in the Scandinavian welfare states, working hours are typically regulated by the government or through central agreements between the organizations in the labor market, independently of wage formation.

In the model specification, this feature is captured by specifying the opportunity density of hours for the female, $g_{1F}(\cdot)$, as

$$\log g_{1F}(h_F) = d_F + \alpha_{19}D_1(h_F) + \alpha_{20}D_2(h_F) \tag{17}$$

where $D_1(h_F)$ is equal to one for full-time hours and zero otherwise, while $D_2(h_F)$ equals one for part-time hours and zero otherwise. For males the corresponding specification equals

$$\log g_{1M}(h_M) = d_M + \alpha_{18}D_1(h_M). \tag{18}$$

The parameters d_F and d_M are determined such that the respective opportunity densities sum up to unity.

We note that (17) and (18) imply that the opportunity densities of hours are assumed to be uniform apart from peaks at full-time for men and at part-time and full-time for women. Unless this or analogous assumptions are made, it is not possible to separate some of the structural coefficients in the systematic part of the utility function from the parameters of the opportunity densities of hours offered. Note that the case with uniformly distributed offered hours corresponds to the traditional textbook framework where agents are free to choose the desired hours of work. As we argue in this paper, a more realistic assumption is that there are more available part-time and full-time hour jobs than jobs with other working hours.

The offered wage opportunity densities are assumed to be the densities of a lognormal distribution function, with expectations:

$$E \log W_k = \beta_0 + \beta_1 s_k + \beta_2 \operatorname{Exp}_k + \beta_3 (\operatorname{Exp}_k)^2 \times 10^{-2}; \qquad k = M, F, \qquad (19)$$

where s_k denotes years of schooling for gender k, Exp_k is experience of gender k, equal to $A_k - s_k - 6$.

Estimation Results

The estimation of the model is based on a procedure suggested by McFadden (1978) which yields results that are close to the full maximum likelihood method; for further details see Dagsvik and Strøm (1995). Note that the opportunity densities are jointly estimated with the parameters of the utility function.

The estimates are reported in Table 1 (utility function and opportunity densities related to hours and job opportunities) and Table 2 (wage opportunity density). The estimates imply that the deterministic part of the utility function is an increasing and quasi-concave function in consumption and leisure.

Now, consider the estimates of the opportunity densities. Note first that g_{0FM}/g_{0M} is to be interpreted as the mean fraction of feasible job opportunities for the married couple, relative to the mean fraction of job opportunities for the male. If the males' and females' opportunity sets are independent, we get $g_{0FM}/g_{0M} = g_{0F}$ and $g_{0FM}/g_{0F} = g_{0M}$. For this to be the case we must have that the interaction term $\alpha_{17} = 0$. According to Table 1, this is not true. Furthermore, we see that the females' market opportunities increase by education. We have not found a similar effect for males and we only report the estimation results when this variable is not included in the specification of the male opportunity density of hours.

Figures 1–3, which display the observed and predicted distributions of hours of work and consumption in 1979, demonstrate that the model reproduces the observed distributions quite well.

Labor Supply Elasticities

In labor supply studies it is common to report elasticities computed from mean sample values, or alternatively based on subsamples of households that are grouped according to some socio-demographic characteristics.

Table 1. *Estimates of the parameters of the utility function and of the opportunity density of hours**

Variables	Coefficients	Estimates 1979
Preferences:		
Consumption	α_1	0.916 (22.4)
	α_2	1.997 (9.7)
Male leisure	α_3	-4.782 (6.7)
	α_4	76.657 (2.4)
	α_5	-38.532 (2.3)
	α_6	5.159 (2.3)
Female leisure	α_7	-0.961 (2.8)
	α_8	258.717 (2.7)
	α_9	-136.624 (2.7)
	α_{10}	19.208 (2.8)
	α_{11}	6.573 (8.1)
	α_{12}	1.967 (5.5)
Leisure interaction term	α_{13}	-3.869 (0.8)
Opportunities:		
Female; $\log(g_{0FM}/g_{0M}) = \alpha_{14} + \alpha_{15}s_F$	α_{14}	-1.164 (1.6)
	α_{15}	0.208 (3.0)
Male; $\log(g_{0FM}/g_{0F}) = \alpha_{16}$	α_{16}	-2.414 (7.4)
Interaction		
Female and male; $\log(g_{0FM}/g_{0F}g_{0M}) = \alpha_{17}$	α_{17}	-1.841 (4.6)
Opportunity densities of hours:		
Full-time peak, males	α_{18}	0.765 (5.8)
Full-time peak, females	α_{19}	0.868 (4.2)
Part-time peak, females	α_{20}	0.407 (3.0)

*Numerical t-values in parentheses.

Table 2. *Wage opportunity densities; simultaneous ML estimates**

Variables	Males	Females
Intercept	2.711 (39.6)	2.730 (3.52)
Education	0.045 (13.3)	0.047 (9.8)
Experience $(\text{Exp } A_k - s_k - 6)$	0.022 (6.4)	0.008 (2.1)
$\text{Exp}^2 \times 10^{-2}$	-0.036 (-6.2)	-0.012 (-1.7)
Standard error	0.101 (36.0)	0.172 (33.6)
R^2	0.23	0.23

*Numerical t-values in parentheses.

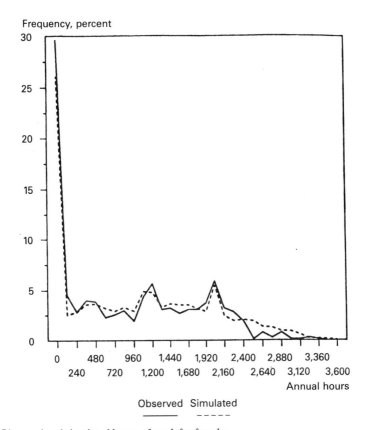

Fig. 1. Observed and simulated hours of work for females.

This is meaningful only when the taste shifters are independent of hours and wages. This is not the case in our model since the taste shifters vary across jobs, and hence across hours and wages; cf. (5). In this model, an increase in hours supplied, say as a response to a higher wage level, will imply a shift of job. Thus we had to take the complete random utility model into account when deriving the elasticities. Hence, we instead computed elasticities of hours of work with respect to the mean wage rate. These elasticities are denoted exact aggregate labor supply elasticities. Note that observed and unobserved heterogeneity in the population as well as the non-convexities of the budget sets, and hours regulations were taken into account when these aggregate elasticities were calculated.

In Table 3 we report aggregate elasticities. The table is divided into three parts. The first part reports the elasticity of the probability of participation with respect to wage, the second the elasticities of hours

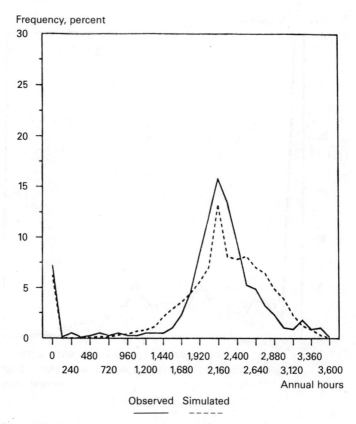

Fig. 2. Observed and simulated hours of work for males.

worked, conditional on participation, while the third reports the elasticities of the unconditional supply of labor. In each part we give elasticities for the 10 percent poorest and richest households, for the 80 percent in the middle and for all households.

Table 3 shows that the elasticities are sharply declining with income. The elasticities of participation tend to be higher than the elasticities of hours supplied, given participation. The elasticites among females are significantly higher than among males, in particular for individuals with middle and higher income.

Increasing the overall wage level by 1 percent yields a direct uncondi- tional Slutsky elasticity of 0.33 for males and of 1.59 for females. When the cross-effects are taken into account, the utility-constant labor supply elasticity is reduced to 0.22 for males and to 1.31 for females.

Most researchers report uncompensated labor supply elasticities that are rather low compared to those we have found, in particular for females.

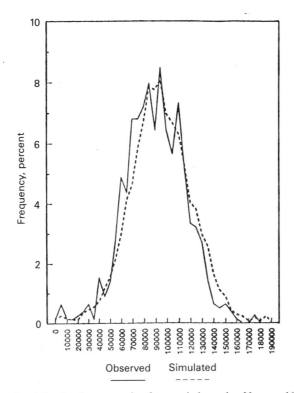

Fig. 3. Observed and simulated consumption for married couples, Norway, 1979.

For example, Blomquist and Hansson-Brusewitz (1990) found labor supply elasticities (hours with respect to wage level) for married women (Sweden) between 0.4 and 0.8. However, exceptions are Arrufat and Zabalza (1986) and Hartog and Theeuwes (1986). Arrufat and Zabalza found an overall elasticity of hours with respect to wage level for married women (U.K.) equal to 2.03, while the elasticity of participation with respect to wage level was equal to 1.41. The corresponding estimates found by Hartog and Theeuwes (the Netherlands) are 3.61 and 1.88. Moreover, Hausman and Ruud (1984) report an elasticity for wives of 0.76. Our male labor supply elasticities are more in line with what others have found; e.g. Blundell and Walker (1986), Meghir (1985) and Pencavel (1987).

V. Policy Simulations

Our methodology for evaluating policy changes is based on EV derived from individual indirect random utilities by means of the model discussed

Table 3. Exact aggregate labor supply elasticities* for males and females, 1979

Type of elasticity		Male elasticities		Female elasticities	
		Own wage elasticities	Cross elasticities	Own wage elasticities	Cross elasticities
Elasticity of the probability of participation	Cournot				
	I	1.89 (0.06)	-1.04 (0.05)	1.85 (0.07)	-1.44 (0.07)
	II	0.09 (0.003)	-0.08 (0.004)	0.66 (0.008)	-0.29 (0.005)
	III	0.03 (0.004)	0.01 (0.003)	0.07 (0.006)	-0.03 (0.011)
	IV	0.29 (0.004)	-0.08 (0.004)	0.83 (0.009)	-0.25 (0.008)
	Slutsky				
	I	2.71 (0.35)	0.41 (0.09)	2.62 (0.28)	0.21 (0.21)
	II	0.07 (0.01)	-0.12 (0.01)	0.73 (0.03)	-0.19 (0.02)
	III	0.01 (0.01)	-0.05 (0.02)	0.03 (0.03)	-0.11 (0.03)
	IV	0.22 (0.02)	-0.08 (0.02)	0.73 (0.03)	-0.16 (0.01)
Elasticity of conditional expectation of total supply of hours	Cournot				
	I	0.29 (0.02)	-0.15 (0.02)	1.04 (0.04)	-1.04 (0.07)
	II	0.07 (0.002)	-0.09 (0.004)	0.78 (0.009)	-0.29 (0.006)
	III	0.03 (0.005)	-0.01 (0.005)	0.12 (0.013)	-0.06 (0.017)
	IV	0.16 (0.002)	-0.07 (0.004)	0.99 (0.007)	-0.26 (0.008)
	Slutsky				
	I	1.11 (0.12)	0.47 (0.11)	2.39 (0.24)	0.42 (0.24)
	II	0.09 (0.02)	-0.05 (0.01)	0.97 (0.05)	-0.17 (0.01)
	III	0.01 (0.01)	-0.02 (0.01)	0.05 (0.01)	-0.04 (0.02)
	IV	0.10 (0.01)	-0.02 (0.01)	0.80 (0.04)	-0.12 (0.01)
Elasticity of unconditional expectation of total supply of hours	Cournot				
	I	2.23 (0.06)	-1.18 (0.05)	3.09 (0.08)	-2.33 (0.11)
	II	0.16 (0.003)	-0.17 (0.004)	1.49 (0.012)	-0.57 (0.009)
	III	0.06 (0.006)	-0.01 (0.004)	0.19 (0.013)	-0.08 (0.017)
	IV	0.45 (0.005)	-0.15 (0.005)	1.82 (0.11)	-0.51 (0.014)
	Slutsky				
	I	4.15 (0.49)	0.88 (0.15)	5.68 (0.58)	0.68 (0.45)
	II	0.16 (0.02)	-0.17 (0.02)	1.77 (0.07)	-0.35 (0.03)
	III	0.02 (0.02)	-0.07 (0.02)	0.07 (0.03)	-0.15 (0.05)
	IV	0.33 (0.02)	-0.11 (0.02)	1.59 (0.05)	-0.28 (0.02)

Note that I = 10 percent poorest household, II = 80 percent in the middle of the consumption distribution, III = 10 percent richest household and IV = all households.
* Standard deviations in parentheses.

above. For expository reasons we focus here on single individuals. The extension to the case of married couples is straightforward. For single individuals it follows (cf. Section II) that the indirect utility has the structure

$$\tilde{V}_i(y, f) = \max_{h, w}(\max_{j \in B_i(h, w)} U_i(f(wh, I) + y, h, j))$$

$$= \max_{h, w}(v(f(wh, I) + y, h) e_i(h, w)) \tag{20}$$

where $e_i(h, w)$ is defined in (5). Moreover, this random term can be expressed as $e_i(h, w) = g_0 g(h, w) \theta_i(h, w)$ when $h, w > 0$, and $e_i(0,0) = \theta_i(0,0)$ when $h = w = 0$, where $\{\theta_i(x, y)\}$ are i.i.d. with cumulative distribution function

$$P(\theta_i(h, w) \le x) = \exp\left(-\frac{1}{x}\right). \tag{21}$$

Hence we can write (20) as

$$\tilde{V}_i(y, f) = \tag{22}$$
$$\max[\max_{h > 0, w > 0} (v(f(wh, I) + y, h) g_0 g(h, w) \theta_i(h, w)), v(f(0, I) + y, 0) \theta_i(0,0)].$$

In words, (20) means that first, utility is maximized with respect to feasible market and non-market opportunities with hours h and wage rate w, subject to the budget constraint

$$C = f(wh, I) + y \tag{23}$$

where y is a given non-taxable amount of money. This gives the conditional indirect utility given (h, w); i.e., the highest utility attainable for the agent, given that hours of work and the wage rate are equal to (h, w), or given that the agent does not work. Second, this conditional indirect utility is maximized with respect to (h, w) which yields the unconditional indirect utility as a function of non-labor income, the tax system, represented by f, and non-taxable income y. This indirect utility also depends on the opportunity density, $g_0 g(\cdot)$, that represents the choice sets $\{B_i(h, w)\}$.

By means of the formalism above, the definition of EV can be expressed as

$$\tilde{V}_i(0, f_1) = \tilde{V}_i(EV, f_0) \tag{24}$$

where f_1 represents the alternative tax system and f_0 represents the initial system.

The policy experiments are performed in a partial equilibrium setting, as in Browning (1987). This means that the opportunity density, $g_0 g(\cdot)$, is kept fixed. In other words, the distribution of offered hours and wage rates associated with feasible jobs is assumed to remain unaffected by changes in the tax rates. For example, if total labor supply increases as a result of tax reforms, then the total number of jobs is assumed to increase so as to maintain a fixed number of job opportunities for each worker.

Since the random terms $\{\theta_i(h, w)\}$ are i.i.d. with a distribution function that does not depend on the structural part of the model, it is easy to use (22) and (24) to perform simulations. In the simulation experiments reported below we generated values of the random terms $\{\theta_i(h, w)\}$ by means of (21).

Consider now the design of the Norwegian personal income tax systems under consideration. The base situation — or the pre-reform tax system — is the tax system as of 1979. The following reforms were investigated: (i) proportional taxation of wage income, (ii) the 1992 tax system and (iii) lump-sum taxes.

The motivation for analyzing these regimes may be explained as follows (see also Section I). First, marginal tax rates as of 1979 were at an all-time high level. Second, marginal tax rates were gradually cut throughout the 1980s and the beginning of the 1990s; the most substantial cut took place in 1992. Third, the slashing of tax rates has gradually moved the tax system towards a proportional tax system for wage income. Fourth, it is not fully satisfactory to use no-taxation or lump-sum taxes as a benchmark case since the latter system cannot be implemented in practice. However, as shown below, the supply-side potential is not much lower with proportional taxes than with lump-sum taxes.

When proportional taxation of wage income replaces the 1979 rules, the tax rate is chosen so as to yield a tax revenue equal to the tax revenue under the 1979 regime. Given this constraint, we simulated the mean gain (mean of EV) relative to mean tax revenue. Moreover, we report additional information on the distribution of individual welfare gains and losses. The extent to which the reform affects the distribution of gross and disposable income is also examined. In doing this we account for both behavioral and non-behavioral effects. Note that in conventional analyses of tax reforms carried out by central authorities, behavioral responses are typically disregarded.

When the 1979 tax system is replaced by the 1992 system, revenues obviously cannot remain unchanged. Thus, we report the mean of the gain from this reform relative to the change in the mean tax revenue.

Proportional Taxes

We applied the model to determine the proportional tax rate which ensures that tax revenue under proportional taxation remains equal to tax revenue under the 1979 system. This rate was found to be 20.1 percent.

Table 4. *Labor supply,* * *tax and income under three different tax regimes; means in 1979 NOK*

	Participation rates percent		Annual hours of work		Household		
					Gross		Disposable
	F	M	F	M	income	Taxes	income
1979 rules	74.2	93.7	1,043	2,132	136,279	40,623	95,656
Proportional taxes	84.3	99.5	1,642	2,790	208,449	40,623	167,825
1992 rules	74.5	96.0	1,178	2,331	156,720	48,809	107,911

*Supply of hours, given participation, is equal to annual hours divided by the participation rates.

Table 4 reports the participation rates and annual hours supplied by gender under the different tax regimes. The table also lists gross household income and disposable income.

The results show that a shift from the 1979 tax rules to proportional taxation of wage income: (i) increases participation rates for females and males by approximately 10 and 6 percentage points, respectively; (ii) increases annual hours supplied, given participation, for females and males by 38 percent and 31 percent, respectively; and (iii) increases gross and disposable household income by 53 percent and 75 percent, respectively. The mean of EV is found to be equal to NOK 25 956 (1979 prices), which amounts to 63.8 percent of the tax revenue under the 1979 rules.

Tables 5a and 5b provide information on the distribution of the gains and losses. When 1979 rules are replaced by proportional taxes, then: (i) as much as 99.4 percent of the population will gain from this reform, while 0.6 percent will lose; (ii) inequality in the distribution of gains proves to be considerably higher than the inequality in the distribution of gross income in 1979; (iii) among the 10 percent of the population that gains the most from the reform, the mean of EV is NOK 45 400 and, for these households, average gross income under the 1979 rules was NOK 182 800 (in contrast, the equivalent amounts for the 10 percent that gains the least are NOK 1 600 and NOK 84 500).

The latter result demonstrates that the magnitude of the gains from the proportional tax reform increases strongly with pre-reform gross household income. The explanation is that among the "poor", the tax reform induces the individuals to work much longer hours, as indicated by the reported elasticities in Table 3, and the gain for these households occurs as a result of increased income and hence consumption. Among the "rich', hours of work are not affected to the same extent. On the other

Table 5A. Equivalent variation, 1979 NOK

| | Equivalent variations | | | | | |
| | Total | Losers | | | Winners | | |
	Mean	Percent of population	Mean	Gini coefficient	Percent of population	Mean	Gini coefficient
Proportional taxes	25,956	0.6	−1,344	—	99.4	26,136	0.303
1992 rules	1,588	42.8	−2,356	0.437	56.8	4,572	0.472

Table 5B. Mean EV and gross household income of the 10 percent who gain most and the 10 percent who gain least from a proportional tax reform, 1979 NOK

	Mean equivalent variation	Gross household income under 1979 rules
The 10 percent who gain most	45,400	182,800
The 10 percent who gain least (lose most)	1,600	84,500

hand, the "rich" benefit greatly from the direct increase in disposable income.

Table 6 reports the Gini coefficients of the distributions of gross and disposable household income. These results demonstrate that the inequality in the distribution of disposable income decreases when proportional taxes replace the progressive 1979 system. This surprising result is due to the fact that the poor have higher labor supply elasticities than the rich. The tax reform induces the poor to choose jobs with much longer hours of work than under the 1979 tax rules.

Even though income inequality decreases due to this reform, the welfare implications, as measured by EV, turn out to be more favorable for the medium-rich and rich households than for the lower-middle and poor households.

The 1992 Tax System

We realize from Table 4 that the 1992 tax reform has a more modest effect on labor supply than proportional taxation. Note, however, that the assumption of a fixed tax revenue is relaxed. The revenue based on the 1992 system turns out to rise by approximately 20 percent which, on average, corresponds to NOK 8186 per household. Despite an increased tax burden, the transition from 1979 to 1992 tax rules yields a positive mean equivalent variation. As reported in Table 4, the mean equivalent variation is equal to NOK 1588 which appears to be considerably lower than the increase in tax revenue. The ratio between the mean equivalent variation and the mean tax increase is equal to 0.194, which turns out to be in accordance with results for the US reported by Browning (1987).

Tables 5A and B show that there is large heterogeneity with regard to gains and losses from this tax reform. As much as 43 percent lose from the reform while the remaining 57 percent are winners. Table 6 shows that the inequality in gross household and disposable income increases.

Table 6. *Inequality in the distributions of gross and disposable income measured by the Gini coefficient**

	Gross income	Disposable income
1979 tax rules	0.196	0.161
	(0.002)	(0.002)
Proportional taxes	0.152	0.152
	(0.001)	(0.001)
1992 tax rules	0.205	0.177
	(0.003)	(0.003)

*Standard deviations in parentheses.

Lump Sum Taxes

In studies of the cost of taxation, lump-sum taxes often serves as the benchmark case with which alternative tax systems are compared. The rationale for doing this is that lump-sum taxes remove all distortive effects of taxation and reveal the supply-side potential of the economy. Since lump-sum taxes cannot be implemented in the economy, it is important to consider alternative reforms (to lump-sum taxes). However, the specific reforms should be evaluated both against the base system of 1979 and against lump-sum taxes in order to reveal the labor supply potential. As shown in Table 7, female labor supply under the 1979 tax rules constitutes 48.2 percent of the non-distortive potential, while in the case of males the figure is 72.2 percent. When proportional taxes replace the 1979 tax system, utilization of the labor supply potential increases considerably for both sexes. In the case of male labor supply it is close to full utilization of its potential, while for females the reform brings utilization up to 76 percent of its potential. The 1992 reform turns out to increase male labor supply to some extent, but much less than the proportional tax system, while female labor supply is closer to the outcome under the 1979 rules. Table 7 also shows how far gross income is from its supply-side potential under the alternative tax systems. Based on the 1979 tax rules, less than 60 percent of the potential turns out to be utilized, while the 1992 reform has increased utilization up to around two-thirds of its potential. We observe, however, that proportional taxes would have brought the economy up to 88 percent of the gross income potential.

VI. Conclusions

The measurement of the welfare effects of tax reforms discussed in this paper is based on a particular empirical labor supply model developed and estimated in Dagsvik and Strøm (1995). In this model labor supply

Table 7. *Mean annual hours of work and gross household income under alternative tax regimes in percent of the corresponding lump-sum results*

| | Annual hours of work | | |
	F	M	Gross household income
1979 tax rules	48.2	72.2	57.7
Proportional taxation	76.0	94.5	88.3
1992 tax rules	54.5	78.9	66.4
Lump-sum taxes Hours, NOK 1979	2,160	2,952	236,197

decisions are viewed as choices between feasible "job packages", where each package is characterized by a wage rate, hours of work and unobserved non-pecuniary attributes. This labor supply model allows for non-convex budget sets, joint decisions of husband and wife, regulations of hours of work, and observed as well as unobserved heterogeneity in preferences and opportunity sets.

In line with others, e.g. Browning (1987), this study applies a partial-equilibrium approach in which the distribution of feasible market and non-market opportunities is kept fixed under various tax-reform experiments. Thus, we are tacitly assuming that supply creates its own demand. In contrast to most studies of the cost of taxation, this study accounts for the effects of observed as well as unobserved heterogeneity when the different reforms are evaluated.

In recent years the degree of progression in the taxation of wage income in Norway has gradually been reduced. Our analysis shows that these gradual reforms may have removed some of the distortion on worker behavior caused by income taxes. However, further reforms towards a proportional tax regime may increase mean welfare and improve efficiency much more. In fact, our results indicate that a proportional tax regime may move the economy close to its supply-side potential as revealed by lump-sum taxation.

The impact on the distribution of welfare gains and losses across households indicates that a proportional tax reform will favor households with incomes between the middle and the top decile of the income distribution far more than the households in the bottom decile. The reason is that the Hicks-compensated labor supply elasticites are much higher among the low-income households than among the high-income households. The proportional tax reform induces the poor to work much more than before and the decreased utility associated with decreased leisure nearly outweighs the benefit from increased disposable income. For the rich, and typically well-educated, the supply elasticities are much lower; they therefore enjoy the increase in income without any large decrease in the utility generated by less leisure.

As regards income distribution, the effect of replacing the 1979 rules by proportional taxes is a reduction in the inequality of disposable household income. However, this surprising result is not inconsistent with the reported distribution of welfare gains. As alluded to above, proportional taxation of wage income induces the poor to work so much harder that the inequality in the distribution of gross income as well as in the distribution of disposable income decreases.

Nearly all households (99.4 percent) gain from replacing the progressive tax system of 1979 by proportional taxation, given a fixed tax revenue. Thus, switching to proportional taxation almost implies a Pareto improvement. The mean welfare gain of the 1979 regime — evaluated against proportional taxation — turns out to be equal to 64 percent of tax revenue. However, our analysis demonstrates that the gains vary strongly with the level of pre-reform 1979 incomes. For instance, if we use a social welfare function that exclusively adds up the equivalent variation of the 10 percent of the households that gain the least, then the mean welfare gain is approximately 4 percent of initial tax revenue. Alternatively, when the social welfare function is based on the equivalent variation of the 10 percent that gain the most, the mean welfare gain increases to approximately 119 percent. These results illustrate the importance of accounting for heterogeneity when evaluating the welfare effects of tax reforms.

References

Arrufat, J. L. & Zabalza, A.: Female labor supply with taxation, random preferences, and optimization errors. *Econometrica 54*, 47–63, 1986.
Atkinson, A. B.: Public economics and the economic public. *European Economic Review 34*, 225–48, 1990.
Auerbach, A. J.: The theory of excess burden and optimal taxation. In A. J. Auerbach & M. Feldstein (eds.), *Handbook of Public Economics*, North-Holland, Amsterdam, 1985.
Ballard, C. L., Shoven, J. B. & Whalley, J.: General equilibrium computations of the marginal welfare costs of taxes in the United States. *American Ecnomic Review 75*, 128–38, 1985.
Ben-Akiva, M. & Lerman, S. R.: *Discrete Choice Analysis*. MIT Press, Cambridge, MA, 1985.
Blomquist, N. S.: The effect of income taxation on the labor supply of married men in Sweden. *Journal of Public Economics 22*, 169–97, 1983.
Blomquist, N. S. & Hansson-Brusewitz, U.: The effect of taxes on male and female labor supply in Sweden. *Journal of Human Resources 25*, 317–57, 1990.
Blundell, R. W. & Walker, I.: A life-cycle consistent empirical model of family labor supply using cross-section data. *Review of Economic Studies 53*, 539–58, 1986.
Blundell, R., Meghir, C., Symons, E. & Walker, I.: Labor supply specification and the evaluation of tax reforms. *Journal of Public Economics 36*, 23–52, 1988.
Browning, E. K.: On the marginal welfare cost of taxation. *American Economic Review 77* (1), 11–23, 1987.
Dagsvik, J. K.: Discrete and continuous choice, max-stable processes and independence from irrelevant attributes. *Econometrica 62*, 1179–205, 1994.
Dagsvik, J. K. & Strøm, S.: Labor supply with non-convex budget sets, hours restrictions and non-pecuniary job attributes. Manuscript, Statistics Norway, Oslo, 1995.
Haneman, W. M.: Applied welfare analysis with qualitative response models. WP 241, Division of Agricultural Sciences, University of California, Berkeley, 1982.
Hausman, J.: Exact consumer's surplus and deadweight loss. *American Economic Review 71* (4), 662–76, 1984.
Hausman, J. & Ruud, P.: Family labor supply with taxes. *American Economic Review 74*, 242–8, 1984.
Hausman, J.: Taxes and labor supply. In A. J. Auerbach & M. Feldstein (eds.), *Handbook of Public Economics*, North-Holland, Amsterdam, 1985.
Hausman, J. A. & Poterba, J. M.: Household behavior and the tax reform act of 1986. *Journal of Economic Perspectives 1*, 101–19, 1987.

Hartog, J. & Theeuwes, J.: Participation and hours of work. *European Economic Review 30*, 833–57, 1986.

Kay, J. A.: The deadweight loss from a tax system. *Journal of Public Economics 13*, 111–19, 1980.

King, M. A.: The empirical analysis of tax reforms. In T. Bewly (ed.), *Advances in Econometrics*, Cambridge University Press, Cambridge, 1987.

Meghir, C.: The specification of labor supply models and the simulation of tax and benefit reforms. Ph.D. thesis, University of Manchester, 1985.

McFadden, D.: Modelling the choice of residentical location. In A. Karlquist, L. Lundquist, F. Snickars & J. J. Weibull (eds.), *Spatial Interaction Theory and Planning Models*, North-Holland, Amsterdam, 1978.

McFadden, D. & Leonard, G. K.: Issues in the contingent valuation of environmental goods: Methodologies for data collection and analysis. In J. Hausman (ed.), *Contingent Valuation*, North-Holland, Amsterdam, 1993.

Pencavel, J.: Labor supply of men: A survey. In O. Ashenfelter & R. Layard (eds.), *Handbook of Labor Economics*, North-Holland, Amsterdam, 1987.

Sandmo, A.: Economists and the welfare state. *European Economic Review 35*, 213–39, 1991.

Vennemo, H.: An applied general equilibrium assessment of the marginal cost of public funds in Norway. In *Five Studies of Tax Policy Using Applied General Equilibrium Models*, Ph.D. thesis, no. 10, University of Oslo, 1992.

Index

194

DATE DUE